Free Video Free Free Video

Essential Test Tips Video from Trivium Test Prep

Dear Customer,

Thank you for purchasing from Trivium Test Prep! We're honored to help you prepare for your GED exam.

To show our appreciation, we're offering a **FREE *GED Essential Test Tips* Video by Trivium Test Prep**.* Our video includes 35 test preparation strategies that will make you successful on the GED. All we ask is that you email us your feedback and describe your experience with our product. Amazing, awful, or just so-so: we want to hear what you have to say!

To receive your **FREE *GED Essential Test Tips* Video**, please email us at 5star@triviumtestprep.com. Include "Free 5 Star" in the subject line and the following information in your email:

1. The title of the product you purchased.
2. Your rating from 1 – 5 (with 5 being the best).
3. Your feedback about the product, including how our materials helped you meet your goals and ways in which we can improve our products.
4. Your full name and shipping address so we can send your **FREE *GED Essential Test Tips* Video**.

If you have any questions or concerns please feel free to contact us directly at 5star@triviumtestprep.com.

Thank you!

– Trivium Test Prep Team

*To get access to the free video please email us at 5star@triviumtestprep.com, and please follow the instructions above.

GED Social Studies Preparation Study Guide 2021-2022

Workbook with Practice Test Questions for the GED Exam

Printed in the United States of America.

Table of Contents

Introduction

Congratulations on choosing to take the GED exam! By purchasing this book, you've taken an important step on your path to earning your high school-equivalency credential.

This guide will provide you with a detailed overview of the GED exam so that you know exactly what to expect on test day. We'll take you through all the concepts covered on the exam and give you the opportunity to test your knowledge with practice questions. Even if it's been a while since you last took a major test, don't worry; we'll make sure you're more than ready!

What is the GED?

The General Educational Development, or GED, test is a high school-equivalency test—composed of four subtests—that certifies that the test-taker has high school-level academic skills. Forty states currently offer the GED test. The four subtests can be taken together or separately, but you must pass all four subtests in order to pass the test overall. Once a test-taker in one of those states passes the exam, then that person becomes eligible to receive a high school-equivalency diploma, which can be used in job applications or in applying to colleges or universities. The test is specifically designed for individuals who did not complete a high school diploma, no matter the reason.

What's on the GED?

The GED test gauges high school-level content knowledge and skills in four areas: Reasoning through Language Arts (RLA), Mathematical Reasoning, Science, and Social Studies. Candidates are expected to be able to read closely, write clearly, edit and understand standard written English as it is used in context, and solve quantitative and algebraic problems. You also must show strong content knowledge in life science, physical science, and Earth and space science as well as civics and government, United States history, geography and the world, and economics.

The test includes a variety of question types, including multiple-choice, drag-and-drop, hot spot, and fill-in-the-blank. The multiple-choice questions are a standard style in which the test-taker selects the best answer among a series of choices. In drag-and-drop questions, the test-taker must select the best answer, click on it, and drag it to the appropriate location. This usually involves sorting items into categories or making associations between different concepts. Hot spot questions require the test-taker to click on a specific area of an image. For fill-in-the-blank questions, the test-taker must type in the word or phrase missing from the statement or question. The Reasoning through Language Arts section also includes some questions in which the test-taker must select the best grammatical or punctuation change from a drop-down list of options as well as extended response questions that require the test-taker to type the answer.

Each subtest is taken separately. You must complete one subtest before moving on to the next. You will have 115 minutes for the math test, ninety minutes for the science test, seventy minutes for the social studies test, and 150 minutes for the Reasoning through Language Arts test.

What's on the GED Exam?

Skills Assessed	Topics	Percentage of Exam*
Reasoning Through Language Arts		
▶ Read closely ▶ Write clearly ▶ Edit and understand the use of standard written English in context	Informational texts	75%
	Literature texts	25%
Mathematical Reasoning		
▶ Understand key mathematical concepts ▶ Demonstrate skill and fluency with key math procedures ▶ Apply concepts to realistic situations	Quantitative problem-solving	45%
	Algebraic problem-solving	55%
Science		
▶ Use scientific reasoning (textually and quantitatively) ▶ Apply scientific reasoning to a variety of realistic situations	Life science	40%
	Physical science	40%
	Earth and space science	20%

Skills Assessed	Topics	Percentage of Exam*
Social Studies		
▶ Textual analysis ▶ Data representation ▶ Inference skills ▶ Problem-solving using social studies content	Civics and government	50%
	United States history	20%
	Economics	15%
	Geography and the world	15%

**Percentages are approximate.*

The Reasoning through Language Arts test assesses your ability to understand a range of texts which can be found in both academic and workplace settings. The test includes literary and informational texts as well as important US founding documents. The texts vary in length from 450 to 900 words. You will be asked to identify details and make logical inferences from—as well as valid claims about—the texts. You also will be asked to define key vocabulary and use textual evidence to analyze the texts in your own words in the form of a written response.

The Mathematical Reasoning test assesses mastery of key fundamental math concepts. Rather than focusing on specific content, the test focuses on reasoning skills and modes of thinking that can be used in a variety of mathematical content areas, specifically algebra, data analysis, and number sense. Questions will assess your ability to make sense of complex problems, use logical thinking to find solutions, recognize structure, and look for and express regularity in repeated reasoning. You also will be evaluated on the precision of your mathematics.

The Science test assesses your mastery of scientific content in life science, physical science, and Earth and space science, as well as your ability to apply scientific reasoning. Each question on the test will focus on one science practice and one content topic. Specifically, questions will relate to two primary themes: Human Health and Living Systems—all concepts related to the health and safety of all living things on the planet—and Energy and Related Systems—all concepts related to sources and uses of energy.

The Social Studies test assesses your mastery of both social studies content and skills. Each question addresses one element of social studies practice and one specific content topic. The primary focus of the test is on American civics and government, with the other three content areas as supplements. The questions address two core themes: Development of Modern Liberties and Democracy—which traces the current ideas of democracy from ancient times to present—and Dynamic Responses in Societal Systems, which addresses how society's systems, structures, and policies have developed and responded to each other.

Unique Question Types

While the majority of the GED exam is made up of multiple-choice questions, it also contains several other types of questions that might be unfamiliar to you. Collectively, these are called "technology-enhanced items" because they require you to interact with a computer. There are four types of these questions: drag-and-drop, hot spot, drop-down or cloze, and fill-in-the-blank. Each type of question is structured a little differently and requires different actions from the test-taker. Each type of question also assesses different skills. While they may seem a little intimidating, once you understand what these questions are testing and how to answer them, you will see they are quite manageable.

DRAG-and-DROP

A drag-and-drop question has three parts: the question or prompt, drop target, and tiles or "draggers." Each tile contains a small image, word, or numerical expression. You will read the question or prompt, and then click the tile you think has the correct answer, drag it to the target area, and then let it go. In some cases, you may be able to put more than one tile in a single target area, or you may be able to put the same tile in multiple target areas. If this is the case, a note included with the question will tell you that. For example, imagine a question says, *Classify the following fruits by color.* There is a response area for yellow, blue, green, and red, and tiles that say *apple*, *strawberry*, *blueberry*, *banana*, and *pear*. You would drag both the apple and strawberry tiles to the red target area. You would also put the apple tile in the green area.

Drag-and-drop questions will differ both in structure and in skills assessed, depending on the subtest. On the Mathematics subtest, drag-and-drop questions are primarily used for constructing expressions, equations, and inequalities. For example, the prompt will include a scenario and an incomplete equation. The tiles will contain various numerical and/or alphabetical variables and operators that could complete the equation. You must then drag the appropriate mathematical element to its spot in the equation. You also could be asked to order the steps in a mathematical process or solution or match items from two different sets.

On the Reasoning Through Language Arts (RLA) subtest, drag-and-drop questions will typically focus on sequencing and classifying to assess comprehension and analysis of a reading passage. Some questions may ask you to order events in a passage based on chronology or to illustrate cause and effect. Or you might be asked to classify evidence based on how it relates to the argument of a passage. Drag-and-drop questions on this subtest will usually incorporate graphic organizers, such as Venn diagrams, timelines, or charts.

On the Social Studies subtest, drag-and-drop questions are primarily used for mapping, classifying, and sequencing. For example, you might be asked to put the steps in a political process in the correct order, or you may be asked to sort actions based on the related constitutional freedom. Alternatively, you could be asked to place correct labels on the continents or use information from a brief text to place data points on a graph or chart.

On the Science subtest, drop-and-drag questions are used primarily for sequencing questions: placing the steps of a biological or chemical process in the correct order. These questions can also be used for classification, like sorting animals into mammals and non-mammals. Like on the RLA subtest, science drag-and-drop questions often utilize graphic organizers, like Venn diagrams.

EXAMPLE

1. The owner of a taco truck decides to use data to determine how many tacos he can make during a two-hour lunch rush. He has determined that the average time it takes to make five tacos is eight minutes.

Complete the equation to show how the taco truck owner determined that he can make seventy-five tacos in two hours.

answer area × answer area = $\frac{75 \text{ tacos}}{2 \text{ hours}}$

$\frac{5 \text{ tacos}}{8 \text{ minutes}}$	$\frac{2 \text{ hours}}{120 \text{ minutes}}$	2 hours
$\frac{8 \text{ minutes}}{5 \text{ tacos}}$	$\frac{120 \text{ minutes}}{2 \text{ hours}}$	5 tacos

HOT SPOT

In a hot spot question, you will be presented with a graphic image. The image is embedded with virtual "sensors" placed at various points. The question will ask you to identify something specific within the image or to select an answer from several listed within the image. You will indicate your selection by clicking on a virtual sensor. For example, the image could be a diagram of the human body. If the question asks where the lungs are located, you would click the chest, activating the sensor there. While hot spot questions are different from a traditional multiple-choice question, they might be easier for you to do. Clicking on part of an image—rather than selecting a choice from A to D—might feel similar to how you express knowledge in the real world.

Hot spot questions appear on every subtest except RLA. On the Mathematics subtest, hot spots are most often used to assess your ability to plot points on coordinate grids, number lines, or scatter plots. For example, the graphic image could be a coordinate grid, and the question would ask you to plot a specific point, like (5, –2). You would then click the spot on the graph associated with (5, –2). Other math questions include identifying specific parts of a scale model, selecting numerical or algebraic expressions that identify parallel equations, or identifying different representations of the same numeric value.

On the Science subtest, hot spot questions may use a graphic image or a block of text. In addition to allowing you to identify information on a model or diagram, they assess your understanding of the relationship between data points or your ability to use data points to support or refute a particular conclusion.

On the Social Studies subtest, hot spots questions often ask you to indicate evidence that supports a particular statement or idea. Like on the Science subtest, you might be asked to demonstrate the relationship between different data points from a short block of text or an image. They are also often used with mapping.

EXAMPLE

2. The square below is based on the eye color of two parents: one with brown eyes and one with green. According to this square, this couple's biological children have a 50 percent chance of having green eyes. Click the sections of the square that support this conclusion.

	A	a
a	Aa	aa
a	Aa	aa

DROP-DOWN (CLOZE)

A drop-down question is an open-stem question, or incomplete statement. This type of question occurs in multiple-choice questions as well. However, in a drop-down question, rather than selecting an answer from the A – D options that appear after the statement, a drop-down box with multiple response options is embedded in the statement. You will select the appropriate word or phrase, which will fill in the blank. You can then read the complete statement to check the accuracy of your response. For example, a question might read, *Bananas are*, followed by a drop-down box with several colors listed—blue, red, yellow, green. You would click yellow, and the statement would then read, *Bananas are yellow*.

On the Mathematics subtest, drop-down questions are most often used to assess math vocabulary or to compare two quantities, in which case the drop-down box will contain less than, greater than, and equal signs. For other drop-down questions, you will be asked to select the correct number to complete a statement.

On the RLA subtest, drop-down questions are used to assess mastery of language skills, such as American English conventions, standard usage, and punctuation. Drop-down questions on this subtest mimic the editing process. So multiple variations of the same phrase will appear in the drop-down box within the text, and you will select the one that is grammatically correct. It is important to read the complete sentence after your selection to ensure your choice makes sense.

On the Science and Social Studies subtests, these questions are also most often used with text. You may be asked to draw a logical conclusion from provided text-based evidence or to make a generalization based on an author's argument.

EXAMPLE

SELECT cleaned the whole kitchen and the upstairs bathrooms before going to bed.

- Karen and me
- Karen and I
- Me and Karen
- I and Karen
- Karen, me

FILL-IN-THE-BLANK (FIB)

A fill-in-the-blank (FIB) question is a combination of a standard item and a constructed response. It is similar to a drop-down question in that it contains an incomplete statement. However, rather than selecting an answer from several options, you type in the answer. Unlike a constructed response, the answer you type will be only one to two words long. Using the example in the drop-down section, if the statement read, *Bananas are*, rather than selecting from several colors, you would simply type *yellow*. FIB can only be used for questions in which the answers have very little variability (so this particular example would not actually appear on the test). Sometimes a question may have more than one blank, requiring you to type two separate responses. FIB questions assess your knowledge without the distraction of incorrect choices.

FIB questions are included in all subtests except the RLA subtest. On the Mathematics subtest, FIB questions may ask you to type a numerical answer to a math problem or to write an equation using the numbers and characters on the keyboard. On the Science subtest, an FIB question may ask you to fill in the specific quantity of something from a graphic representation of data or for a response to a specific calculation.

On the Social Studies subtest, FIB questions are used to assess your understanding of a concept or key vocabulary. Often there will be brief text from which you will have to infer the concept or vocabulary. Other questions will ask you to identify specific information—from a chart, graph, or map—that supports or demonstrates a concept, idea, or trend.

EXAMPLE

Type the appropriate year into the box.

The percent of eligible voters who actually voted in [ ] was eight percent lower than in 2004.

How is the GED Scored?

You will receive your scores on your GED tests within twenty-four hours of completing the exam.

The number of raw points each question is worth depends on the number of required answers for that question. For example, a question that requires the test-taker to select two items from a drop-down menu would be worth two raw points.

The two science constructed-response questions are scored on a three-point scale. Scores are based on scientific reasoning, the application of relevant scientific skills, and the quality of the evidence or support provided.

The written component of the Reasoning through Language Arts subtest is scored on three traits: analysis of arguments and use of evidence, development of ideas and structure, and clarity and command of standard English. Each trait can earn a raw score of up to two points.

The number of questions can vary between versions of the exam but the number of raw points remains constant. There are sixty-five raw score points on the Reasoning through Language Arts exam, forty-nine on the Mathematical Reasoning exam, forty on the Science exam, and thirty on the Social Studies exam. The total number of raw points earned is then scaled to a score between 100 and 200. You must earn at least 145 scaled score points in order to qualify for your high school equivalency credential. A score of at least 165 qualifies you as College Ready, and a score of 175 or higher qualifies you as College Ready + Credit, meaning you could qualify to receive college credit.

Each test is scored independently, and points from one test cannot affect the point value of another. You must pass each subtest in order to qualify for your high school-equivalency credential.

There is no guessing penalty on the GED exam, so you should always guess if you do not know the answer to a question.

How is the GED Administered?

The GED exam is a computer-based test offered at a wide range of sites throughout the United States and the world. To find a test center near you, check with Pearson VUE.

You will need to print your registration ticket from your online account and bring it, along with your identification, to the testing site on test day. Some test centers will require other forms or documentation, so make sure to check with your test center in advance. No pens, pencils, erasers, printed or written materials, electronic devices or calculators are allowed. An online scientific calculator will be provided to you at the time of the test as well as a formula reference sheet for the math test. Check in advance with your testing center for specific testing guidelines, including restrictions on dress and accessories.

You may take the subtests all on the same day or individually on separate days. There is no required order for completing the test. Certain jurisdictions may apply limits to the amount of time available for completing all four tests.

There are three versions of each test, so if you want to retake the test, you can do so right away up to two times. You will receive a different version of the test each time. If you still need to retake the test after the third time, you must wait sixty days. Ultimately, you may take each test up to eight times a year. If you do not pass one subtest, you are not required to retake all of the tests—only the one you failed.

About This Guide

This guide will help you to master the most important test topics and also develop critical test-taking skills. We have built features into our books to prepare you for your tests and increase your score. Along with a detailed summary of the test's format, content, and scoring, we offer an in-depth overview of the content knowledge required to pass the test. In the review you'll find sidebars that provide interesting information, highlight key concepts, and review content so that you can solidify your understanding of the exam's concepts. You can also test your knowledge with sample questions throughout the text and practice questions that reflect the content and format of the GED. We're pleased you've chosen Accepted, Inc. to be a part of your journey!

CHAPTER ONE
United States History

North America Before European Contact

Prior to European colonization, diverse Native American societies controlled the continent; they would later come into economic and diplomatic contact, and military conflict, with European colonizers and United States forces and settlers.

Major civilizations that would play an important and ongoing role in North American history included the **Iroquois** and **Algonquin** in the Northeast. Both of those tribes would also be important allies of the English and French, respectively, in future conflicts, in that part of the continent.

Later, the young United States would come into conflict with the **Shawnee**, **Lenape**, **Kickapoo**, **Miami**, and other tribes in the Midwest during early western expansion. These tribes formed the Northwest Confederacy to fight the United States.

In the South, major tribes included the **Chickasaw**, **Choctaw**, and **Creek** (Muscogee), who were the descendants of the **Mississippi Mound Builders** or Mississippian cultures, societies that built mounds from around 2,100 to 1,800 years ago as burial tombs or the bases for temples. It is thought that the **Cherokee** migrated south to present-day Georgia sometime long before European contact, where they remained until they were forcibly removed in 1832.

Farther west, tribes of the Great Plains like the **Sioux**, **Cheyenne**, **Apache**, **Comanche**, and **Arapaho** would later come into conflict with American settlers as westward expansion continued. Traditionally nomadic or semi-nomadic, these tribes depended on the **buffalo** for survival.

The **Navajo** controlled territory in the Southwest. The Navajo were descendants of the **Ancestral Pueblo** or **Anasazi**, who had settled in the Four Corners area.

In the Pacific Northwest, fishing was a major source of sustenance, and Native American peoples like the **Coast Salish** and **Chinook** created and used canoes to engage in the practice.

Ultimately, through both violent conflict and political means, Native American civilizations lost control of most of their territories and were forced onto reservations by the United States. Negotiations continue today over rights to land and opportunities and reparations for past injustices.

Colonial North America

The Americas were quickly colonized by Europeans after Christopher Columbus first laid claim to them for the Spanish, and the British, French, and Spanish all held territories in North America throughout the sixteenth, seventeenth, eighteenth, and nineteenth centuries.

Spanish ***conquistadors*** explored what is today the Southwestern United States, claiming land inhabited by local tribes for Spain. Spanish colonization not only included the control and settlement of land but also the mission to spread Christianity. The Spanish Crown granted ***encomiendas***, land grants to individuals to establish settlements, allowing the holder to ranch or mine the land and demand tribute and forced labor from local Native peoples.

Forced labor and diseases like **smallpox** had decimated Native American populations in Mexico and the Southwest. Consequently, to exploit these resource-rich lands, Spanish colonizers took part in the European-driven **trans-Atlantic slave trade**, kidnapping African people or purchasing them on the West African coast, bringing them to the Americas, and forcing them into slavery in mines and plantations in the Western Hemisphere.

DID YOU KNOW?
Eventually France would control much of the Great Lakes and the Mississippi region through Louisiana and New Orleans, valuable trade routes. French explorers included **Jacques Cartier** and **Samuel de Champlain**, who founded New France.

Unlike Spain, which sought not only profit but also to settle the land and convert Native Americans to Christianity, France was mainly focused on trade. French explorers reached the Northeast and the eastern Great Lakes region as early as the seventeenth century in search of fur and beaver pelts.

While the Spanish and French arrived generally as single men for trade, who would intermarry with local inhabitants, the English brought their families and settled in North America, with the goal of establishing agricultural settlements. In the sixteenth century, Sir Walter Raleigh established the Roanoke colony in present-day Virginia; while this settlement disappeared by 1590, interest in colonization reemerged as **joint-stock companies** sought royal charters to privately develop colonies on the North American Atlantic coast.

The first established colony, **Jamestown**, was also located in Virginia, which became so profitable that the English Crown took it over as a colony in 1624. Tobacco and rice grew in Virginia, the Carolinas, and Georgia. Appropriate for plantation farming, these crops required unskilled labor, and the southern colonies became socially stratified, with a society composed mainly of large numbers of enslaved Africans, indentured servants, and landowners.

In New England, **Separatists**, members of the Church of England who believed it had strayed too far from its theological roots, had come to North America seeking more religious freedom. The first group of Separatists, the Pilgrims, arrived on the *Mayflower* in 1620 and had drawn up the **Mayflower Compact**, guaranteeing government by the consent of the governed. They were later joined by the **Puritans**, who had been persecuted in England. These philosophies would later inform the American Revolution.

Despite differences from the South, social stratification existed in New England as well: according to Puritan belief, wealth and success showed that one was a member of the **elect**, or privileged by God. Poorer farmers were generally tenant farmers; they did not own land and rarely made a profit.

The North American colonial economy was part of the **Atlantic World**, taking part in the **triangular trade** between the Americas, Africa and Europe, where people from Africa who were enslaved were exchanged in the Americas for raw materials shipped to Europe to be processed into goods for the benefit of the colonial powers. Sometimes those goods were also exchanged for slaves in Africa. In this way, North America was part of the **Columbian Exchange**, the intersection of goods and people throughout the Atlantic World.

DID YOU KNOW?
The mid-Atlantic colonies were also founded on the basis of religious tolerance in the Quaker spirit inspired by the Quaker William Penn.

British policy toward the Colonies had been one of **salutary neglect**, allowing them great autonomy. However, an emerging culture of independence in the Thirteen Colonies caught the attention of the British Crown; it passed the **Navigation Acts** in 1651 to prevent colonial trade with any other countries. An early sign of colonial discontent, **Bacon's Rebellion** in 1676 against Governor Berkeley of Virginia embodied the growing resentment of landowners, who wanted to increase their own profit rather than redirect revenue to Britain.

American colonists were also increasingly influenced by Enlightenment thought. John Locke's ***Second Treatise*** was published in 1689; critical of absolute monarchy, it became popular in the Colonies. Locke argued for **republicanism**: that the people must come together to create a government for the protection of themselves and their property, thereby giving up some of their natural rights. However, should the government overstep its bounds, the people have the right to overthrow it and replace it.

In the mid-eighteenth century, a sense of religious fervor called the **Great Awakening** spread throughout the Colonies; people became devoted to God beyond the confines of traditional Christianity. The Great Awakening helped develop a more singularly

North American religious culture. It also created a divide between traditional European Christianity and emerging North American faiths.

Meanwhile, North America served also as a battleground for France and England, already in conflict in Europe and elsewhere. In the mid-seventeenth century, the two colonial powers fought the proxy Beaver and Chickasaw wars in alliances with Native American tribes in the Northeast and Southeast.

The Seven Years' War broke out in Europe in 1756; this conflict between the British and French in North America was known as the **French and Indian War**. Following defeats by strong colonial military leaders like **George Washington** and despite its strong alliances and long-term presence on the continent, France eventually surrendered. Britain gained control of French territories in North America—as well as Spanish Florida—in the 1763 **Treaty of Paris** which ended the Seven Years' War. In the Proclamation of 1763, Britain also promised Native American tribes that it would not expand its colonies farther west.

Revolution and the Early United States

As a result of the French and Indian War and subsequent unrest, Britain once again discarded its colonial policy of salutary neglect. Furthermore, Britain was in desperate need of cash, as the war had nearly bankrupted the country. The Crown sought ways to increase its revenue from the Colonies.

King George III enforced heavy taxes and restrictive acts in the colonies to generate income for the Crown and punish disobedience. These included the **Sugar Act** in 1764 and the **Quartering Act**, requiring colonists to provide shelter to British troops stationed in the region.

The 1765 **Stamp Act**, the first direct tax on the colonists, triggered more tensions. Any document required a costly stamp, the revenue reverting to the British government.

As a result, colonists began boycotting British goods and engaging in violent protest. In response, officials enforced the punitive **Townshend Acts** which imposed more taxes and restrictions on the colonies. Samuel Adams continued to stir up rebellion with his **Committees of Correspondence**, which distributed anti-British propaganda.

Protests against the Quartering Act in Boston led to the **Boston Massacre** in 1770, when British troops fired on a crowd of protesters. By 1773, colonists protested the latest taxes on tea levied by the **Tea Act** in the famous **Boston Tea Party** by dressing as Native Americans and tossing tea off a ship in Boston Harbor. In response, the government passed the **Intolerable Acts**, closing Boston Harbor and bringing Massachusetts back under direct royal control.

In response to the Intolerable Acts, colonial leaders met in Philadelphia at the **First Continental Congress** in 1774 and issued the ***Declaration of Rights and***

Grievances, presenting colonial concerns to the King, who ignored it. However, violent conflict began in 1775 at **Lexington and Concord**, when American militiamen (**minutemen**) had gathered to resist British efforts to seize weapons and arrest rebels in Concord. On June 17, 1775, the Americans fought the British at the **Battle of Bunker Hill**; despite American losses, the number of casualties the rebels inflicted caused the king to declare that the colonies were in rebellion. Troops were deployed to the colonies; the Siege of Boston began.

In May 1775, the **Second Continental Congress** met at Philadelphia to debate the way forward. Debate between the wisdom of continued efforts at compromise and negotiations and declaring independence continued. **Thomas Paine** published his pamphlet ***Common Sense***; taking Locke's concepts of natural rights and the obligation of a people to rebel against an oppressive government, it popularized the notion of rebellion against Britain.

By summer of 1776, the Continental Congress agreed on the need to break from Britain; on July 4, 1776, it declared the independence of the United States of America and issued the **Declaration of Independence**, drafted mainly by **Thomas Jefferson** and heavily influenced by Locke. Pro-revolution Americans were known as **Patriots**; those against were **Tories**. The American Revolution had begun.

George Washington was appointed head of the Continental Army and led a largely unpaid and unprofessional army; despite early losses and the military and financial superiority of the British, Washington and the colonists gained ground due to strong leadership, superior knowledge of the land, and international support. In the 1783 **Treaty of Paris**, the United States was recognized as a country. The American Revolution would go on to inspire revolution around the world.

Joy in the victory over Great Britain was short-lived. Fearful of tyranny, the Second Continental Congress had provided for only a weak central government, adopting the **Articles of Confederation** to organize the Thirteen Colonies—now states—as a loosely united country. However, it soon became clear that the Articles of Confederation were not strong enough to keep the nation united.

Alexander Hamilton and **James Madison** called for a **Constitutional Convention** to write a Constitution as the foundation of a stronger federal government. Madison and other **Federalists** like **John Adams** believed in **separation of powers**, republicanism, and a strong federal government.

Despite the separation of powers provided for in the Constitution, **Anti-Federalists** like **Thomas Jefferson** called for even more limitations on the power of the federal government. The first ten amendments to the Constitution, or the **Bill of Rights**, a list of guarantees of American freedoms, was a

DID YOU KNOW?

The new country was heavily in debt. Currency was weak, and high taxes led to instability in the form of minor rebellions like **Shays' Rebellion**, a revolt of indebted farmers, and the **Whiskey Rebellion**. Furthermore, debt and disorganization made the country appear weak and vulnerable to Great Britain and Spain. If the United States was to remain one country, it needed a stronger federal government.

concession to the anti-Federalists, who would later become the **Democratic-Republican Party** (eventually, the Democratic Party).

In order to convince the states to ratify the Constitution, Hamilton, Madison, and John Jay wrote the ***Federalist Papers***, articulating the benefits of federalism. Likewise, the Bill of Rights helped convince the hesitant. In 1791, the Constitution was ratified. **George Washington** was elected president, with John Adams serving as vice president; Washington appointed Hamilton as Secretary of the Treasury and Jefferson as Secretary of State.

Federalists favored taxation and centralized financial management, which Anti-Federalists—who became known as **Democratic-Republicans**—vehemently opposed. The US tried to remain neutral in international affairs but was accosted by Britain and France at sea and in conflict in the Northwest Indian Wars.

In President Washington's **Farewell Address**, he recommended the United States follow a policy of neutrality in international affairs, setting a precedent for early American history. Vice President John Adams, a Federalist, became the second president.

During the Adams administration, the Federalists passed the harsh **Alien and Sedition Acts** that increased executive power. Divisions between the Federalists and the Democratic-Republicans were deeper than ever and the presidential elections of 1800 were tense and controversial; nevertheless, Thomas Jefferson was elected to the presidency in 1801 in a historical non-violent transfer of power.

Jefferson shrank the federal government. The Alien and Sedition Acts were repealed. Economic policies favored small farmers and landowners, in contrast to Federalist policies, which supported big business and cities. However, Jefferson also oversaw the **Louisiana Purchase**, which nearly doubled the size of the United States. This troubled

Figure 1.1. Louisiana Purchase

some Democratic-Republicans, who saw this as federal overreach, but the Louisiana Purchase would be a major step forward in westward expansion.

Continuing British provocation at sea and in the northwest led to the **War of 1812**. Growing nationalism in the United States pressured Madison into pushing for war after the **Battle of Tippecanoe** in Indiana, when **General William Henry Harrison** fought the **Northwest Confederacy**, a group of tribes led by the Shawnee leader **Tecumseh**. Despite the Confederacy's alliance with Britain, the United States prevailed. Congress declared war under Madison with the intent to defend the United States, end chaotic trade practices and treatment of Americans on the high seas, and penetrate British Canada.

The war resulted in no real gains or losses for either the Americans or the British. Yet at the war's end, the United States had successfully defended itself as a country and reaffirmed its independence. Patriotism ran high.

With the Louisiana Purchase, the country had almost doubled in size. In the nineteenth century, the idea of **manifest destiny**, or the sense that it was the fate of the United States to expand westward and settle the continent, prevailed. The **Monroe Doctrine**, James Monroe's policy that the Western Hemisphere was "closed" to any further European colonization or exploration, asserted US hegemony in the region.

Westward expansion triggered questions about the expansion of slavery, a divisive issue. Slavery was profitable for the southern states which depended on the plantation economy, but increasingly condemned in the North with the growing **abolitionist** movement. The **Missouri Compromise**, also known as the **Compromise of 1820**, allowed Missouri to join the union as a slave state, but provided that any other states north of the **thirty-sixth parallel (36°30')** would be free. However, more tension and compromises over the nature of slavery in the West were to come.

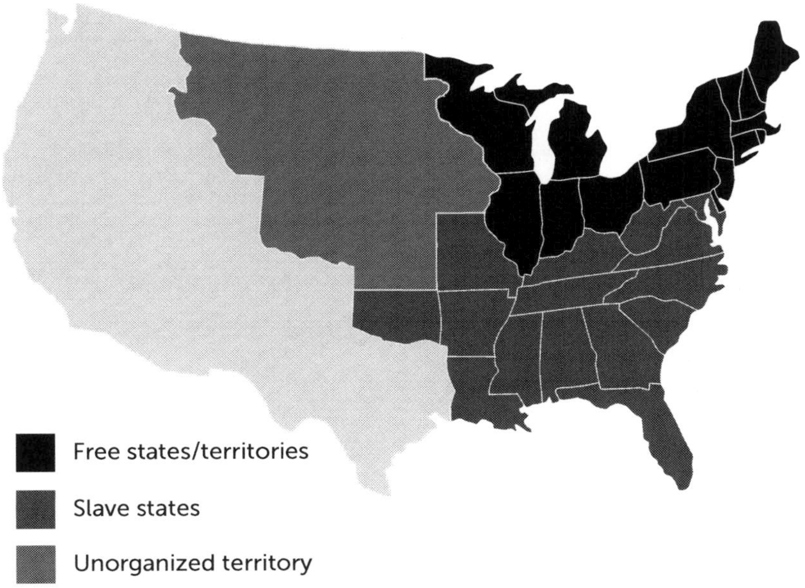

Figure 1.2. Missouri Compromise

Demographics were changing throughout the early nineteenth century. Technological advances such as the **COTTON GIN** had allowed exponential increases in cotton; therefore, more persons were enslaved than ever before, bringing more urgency to the issue of slavery. In addition, **IMMIGRATION** from Europe to the United States was increasing—mainly Irish Catholics and Germans. Reactionary **NATIVIST** movements like the **KNOW-NOTHING PARTY** feared the influx of non-Anglo Europeans, particularly Catholics, and discrimination was widespread, especially against the Irish. Other technological advances like the **RAILROADS** and **STEAMSHIPS** were speeding up westward expansion and improving trade throughout the continent; a large-scale **MARKET ECONOMY** was emerging. With early industrialization and changing concepts following the Second Great Awakening, women were playing a larger role in society, even though they could not vote.

Most states had extended voting rights to white men who did not own land or substantial property: **UNIVERSAL MANHOOD SUFFRAGE.** Elected officials would increasingly come to better reflect the electorate, and the brash war hero Andrew Jackson was popular among the "common man." During this period, the **TWO-PARTY SYSTEM** also emerged.

Jackson's popularity with the "common man," white, male farmers and workers who felt he identified with them, and the fact that owning property was no longer a requirement to vote, gave him the advantage and a two-term presidency. Jackson rewarded his supporters, appointing them to important positions as part of the **SPOILS SYSTEM.**

Jackson's administration faced economic crises that exacerbated divisions between northern, industrial interests that supported tariffs, and southern, agrarian interests that opposed them. Jackson also supported further continental expansion, which brought conflict with Native Americans. The 1830 **INDIAN REMOVAL ACT** forced thousands of people to travel mainly on foot, with all of their belongings, to Indian Territory (today, Oklahoma) on the infamous **TRAIL OF TEARS**, to make way for white settlers.

EXAMPLE

1. What advantage did the colonists have in the American Revolution?

A) vast financial wealth and resources

B) superior weaponry and equipment

C) strong leadership and knowledge of the terrain

D) a professional military and access to mercenaries

Civil War and Westward Expansion

In 1845, Texas, which had declared independence from Mexico in 1836, joined the Union; this event, in the context of US westward expansion, triggered the **MEXICAN-**

American War. As a result, the United States obtained territory in the Southwest, including gold-rich California. The population of California would grow rapidly with the **gold rush** as prospectors in search of gold headed west to try their fortunes. However, Californians of Hispanic descent who had lived in the region under Mexico lost their land and also suffered from racial and ethnic discrimination.

Meanwhile, social change in the Northeast and growing Midwest continued. As the market economy and early industry developed, so did an early **middle class**. Activists like **Susan B. Anthony** and **Elizabeth Cady Stanton** worked for women's rights. Women were also active in the temperance movement.

Reform movements continued to include abolitionism, which ranged from moderate to radical. An activist leader and writer, slave **Frederick Douglass** publicized the movement along with the American Anti-Slavery Society and publications like Harriet Beecher Stowe's *Uncle Tom's Cabin*. The radical abolitionist **John Brown** led violent protests against slavery.

Competing factions in Congress had continued to battle over the expansion of slavery, resulting in the unsuccessful 1846 **Wilmot Proviso**; the **Compromise of 1850**, which admitted the populous California as a free state; and the **Fugitive Slave Act**, which allowed slave owners to pursue escaped slaves to free states and recapture them. Congress passed the **Kansas-Nebraska Act of 1854** effectively repealing the Missouri Compromise. Violence broke out in Kansas between pro- and anti-slavery factions in what became known as **Bleeding Kansas**.

In 1856, an escaped slave, **Dred Scott**, took his case to the Supreme Court to sue for freedom. The Court upheld the Fugitive Slave Act, nullified the Missouri Compromise, and essentially decreed that African Americans were not entitled to rights under US citizenship.

In 1858, a series of debates between Illinois senate candidates, Republican **Abraham Lincoln** and Democrat **Stephen Douglas**, showed the deep divides in the nation over slavery and states' rights. During the **Lincoln-Douglas Debates**, Lincoln spoke out against slavery, while Douglas supported the right of states to decide its legality on their own. In 1860, Lincoln was elected to the presidency. Given Lincoln's outspoken stance against slavery, South Carolina seceded immediately thereafter, followed by Mississippi, Alabama, Florida, Louisiana, Georgia, and Texas. They formed the Confederate States of America, or the **Confederacy**, on February 1, 1861.

Shortly after secession, Confederate forces attacked Union troops in Charleston Harbor, South Carolina; the **Battle of Fort Sumter** sparked the Civil War. As a result, Virginia, Tennessee, North Carolina, and Arkansas seceded and joined the Confederacy.

The Confederacy had experienced military leadership and vast territory. The Union had a larger population (strengthened by

DID YOU KNOW?
Gettysburg, Pennsylvania, was the site of the bloodiest battle in US history up to that point. President Lincoln later delivered the Gettysburg Address there, in which he framed the Civil War as a battle for human rights and equality.

immigration) and stronger industrial capacity (including weapons-making capacity). Both sides believed the conflict would be short-lived; however it became clear that the war would not end quickly.

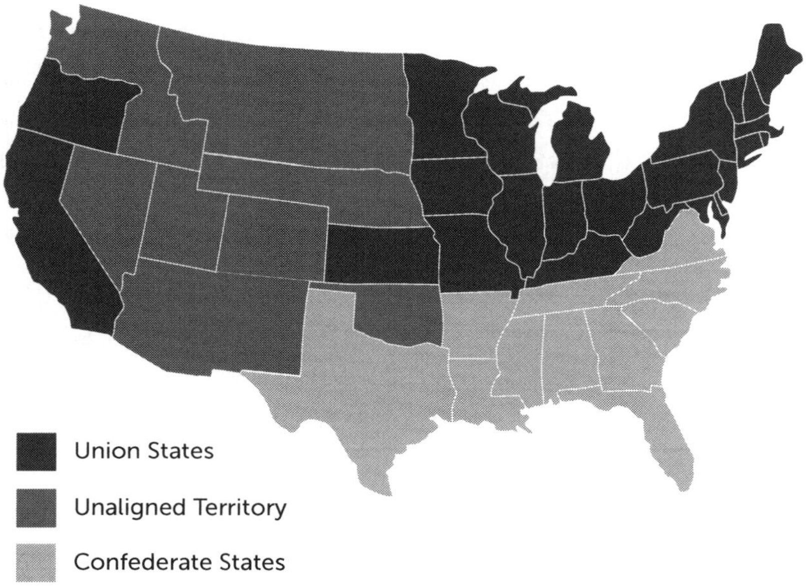

Figure 1.3. Union and Confederacy

The Union developed a blockade to prevent the Confederacy from trading internationally, since the South depended on international cotton trade for much of its income. Several years of bloody battles and economic stagnation resulted in Confederate surrender at Appomattox, Virginia, on April 9, 1865, where General Lee surrendered to General Grant. The war ended shortly after and **Reconstruction** began.

On January 1, 1863, President Lincoln had already decreed the end of slavery in the rebel states with the **Emancipation Proclamation**. Before his assassination just a few days after Confederate surrender, Lincoln had crafted the **Ten Percent Plan** permitting a Southern state's readmission to the Union if ten percent of the population swore allegiance to the Union. However Lincoln's vice president, Andrew Johnson, enforced Reconstruction weakly and the white supremacist **Ku Klux Klan** emerged; likewise, states developed the oppressive **Black Codes** to limit the rights of African Americans.

Congress passed the **Civil Rights Act** in 1866, granting citizenship to African Americans and guaranteeing African American men the same rights as white men (later reaffirmed by the **Fourteenth Amendment**). Eventually former Confederate states also had to ratify the 1865 **Thirteenth Amendment**, which abolished slavery; the **Fourteenth Amendment**, which upheld the provisions of the Civil Rights Act; and the **Fifteenth Amendment**, which in 1870 granted African American men the right to vote.

In 1867, a Republican-led Congress passed the **Reconstruction Acts**, placing former Confederate states under the control of the US Army, effectively declaring martial law, but modernizing Southern education systems, tax collection, and infrastructure. The **Freedmen's Bureau** was tasked with assisting freed slaves in the South.

While enslaved African Americans had been freed, many were not aware of this; others still remained voluntarily or involuntarily on plantations. All slaves were eventually freed; however, few had education or skills. Furthermore, oppressive social structures remained: the **Jim Crow laws** enforced **segregation** in the South. In 1896, the Supreme Court upheld segregation in ***Plessy v. Ferguson*** when a mixed-race man, Homer Plessy, was forced off a whites-only train car. When Plessy challenged the law, the Court held that segregation was, indeed, constitutional; according to the Court, *separate but equal* did still ensure equality under the law. This would remain the law until ***Brown v. Board of Education*** in 1954.

Resentment over the Reconstruction Acts never truly subsided, and military control of the South finally ended with the **Compromise of 1877**, which resolved the disputed presidential election of 1876, granting Rutherford B. Hayes the presidency and removing Union troops from the South.

While the Civil War raged, and during the chaotic post-war Reconstruction period, settlement of the West continued. California had already grown in population due to the gold rush. In the mid-nineteenth century, **Chinese immigrants** came in large numbers to California. While Chinese Americans faced racism, Americans of European descent were encouraged to settle the Frontier by the **Homestead Act of 1862**. Meanwhile, ranching and herding cattle became popular and profitable. White settlers also hunted the buffalo; mass buffalo killings threatened Native American survival.

DID YOU KNOW?

Americans of Asian descent moved beyond California and settled in western cities like Denver. They were an important part of the labor force that built the transcontinental railroads.

Meanwhile, the Great Plains and Rockies were already populated with the Sioux, Cheyenne, Apache, Comanche, Arapaho, Pawnee, and others. Conflict between Native American tribes and white settlers was ongoing. The **Ghost Dance Movement** united Plains tribes in a spiritual movement and in the belief that whites would eventually be driven from the land. In 1890, the military forced the Sioux to cease this ritual; the outcome was a massacre at **Wounded Knee** and the death of the Sioux chief, **Sitting Bull.**

In 1887, the **Dawes Act** ended federal recognition of tribes, withdrew tribal land rights, and forced the sale of reservations—tribal land. It also dissolved Native American families: children were sent to boarding schools, where they were forced to assimilate to the dominant American culture.

Back in the Northeast, the market economy and industry were flourishing. The **Gilded Age** saw an era of rapidly growing income inequality, justified by theories like **Social Darwinism** and the **Gospel of Wealth**, which argued that the wealthy had been made rich by God and were socially more deserving of it.

EXAMPLE

2. Following the Civil War, the United States ratified the Thirteenth, Fourteenth and Fifteenth Amendments to the Constitution. What did these amendments guarantee?

A) an end to slavery, equal rights for all Americans, and voting rights for all Americans, respectively

B) an end to slavery, equal rights for all Americans, and voting rights for all African Americans, respectively

C) an end to slavery, equal rights for all American men, and voting rights for all African American men, respectively

D) an end to slavery, equal rights for Americans, and voting rights for African American men, respectively

Industrialization and the Progressive Era

Following the war, the **INDUSTRIAL REVOLUTION** accelerated in the United States. The Industrial Revolution had begun on the global level with textile production in Great Britain, had been fueled in great part by supplies of Southern cotton, and was evolving in the United States with the development of heavy industry—what would come to be called the **SECOND INDUSTRIAL REVOLUTION**. Westward expansion required railroads; railroads required steel, and industrial production required oil: all these commodities spurred the rise of powerful companies like John D. Rockefeller's Standard Oil and Andrew Carnegie's US Steel.

The creation of **MONOPOLIES** and **TRUSTS** helped industrial leaders consolidate their control over the entire economy. **MONOPOLIES** let the same business leaders control the market for their own products. Business leaders in varying industries (monopolies) organized into **TRUSTS**, ensuring their control over each other's industries.

With limited governmental controls or interference in the economy, American **CAPITALISM**—the free market system—was dominated by the elite. Government corruption led only to weak restrictive legislation like the **INTERSTATE COMMERCE ACT** of 1887, which was to regulate the railroad industry, and the **SHERMAN ANTITRUST ACT** (1890), which was intended to break up monopolies and trusts, in order to allow for a fairer marketplace. However, these measures would remain largely toothless until President Theodore Roosevelt's "trust-busting" administration in 1901.

To continue fueling economic growth, the United States needed more markets abroad. ***NEW IMPERIALISM*** described the US approach to nineteenth and early twentieth century imperialism as practiced by the European powers. Rather than controlling territory as the European powers did, the US sought economic connections with countries around the world.

While the free markets and trade of the **CAPITALIST** economy spurred national economic and industrial growth, the **WORKING CLASS**, many of whom were immigrants, suffered from dangerous working conditions and other abuses. As the railroads expanded westward, white farmers, Native Americans, and Mexican Americans suffered: they lost their land to corporate interests. African Americans in the South, though freed from slavery, were also struggling under **SHARECROPPING**, in which many worked the same land owned by former slaveholders, leasing land and equipment at unreasonable rates and unable to profit.

The **PEOPLE'S (POPULIST) PARTY** formed in response to corruption and industrialization injurious to farmers (later, it would also support reform in favor of the working class and women and children). Farmers were also concerned about fiscal policy and debt.

At the same time, the **LABOR MOVEMENT** emerged to support mistreated industrial workers in urban areas using **STRIKES** and **COLLECTIVE BARGAINING** to gain protections and fair pay for the unskilled workers who had come to cities seeking industrial jobs. With the continual rise of the **MIDDLE CLASS**, women took a more active role in advocating for the poor and for themselves. Women activists also aligned with labor and the emerging **PROGRESSIVE MOVEMENT** to ensure better treatment for workers and immigrants.

With the Progressive **THEODORE ROOSEVELT'S** ascension to the presidency in 1901, the Progressive Era reached its apex. The ***TRUST-BUSTER*** Roosevelt broke up monopolies and obtained fairer treatment for workers. The Progressive Era also saw a series of acts to protect workers, health, farmers, and children.

DID YOU KNOW?

Jacob Riis' groundbreaking book and photo essay *How the Other Half Lives* revealed the squalor and poverty the poor urban classes endured, leading to more public calls for reform. Check it out to get a better understanding of life in the early twentieth century and prepare for images you might see on GED questions. It's available online for free!

Roosevelt also continued overseas expansion following McKinley's **SPANISH-AMERICAN WAR** (1898 – 1901), in which the US gained control over Spanish territory in the Caribbean, Asia, and the South Pacific. The **ROOSEVELT COROLLARY** to the Monroe Doctrine promised US intervention in Latin America in case of European aggression, asserting US dominance in the region.

EXAMPLE

3. Workers organized labor unions for all of the following reasons EXCEPT

- **A)** not being paid fairly for their work
- **B)** shifts that were frequently twelve to fourteen hours a day
- **C)** to overthrow capitalists like Carnegie and Rockefeller
- **D)** dangerous working conditions

The United States Becomes a Global Power

Debate had arisen within the US between **INTERVENTIONISM** and **ISOLATIONISM**—whether the US should intervene in international matters or not. Interventionists believed in spreading US-style democracy, while isolationists believed in focusing on development at home. This debate became more pronounced with the outbreak of World War I in Europe.

Several inflammatory events triggered US intervention in WWI. With victory in 1918, the US had proven itself a superior global military and industrial power. Interventionist **PRESIDENT WOODROW WILSON** played an important role in negotiating the peace. However, divisions between interventionists and isolationists continued.

On the home front, fear of homegrown radicals—particularly of communists and anarchists—and xenophobia against immigrants led to the **RED SCARE** in 1919 and a series of anti-immigration laws. In response to widespread xenophobia and a sentiment of isolationism following the First World War, Congress limited immigration specifically from Asia, Africa, Eastern Europe, and Southern Europe with the racist **EMERGENCY QUOTA ACT** of 1921 and **NATIONAL ORIGINS ACT** of 1924.

The **GREAT MIGRATION** of African Americans to the North that had begun after the Civil War continued, but tensions increased with urban race riots in 1919. In the South, the Ku Klux Klan was growing in power, and blacks faced intimidation, violence, and death. **LYNCHINGS**, in which African Americans were kidnapped and murdered, sometimes publicly, occurred frequently. At the same time, African American culture flourished with the **HARLEM RENAISSANCE** and become an integral part of a growing American popular culture.

Following WWI, the United States had experienced an era of consumerism and corruption. The government sponsored **LAISSEZ-FAIRE** policies and supported **MANUFACTURING**, flooding markets with cheap consumer goods. Union membership suffered; so did farmers, due to falling crop prices. While mass-production helped the emerging middle class afford more consumer goods and improve their living standards, many families resorted to **CREDIT** to fuel consumer spending. These risky consumer loans, **OVERSPECULATION** on crops and the value of farmland, and weak banking protections helped bring about the **GREAT DEPRESSION**. On October 29, 1929, or ***BLACK TUESDAY***, the stock market collapsed. During the same time period, a major drought occurred in the Great Plains, affecting farmers throughout the region. Millions of Americans faced unemployment and poverty.

DID YOU KNOW?

Japanese-Americans faced oppression and discrimination at home simply due to their race. Forced into internment camps, Japanese Americans challenged this violation of their rights in *Korematsu v. US*; however, the Supreme Court ruled that this forced displacement was constitutional. In 1988, the US government apologized for its actions.

Following weak responses by the Hoover administration, **FRANKLIN DELANO ROOSEVELT** was elected to the presidency in 1932. FDR offered Americans a ***NEW DEAL***: a plan to bring the country out of the Depression. During the ***First Hundred Days*** of FDR's administration, a series of emergency acts (known as an ***alphabet soup*** of acts due to their many acronyms) was passed for the immediate repair of the banking system. A number of acts also provided relief to the poor and unemployed.

Figure 1.4. Soup Kitchen During the Great Depression

The entire world suffered from the Great Depression, and Europe became increasingly unstable. With the rise of the radical Nazi Party in Germany, the Nazi leader Adolf Hitler led German takeovers of several European countries and became a threat to US allies, bombing Britain. However, the United States, weakened by the Great Depression and reluctant to engage in international affairs due to continuing public and political support for isolationism, remained militarily uncommitted in the war.

After the Japanese attack on **Pearl Harbor** on December 7, 1941, the US entered World War II on the side of the Allies in Europe and the Pacific. The war ended with Japanese surrender in 1945 after the US bombed the Japanese cities **Hiroshima** and **Nagasaki**, the only times that **atomic weapons** have been used in conflict. With most of Europe destroyed, the victorious United States and the Soviet Union emerged as the two global **superpowers**.

The US-led **Marshall Plan** was a program to rebuild Europe, but the USSR consolidated its presence and power in eastern European countries, forcing them to reject aid from the Marshall Plan. This division would destroy the alliance between the Soviets and the West, leading to the **Cold War** between the two superpowers and the emergence of a **bipolar world**.

With the collapse of the relationship between the USSR and the US, distrust and fear of **communism** grew. Accusations of communist sympathies against public figures ran rampant during the **McCarthy Era** in the 1950s, reflecting domestic anxieties.

President Harry S. Truman's **Truman Doctrine** stated that the US would support any country threatened by authoritarianism (communism), leading to the **Korean War** (1950 – 1953), a conflict between the US and Soviet-backed North Korean forces, which ended in a stalemate. The policy of **containment**, to contain Soviet (communist) expansion, defined US foreign policy. According to **domino theory**, once one country fell to communism, others would quickly follow.

Meanwhile, in Southeast Asia, communist forces in North Vietnam were gaining power. Congress never formally declared war in Vietnam but gave the president authority to intervene militarily there through the **Gulf of Tonkin Resolution** (1964). However, the resulting protracted conflict—the **Vietnam War**—also led to widespread domestic social unrest.

EXAMPLE

4. How did the United States change in the 1920s?

A) The Great Migration ceased.

B) African American culture became increasingly influential.

C) The Great Depression caused high unemployment.

D) Thanks to the New Deal, millions of Americans found jobs.

Postwar and Contemporary United States

During the 1960s, the US experienced social and political change, starting with the election of the young and charismatic **John F. Kennedy** in 1960. Kennedy and his successor after his assassination, **Lyndon B. Johnson**, embraced **liberalism**, believing that government should fight poverty at home, and play an interventionist role abroad (in this era, by fighting communism). **Johnson**'s administration envisioned a **Great Society**, passing legislation in support of the poor and of civil rights in the tradition of the Progressives. Johnson launched a **War on Poverty**, passing reform legislation to support the poor, providing housing, health care, and education.

The **Civil Rights Movement**, led by activists like the **Rev. Dr. Martin Luther King, Jr.** and **Malcolm X**, fought for African American rights in the South, including the abolition of segregation, and also for better living standards for blacks in northern cities. Civil rights came to the forefront with the 1954 Supreme Court case ***Brown v. Board of Education***, when the Court found segregation unconstitutional.

Civil rights became a major domestic political issue with widespread public support. Civil rights workers organized the **March on Washington** in 1963, when Dr. King delivered his famous ***I Have a Dream*** speech. In 1964, Congress passed the **Civil Rights Act**, which outlawed segregation. However, African Americans' voting rights were still not sufficiently protected. In 1965, led by President Lyndon B. Johnson, Congress passed the **Voting Rights Act**, which forbade restrictions impeding the ability of African Americans to vote.

Figure 1.5. March on Washington

The Civil Rights Movement extended beyond the Deep South. **Cesar Chavez** founded the **United Farm Workers (UFW)**, which organized Hispanic and migrant farm workers in California and the Southwest to advocate for unionizing and collective bargaining. The Civil Rights Movement also included **feminist** activists who fought for fairer treatment of women in the workplace and for women's reproductive rights. The

American Indian Movement (AIM) addressed injustices and discrimination suffered by Native Americans, achieving more tribal autonomy. The 1969 **Stonewall riots** occurred in New York City in response to police repression of the gay community. These riots and subsequent organized activism are seen as the beginning of the LGBT rights movement.

DID YOU KNOW?

At the same time, LBJ's overseas agenda in Vietnam was increasingly unpopular due to high casualties, the draft (which forced young American males to fight overseas) and what seemed to many to be the purposelessness of the war. Protests swept the nation against the war, and popular counterculture usurped government authority and challenged traditional values.

Conservatism strengthened in response to the heavy role of government in public life throughout the 1960s, high rates of government spending, and social challenges to traditional values. During the administration of the conservative President **Richard Nixon**, the conflict in Vietnam ended and a diplomatic relationship with China began. Nixon also oversaw economic reforms. However, the **Watergate scandal**, when the president was involved in a break-in at the headquarters of the **Democratic National Committee**, forced Nixon to resign. Nixon's resignation further destroyed many Americans' faith in their government.

After political and economic instability in the 1970s, the conservative president **Ronald Reagan** championed domestic tax cuts and an aggressive foreign policy against the Soviet Union. However, tax cuts forced Congress to cut or eliminate social programs that benefitted millions. Enormous military investment—the **arms race** with the Soviet Union—helped bring about the end of the Cold War with the 1991 fall of the USSR and later, a new era of globalization. It also increased government debt. Finally, the Reagan Revolution ushered in an era of conservative values in the public sphere.

With the collapse of the Soviet Union, the balance of international power changed. The bipolar world became a unipolar world, and the United States was the sole superpower. US intervention in the Middle East during the **Gulf War**, or **Operation Desert Storm** (1991)—cemented its status as the world's sole superpower.

With the election of President **Bill Clinton** in 1992, the US took an active role in international diplomacy. Society became increasingly liberal. Technology like the **internet** facilitated national and global communication, media, and business; minority groups like the LGBT community engaged in more advocacy; and environmental issues became more visible.

As part of **globalization**, the facilitation of global commerce and communication, the Clinton administration prioritized free trade. The United States signed the **North American Free Trade Agreement (NAFTA)** with Mexico and Canada, removing trade restrictions throughout North America. Many American jobs went overseas, especially manufacturing jobs, where labor was cheaper, benefitting companies but causing unemployment. Furthermore, globalization began facilitating the movement of people as methods of communication and transportation transformed. **Immigration reform** would be a major issue into the twenty-first century.

By the end of the twentieth century, the United States had established itself as the dominant global economic, military, and political power. Due to its role in global conflict from the Spanish-American War onward, the US had established a military presence worldwide. The US dominated global trade. American popular culture was widely popular.

However, globalization also facilitated global conflict. On **September 11, 2001 (9/11)**, the terrorist group **al Qaeda** attacked the US, triggering an aggressive military and foreign policy under the administration of President **George W. Bush**, who declared a ***War on Terror***, an open-ended global conflict against terrorist organizations and their supporters. The US attacked al Qaeda bases in Afghanistan. President Bush believed in the doctrine of **preemption**, that if the US was aware of a threat, it should preemptively attack the source of that threat. Preemption would drive the invasion of Iraq in 2003.

At home, Congress passed the **USA Patriot Act** to respond to fears of more terrorist attacks on US soil. This legislation gave the federal government unprecedented—and, some argued, unconstitutional—powers of surveillance over the American public.

Despite the tense climate, social liberalization continued in the US. Following the Bush administration, during which tax cuts and heavy reliance on credit helped push the country into the **Great Recession**, the first African American president, **Barack Obama**, was elected in 2008. Under his presidency, the US emerged from the recession, ended its occupations of Iraq and Afghanistan, passed the Affordable Care Act, which reformed the healthcare system, and legalized same-sex marriage. The Obama administration also oversaw the passage of consumer protection acts, increased support for students, and safety nets for homeowners.

Yet change persists in the United States. In 2016, the country was deeply divided as the television personality and real estate developer **Donald Trump** was elected president on a platform of conservatism and isolationism. However his opponent, former senator and Secretary of State **Hillary Rodham Clinton**, won the popular vote. Many Americans viewed Trump as racist and sexist, and grassroots opposition movements developed. Still, his supporters remained committed. Some argued he understood the harms of rising income inequality better than Clinton, despite her work to support the poor and working class. Some researchers believe the election showed deeper divisions among Americans than had previously been understood.

EXAMPLE

5. Which of the following BEST describes the approach taken by the Reagan administration to counter the Soviet Union?

A) bilateral diplomacy

B) direct military confrontation

C) engagement in multilateral pact such as the United Nations

D) escalation of arms production and proxy warfare

Test Your Knowledge

Read the question, and then choose the most correct answer.

1. Which of the following was a major difference between British and French colonization of the Americas?

A) French colonists tended to be single men who intermarried with local residents, while British colonists brought their entire families to settle permanently, forming insular communities.

B) British colonists tended to be single men who intermarried with local residents, while French colonists brought their entire families to settle permanently, forming insular communities.

C) French colonists were more likely to form alliances with Native American tribes, while the British shunned them.

D) British colonists had more economic interests in the Americas than the French did.

2. Why was the Mayflower Compact an important contribution to the foundation of American government?

A) It provided for equal treatment of all Christians under the law.

B) It was the first treaty between European settlers (the Pilgrims) and Native Americans.

C) It laid out terms for government with the consent of the governed.

D) It allowed people of all faiths to practice their religions freely under the law.

3. What advantage did the colonists have in the American Revolution?

A) vast financial wealth

B) superior weaponry

C) strong leadership and knowledge of the terrain

D) a professional military and access to mercenaries

4. How did the views of the Federalists and the Anti-Federalists differ during the Constitutional Convention?

A) The views of the Federalists and Anti-Federalists did not significantly differ at the Constitutional Convention.

B) The Anti-Federalists did not believe in a Constitution at all, while the Federalists insisted on including the Bill of Rights.

C) The Anti-Federalists favored a stronger Constitution and federal government, while Federalists were concerned that states would risk losing their autonomy.

D) The Federalists favored a stronger Constitution and federal government, while Anti-Federalists were concerned that states would risk losing their autonomy.

5. Why was the Louisiana Purchase controversial?

   A) Observers feared it would destabilize the relationship between the United States and France.

   B) Many people were concerned about federal overreach, given the scope of the purchase.

   C) Americans worried about maintaining stable relationships with the Native Americans living west of the Mississippi River.

   D) Citizens thought the United States could not control the enormous amount of land it had gained.

6. What was an important consequence of the War of 1812?

   A) The United States gained territory from Britain in the Northeast, including the state of Maine.

   B) The United States captured military technology from British troops fleeing the unsuccessful siege of Washington, DC.

   C) The United States purchased the Port of New Orleans from the French.

   D) The United States developed a sense of a strong national identity following its successful expulsion of the British and defense of its borders.

7. What was one reason for the election of Andrew Jackson to the presidency?

   A) Jackson was able to find a solution to the first Nullification Crisis.

   B) Allowing white men who did not own property to vote was a boon to Jackson, who was popular with the "common man."

   C) Jackson's popularity with landowners in Northern states guaranteed him the funds he needed to win the presidency.

   D) Jackson and his vice president, John C. Calhoun, were a strong and popular team when running for election.

8. Although women did not gain the right to vote until the ratification of the Nineteenth Amendment in 1920, activists like Elizabeth Cady Stanton and Susan B. Anthony began advocating for women's rights as early as the Seneca Falls Convention of 1848. Why did the women's movement gain traction in the mid-nineteenth century?

   A) European literary thought supporting women's rights became popular in the northern states.

   B) As the abolitionist movement grew, abolitionists also came to oppose the oppression of women, recognizing their limited rights under the law and in society.

   C) The development of a middle class gave some women the time and the means to engage in progressive activism.

   D) Women settling the Frontier became increasingly vocal about equality at a national level, since men and women were nominally equal in many remote, isolated western settlements.

9. The Mexican-American War resulted in which of the following gains for the United States?
   A) territory south of the Rio Grande
   B) the Southwest and California
   C) Oregon and Washington State
   D) western land including Idaho

10. Immigration to the United States, particularly from famine-hit Ireland, increased in the nineteenth century. What was one widespread response?
   A) the nativist movement, which promoted the rights of Native Americans
   B) the "Know-Nothing" movement, a nativist, anti-immigrant, anti-Catholic society
   C) the "Know-Nothing" movement, a nativist, anti-immigrant, anti-Protestant society
   D) the privileging of Chinese immigrants over white Irish immigrants

11. What did the Missouri Compromise accomplish?
   A) It admitted Missouri as a free state.
   B) It admitted California as a free state.
   C) It allowed slavery in New Mexico and Utah to be decided by popular sovereignty.
   D) It banned slavery north of the thirty-sixth parallel, so that new states formed in northern territories would be free.

12. How did the Lincoln-Douglas Debates impact the nation before the 1860 presidential election?
   A) They reflected the national mood: that the country was deeply divided over the question of slavery and whether states had the right to determine its legality.
   B) They reflected the national mood: that the country was deeply divided over the question of slavery—Lincoln called for abolition, while Douglas favored the practice.
   C) They reinvigorated the debate over slavery, which had been overshadowed by debate over states' rights.
   D) They reinvigorated the debate over states' rights, which had been overshadowed by debate over slavery.

13. In the Emancipation Proclamation, President Lincoln declared an end to slavery
   A) in Kentucky and Missouri.
   B) in the Union only.
   C) in slave states that had not seceded from the Union.
   D) in the rebel states.

14. What assets did the Confederacy have during the Civil War?

A) The Confederacy had superior weaponry and production resources.

B) The Confederacy maintained brisk trade with Europe, enabling it to fund the war.

C) The Confederacy benefitted from strong military leadership and high morale among the population.

D) The Confederacy's strong infrastructure allowed it to transport supplies and people efficiently throughout the South.

Read the following excerpt from Jefferson Davis' speech explaining his retirement from the US Senate to join Mississippi as it seceded from the United States. He would go on to become the president of the Confederacy. Answer the questions that follow.

It has been a conviction of pressing necessity, it has been a belief that we are to be deprived in the Union of the rights which our fathers bequeathed to us, which has brought Mississippi into her present decision.

She has heard proclaimed the theory that all men are created free and equal, and this made the basis of an attack upon her social institutions; and the sacred Declaration of Independence has been invoked to maintain the position of the equality of the races. That Declaration of Independence is to be construed by the circumstances and purposes for which it was made. The communities were declaring their independence...that there was no divine right to rule; that no man inherited the right to govern; that there were no classes by which power and place descended to families, but that all stations were equally within the grasp of the body-politic.

These were the great principles they announced; these were the purposes for which they made their declaration... They have no reference to the slave; else, how happened it that among the items of arraignment made against George III was that he endeavored to do just what the North has been endeavoring of late to do—to stir up insurrection among our slaves? Had the Declaration announced that negroes were free and equal, how was the prince to be arraigned for stirring up insurrection among them?

...When our Constitution was formed, the same idea was rendered more palpable, for there we find provision made for that very class of persons as property; they were not put upon the footing of equality with white men...but, so far as representation was concerned, were discriminated against as a lower caste, only to be represented in the numerical proportion of three-fifths.

– Jefferson Davis, *On Retiring from the Senate*, US Congress, Senate, Congressional Globe, 36th Congress, 2nd Session, p. 487.

15. How does Jefferson Davis use American history to justify slavery?

A) He argues that the Declaration of Independence asserted *political* equality rather than *racial* equality. He believed that no men (presumably no white men) had the right to rule over others (presumably other white men).

B) He reminds the Senate of the Three-Fifths Compromise, in which the states agreed that to count a state's population, slaves would count as three-fifths of a person (although they could not vote).

C) He reminds the Senate that King George III was accused of inciting rebellion among slaves to weaken the Revolution.

D) all of the above

16. How does Jefferson Davis describe the society of Mississippi?

A) Mississippi believed that all men were free and equal.

B) Mississippi's social institutions were based on the premise that all men were NOT free and equal.

C) Mississippi's social institutions were based on freedom and equality for all people, women and men.

D) Mississippi did not support the Declaration of Independence.

Read the following sentence from the speech and answer the question that follows.

It has been a conviction of pressing necessity, it has been a belief that we are to be deprived in the Union of the rights which our fathers bequeathed to us, which has brought Mississippi into her present decision.

17. Given how Jefferson Davis develops the text that follows this sentence, which of the following BEST explains the specific rights that Mississippi fears it will lose under the Union?

A) the right to secede from the Union

B) the right to make its own laws

C) the right to legally enslave black people

D) the right to trade internationally

18. What did the Reconstruction Acts do?

A) They immediately improved conditions for African Americans in the South.

B) They rapidly benefitted the Southern economy.

C) They were widely considered fair in Congress and by Southerners.

D) They imposed Northern military control over the South.

19. How did the US government break down tribal bonds and weaken Native American societies?

A) through policies of assimilation

B) by forcing Native American children to go to white schools and reject their cultures

C) by forcing Native Americans to move onto reservations

D) all of the above

20. The Interstate Commerce Act and the Sherman Anti-Trust Act

A) immediately went into effect to regulate the railroad industry and break up monopolies.

B) remained largely toothless until the First World War.

C) remained largely toothless until the administration of Theodore Roosevelt.

D) immediately went into effect to promote congressional efforts to regulate interstate commerce.

21. The United States remained relatively neutral in international conflicts for much of its early history. Which of the following conflicts is considered to be its first major assertion of international power overseas?

A) the Spanish-American War

B) the First World War

C) the Texan Revolution

D) the War of 1812

22. The United States entered WWI largely because of which of the following?

A) the Zimmerman Telegram

B) the rise of Nazi Germany

C) the assassination of Franz Ferdinand

D) the attack on the *Lusitania*

23. Segregation was found unconstitutional by which of the following Supreme Court decisions?

A) *Brown v. Board of Education*

B) *Plessy v. Ferguson*

C) *Scott v. Sanford*

D) *Korematsu v. US*

24. What was the relevance of the Gulf of Tonkin Resolution?

A) It gave Congress the power to declare war against the North Vietnamese forces.

B) It authorized the president to take military action against North Vietnamese forces.

C) It authorized the military to take action against North Vietnamese forces.

D) It authorized the president to take military action against South Vietnamese forces.

25. What was the significance of the Voting Rights Act of 1965?

A) It gave African Americans the right to vote in the segregated states.

B) It gave Americans under the age of twenty-one the right to vote.

C) It ended segregation in voting.

D) It ended restrictions that prevented African Americans from voting in many states with histories of institutionalized racism.

26. How did Cesar Chavez and the United Farm Workers impact Hispanic Americans?

A) They supported Mexicans who wanted to join the Bracero program and become guest workers in the United States.

B) They supported Mexican American agricultural workers in California and the Southwest and provided a foundation for later advocacy groups working for Hispanic Americans.

C) They worked on behalf of Texas farmers to coordinate agreements with agricultural workers from Mexico.

D) They worked on behalf of the California state government to negotiate temporary worker agreements with Mexico.

27. Which of the following events is generally considered to mark the beginning of the movement for LGBT civil rights in the United States?

A) the first Gay Pride marches in New York, Chicago, and San Francisco

B) the election of Harvey Milk to the San Francisco Board of Supervisors

C) activism and dialogue surrounding the AIDS crisis

D) the Stonewall Riots in New York City

28. Which of the following best explains the impact of the Watergate scandal on the United States?

A) President Nixon was impeached.

B) President Nixon declined to seek a second term of office.

C) Americans lost faith in the federal government.

D) Americans began supporting third party candidates more.

29. NAFTA accomplished which of the following?

A) opened borders between the U.S., Canada, and Mexico, allowing for free movement of goods and people between these three countries

B) initiated free trade between the US, Mexico, and Canada, facilitating and strengthening trade between these three countries

C) created a union similar to the European Union in North America, in which Canada, Mexico, and the U.S. shared similar policy goals and consulted each other on matters of shared concern

D) established common immigration procedures between Mexico, the US, and Canada

30. What was a consequence of Operation Desert Storm, the 1991 Gulf War?

A) The United States occupied Iraq.

B) Iraq occupied Kuwait under an international agreement.

C) The United States became the world's sole superpower.

D) The United States and the former Soviet Union, now represented by the Russian Federation, improved their cooperation at the United Nations.

Answer Key

EXAMPLES

1. **C) is correct.** The colonial military had strong leaders and an intimate knowledge of the terrain; many of its military leaders were born and raised in North America.

2. **D) is correct.** The Thirteenth Amendment abolished slavery; the Fourteenth Amendment promised equal protection under the law to all U.S. citizens; the Fifteenth Amendment ensured that (male) African Americans and former slaves could vote.

3. **C) is correct.** Labor unions sought improved working conditions, not the overthrow of capitalism.

4. **B) is correct.** The Harlem Renaissance is one example of the emergence of African American culture in the public imagination; as US popular culture developed, African American contributions had a strong influence.

5. **D) is correct.** The Reagan administration focused on arms buildup, weapons spending, and supporting anti-Soviet movements around the world.

TEST YOUR KNOWLEDGE

1. **A) is correct.** French colonists were generally single men seeking profit; if they stayed, they were more likely than the British to intermarry.

   B) is incorrect. The British were more likely to establish settler colonies; entire families settled and formed communities in the colonies.

   C) is incorrect. Both the British and the French formed strategic alliances with tribes as was expedient.

   D) is incorrect. Both the British and the French had major economic interests in the Americas.

2. A) is incorrect. The Mayflower Compact was written by one Christian group—Separatists.

   B) is incorrect. The Mayflower Compact articulated terms of governance among European settlers; it was not a treaty with other parties.

   C) is correct. As a governing document, the Mayflower Compact was notable in that it provided for governance with the consent of the governed, a departure from British rule.

   D) is incorrect. The Mayflower Compact was written by Separatists.

3. A) is incorrect. While some colonists were quite wealthy, colonial wealth paled in the face of British wealth.

   B) is incorrect. The colonists did not have superior weaponry.

   C) is correct. The colonial military did have strong leaders, and an intimate knowledge of the terrain, many having been born there.

   D) is incorrect. Britain had an experienced military with substantial experience fighting in Europe and elsewhere. In addition, King George III hired Hessian mercenaries from Germany to supplement British troops.

4. A) is incorrect. The views of the Federalists and Anti-Federalists differed a great deal.

   B) is incorrect. The Bill of Rights was a compromise measure; it was not originally a Federalist contribution.

   C) is incorrect. The reverse was true.

   D) is correct. The Federalists were the driving force behind a stronger Constitution that would empower the United States federal government. The Anti-Federalists favored state sovereignty and ensured the passage of the Bill of Rights to protect certain rights not explicitly guaranteed in the Constitution itself.

5. A) is incorrect. France and the early United States had a complex relationship, but this was not the central reason for US anxiety over the Louisiana Purchase.

   B) is correct. Despite Jefferson's position as an Anti-Federalist Democrat, he had used executive powers as president to negotiate the purchase without congressional consultation, considered by many to be federal overreach.

   C) is incorrect. The needs of Native Americans were not a pressing issue for most Americans; many considered strategic control of land and, eventually, westward expansion, to be necessary.

D) is incorrect. This was not the most pressing concern for most Americans, who were still preoccupied with preventing a dictatorship.

6. A) is incorrect. The United States did not win any territory in the War of 1812.

B) is incorrect. The United States made no major gains in military technology.

C) is incorrect. The United States already controlled New Orleans.

D) is correct. A spirit of patriotism pervaded among many Americans, given that the country had successfully held off the British.

7. A) is incorrect. This did not occur until after Jackson had been elected president.

B) is correct. Jackson was extremely popular among the lower classes and rural farmers of the South; universal manhood suffrage expanded the electorate, giving him a huge advantage.

C) is incorrect. Jackson was unpopular with the elite landowners of the North.

D) is incorrect. Jackson and Calhoun were fierce rivals with a poor personal and professional relationship.

8. A) is incorrect. There was no major literary movement explicitly supporting women's rights (although significant women writers like Jane Austen and the Bronte sisters wrote novels with strong female characters).

B) is incorrect. While some abolitionists also believed in improving women's rights, women's suffrage was not part of the abolitionist platform.

C) is correct. Middle and upper-middle class women had more time for activism and charity, as they did not have to work.

D) is incorrect. Women's status on the Frontier may have varied, but Frontier women did not play a major political role in the nineteenth century women's rights movement.

9. A) is incorrect. The United States never controlled the land south of the Rio Grande, which remains part of Mexico to this day.

B) is correct. Following the war, the United States took control of the Southwest (today, Arizona, New Mexico, and adjacent areas), as well as California.

C) is incorrect. These areas came under US control in the 1846 Oregon Treaty with the British.

D) is incorrect. Idaho emerged from portions of the Washington and Dakota Territories.

10. A) is incorrect. Nativists promoted the rights of white Americans who had been born in North America and whose families had been born there for generations, not Native Americans.

B) is correct. The Know-Nothings were an underground nativist and anti-immigrant group.

C) is incorrect. The Know-Nothings were particularly anti-Catholic, not anti-Protestant; immigrants from Ireland and Southern Europe were mainly

Catholic, while white Americans were mainly Protestant.

D) is incorrect. Chinese and other Asian immigrants were rarely, if ever, privileged over white immigrants.

11. A) is incorrect. The Missouri Compromise allowed slavery in Missouri.

B) is incorrect. California was not admitted as a state until 1850.

C) is incorrect. This was a feature of the Compromise of 1850.

D) is correct. The Missouri Compromise prohibited slavery north of the thirty-sixth parallel in new US territories, permitting slavery in Missouri.

12. **A) is correct.** The Lincoln-Douglas Debates showed how divided the country was over slavery.

B) is incorrect. Douglas was not so much in favor of slavery as he was a proponent of states' rights.

C) is incorrect. Slavery and states' rights were intertwined.

D) is incorrect. The question of slavery was at the root of the debate over states' rights.

13. A) is incorrect. The Emancipation Proclamation applied to rebel states; Missouri and Kentucky did not secede.

B) is incorrect. Lincoln freed the slaves in the Confederacy with the Emancipation Proclamation, not in the Union.

C) is incorrect. The Emancipation Proclamation applied to the rebel states.

D) is correct. The Emancipation Proclamation freed the slaves in the Confederacy.

14. A) is incorrect. The South's technological resources were inferior to those of the North.

B) is incorrect. European countries ceased trade with the South, finding alternative sources of cotton in protest of slavery.

C) is correct. The Confederacy had excellent military leaders; many Confederate leaders and much of the population strongly believed in the right of states to make decisions without federal interference, not only about slavery but also about trade and other issues.

D) is incorrect. The Confederacy had limited infrastructure.

15. A) is incorrect. Davis does argue that the Declaration of Independence asserted political equality, rather than racial equality, but this is not the only correct answer.

B) is incorrect. Davis does invoke the Three-Fifths Compromise, in which the states agreed that to count a state's population, slaves would count as three-fifths of a person (although they could not vote).

C) is incorrect. Davis does recall the accusations against King George III, but there is a better answer here.

D) is correct. Davis referred to all these points in his speech.

16. A) is incorrect. Davis claims the opposite.

B) is correct. Davis justifies his departure based upon the right of Mississippi as a state to maintain a society based on the premise that all men were *not* free and equal.

C) is incorrect. Davis claims the opposite, and he does not even mention women.

D) is incorrect. Davis invokes the Declaration of Independence to support his argument.

17. A) is incorrect. Davis invokes Mississippi's right to a society based on inequality; he does not express fears of being unable to secede.

B) is incorrect. Davis is worried about more than just Mississippi's right to make its own laws; he sees new interpretations of the law as a threat to Mississippi's social fabric.

C) is correct. Davis asserts that Mississippi has the right to maintain slavery, since "the theory that all men are created free and equal, and this made the basis of an attack upon her social institutions."

D) is incorrect. Davis is concerned about the interpretation of the Declaration of Independence to mean that all people, regardless of race, enjoy equality. He is not fearful of Mississippi's right to trade internationally.

18. A) is incorrect. Conditions for most freed slaves did not immediately improve; they continued to face widespread violence and discrimination.

B) is incorrect. With damage to agricultural land and existing infrastructure, the Southern economy and many Southerners suffered; Reconstruction programs did not immediately take effect.

C) is incorrect. Radical Republicans felt that the Reconstruction Acts did not go far enough in punishing the South; others in Congress felt they were too harsh. Likewise, many in the South felt they were unfair.

D) is correct. The Reconstruction Acts effectively placed the South under martial law.

19. A) is incorrect. Assimilation destroyed many people's connection with their cultures and traditions, but this answer choice is incomplete in the context of the other options.

B) is incorrect. Again, forcing children to leave their families for white schools destroyed their connection with their languages, cultures, and traditions. Moreover, these actions injured their personal bonds with their families and communities—further weakening tribal societies. However, this answer choice is insufficient, given the other answer choices available.

C) is incorrect. Forcing people to leave their homelands for assigned living spaces on reservations fostered social breakdown by interrupting traditional connections with land and dispossessing people of their homes. Again, however, this answer choice is incomplete.

D) is correct. All of the above are true.

20. A) is incorrect. The Interstate Commerce Act and the Sherman Anti-Trust Act were ineffective until the Roosevelt administration; they were even used to break up labor unions and farmer's organizations rather than for their intended purpose.

B) is incorrect. During Theodore Roosevelt's presidency, the

Interstate Commerce Act and the Sherman Anti-Trust Act were finally used to break up monopolies and to ensure a fairer marketplace.

C) is correct. It was not until Theodore Roosevelt came into office that these acts were effectively used for their intended purpose: to create a fair market in the United States by eliminating trusts and monopolies.

D) is incorrect. They were not immediately implemented.

21. **A) is correct.** The United States was the aggressor in the Spanish-American War—it was never definitively proven that the *Maine* was actually attacked by Spain. Furthermore, the war was fought in several different theaters worldwide.

B) is incorrect. The First World War took place after all these conflicts.

C) is incorrect. The Texan Revolution occurred before Texas joined the United States.

D) is incorrect. The War of 1812 was partially due to British provocations and took place entirely on US and British Canadian soil.

22. **A) is correct.** The Zimmerman Telegram, a German offer to assist Mexico in attacking the U.S., forced the United States to enter WWI, following a series of other German provocations.

B) is incorrect. Nazi Germany did not exist until the 1930s.

C) is incorrect. While the assassination of Franz Ferdinand triggered the First World War in Europe, the United States did not enter the conflict until later.

D) is incorrect. The attack on the *Lusitania* angered many Americans but did not alone trigger U.S. entry into the conflict.

23. **A) is correct.** *Brown v. Board of Education* found that keeping races separate (in this case, in segregated schools) could not ensure that all people would receive equal treatment, and that segregation was therefore unconstitutional.

B) is incorrect. *Plessy v. Ferguson* upheld segregation.

C) is incorrect. *Scott v. Sandford* upheld and strengthened the Fugitive Slave Act, thereby upholding the Kansas-Nebraska Act and effectively abolishing the Missouri Compromise.

D) is incorrect. *Korematsu v. US* ruled the constitutionality of the Japanese internment camps during WWII.

24. A) is incorrect. The Gulf of Tonkin Resolution allowed the president flexibility in committing forces. According to the Constitution, Congress has the power to declare war.

B) is correct. The Gulf of Tonkin Resolution gave the president power to commit military troops in Vietnam without Congressional authorization.

C) is incorrect. The president is the Commander in Chief, and Congress empowers the president to take lengthy military action.

D) is incorrect. The United States was allied with South Vietnamese forces.

25. A) is incorrect. Black men gained the right to vote with the Fifteenth

Amendment; black women could vote after the ratification of the Nineteenth Amendment (although in practice, African American men and women were often denied this right).

B) is incorrect. Americans eighteen years of age and older were able to vote after the ratification of the Twenty-Sixth Amendment.

C) is incorrect. Segregation in public places ended with the Civil Rights Act.

D) is correct. The Voting Rights Act abolished discriminatory restrictions that prevented African Americans from exercising their right to vote.

26. A) is incorrect. Cesar Chavez and the UFW organized Mexican and Mexican American workers already present in the United States. They focused on the rights of workers in the United States.

B) is correct. Cesar Chavez and the UFW advocated for the rights of Mexican and Mexican American farmworkers in the United States, who were often disadvantaged. The activism of the UFW set a precedent for later advocacy in support of Hispanic Americans.

C) is incorrect. Cesar Chavez and the UFW were mainly active in California and the Southwest, not Texas. Furthermore, they advocated for workers, not farmers.

D) is incorrect. Cesar Chavez and the UFW did not work for any government; they organized and supported farm workers in the United States.

27. A) is incorrect. Gay Pride rallies and marches were not major features of the public landscape until after the Stonewall Riots.

B) is incorrect. Milk's election was an important development in LGBT rights as openly gay public figures were rare, but his election occurred after the Stonewall Riots.

C) is incorrect. Again, the public discourse and activism that resulted from the AIDS crisis helped bring LGBT issues into the mainstream public sphere, but these events happened in the 1980s and 1990s.

D) is correct. Generally viewed as the beginning of the LGBT rights movement, the Stonewall Riots occurred in response to ongoing police harassment of the gay community in New York City and resulted in a more organized push for civil rights.

28. A) is incorrect. President Nixon resigned.

B) is incorrect. Watergate unfolded during Nixon's second term.

C) is correct. Watergate destroyed many Americans' trust in the government, which had already been weakened after the turbulent 1960s and the Vietnam War.

D) is incorrect. Watergate did not change the two-party system.

29. A) is incorrect. NAFTA permitted free trade among the three countries, but national borders remain, and movement of people is restricted.

B) is correct. NAFTA is a free trade agreement among the three countries.

C) is incorrect. NAFTA is not a political agreement; it is an economic one.

D) is incorrect. NAFTA is not an immigration agreement; it addresses international trade.

30. A) is incorrect. The United States did not occupy Iraq until the 2003 Iraq War.

B) is incorrect. Iraq was driven from Kuwait in 1991 by US-led forces.

C) is correct. Having led the coalition that defeated Iraq in the 1991 Gulf War, the United States proved its position as the sole superpower after the collapse of the Soviet Union.

D) is incorrect. The relationship between the United States and the Russian Federation, while not destabilized by the Gulf War, did not necessarily improve because of it.

CHAPTER TWO
Civics and Government

The Constitution

Any study of the United States government must begin with its founding document: the **Constitution**. It was written as both an expression of ideals and as a practical framework for the functioning of the country. Designed to be a "living document," the Constitution and how it is interpreted has changed in the almost 230 years since it was written. However, its core principles have not. They continue to serve as the foundation and guiding light of American government and politics. In order to understand the government that emerged from the US Constitution, it is necessary to understand its historical context.

HISTORICAL BACKGROUND

In 1781 the Second Continental Congress had convened to organize a government for the emerging nation. The colonies had broken away from Britain because of what they viewed as the oppressive rule of an overbearing central government. As a result, the first government they created, whose framework was called the **Articles of Confederation**, was intentionally weak. Called a "firm league of friendship," it was designed to create a loose confederation between the colonies (now states) while allowing them to retain much of their individual sovereignty.

As a result, the Articles established a political system which consisted of a **unicameral legislature** (only one house) with extremely limited authority. The Congress of the Confederation, as it was called, did not have the power to levy taxes or raise an army. Any laws had to be passed by a two-thirds vote, and any changes to the Articles had to be passed unanimously—essen-

DID YOU KNOW?

While influenced by philosophy, the Constitution is actually a very practical document. It lays out the overarching structure of the government. However, each decision made about the structure of the government was an attempt to either prevent the re-emergence of tyranny or fix the mistakes of the first, failed government.

tially an impossible feat. The legislature was intentionally subordinate to the states. Representatives were selected and paid by state legislatures.

It quickly became clear that this government was too weak to be effective, and by 1787 the new government of the United States was already in crisis. Without the power to levy taxes, the federal government had no way to alleviate its debt burden from the war. In addition, without an organizing authority, states began issuing their own currencies and crafting individual trade agreements with foreign nations, halting trade and sending inflation through the roof. Without a national judicial system, there was no mechanism to solve the inevitable economic disputes.

Discontent was particularly strong among farmers, who were losing their property at devastating rates. Violence exploded in 1786 when Daniel Shays led a rebellion against Massachusetts tax collectors and banks. Unable to raise an army, the Congress of the Confederation was powerless to intervene. The rebellion was finally suppressed when citizens of Boston contributed funds to raise a state militia. **SHAYS' REBELLION** made it clear that the new government was unable to maintain order.

A convention of the states was called to address problems in the young United States. At the **CONSTITUTIONAL CONVENTION** in 1787, a decision was made to completely throw out the old Articles and write a new governing document from scratch. There were five main goals for the new Constitution:

1. the protection of property
2. granting increased, but limited, power to the federal government
3. the protection of and limitations on majority rule
4. the protection of individual rights
5. the creation of a flexible framework for government

Each of these reflects the desire to balance authority and liberty, the core of the framework of the American government.

DID YOU KNOW?

It was clear that a stronger central government was needed. However, the states did not want a central government that was so strong that it would oppress the states or the people. The solution? Increase the power of the government, but prevent the concentration of power by *dividing* it.

The federal government was reorganized under the Constitution, shifting from a one-body political system to a three-branch system as conceived by the Enlightenment philosopher **MONTESQUIEU**. In addition to a now bicameral (two house) legislature, a legitimate executive branch was added as well as a judicial. Following Montesquieu's model of **SEPARATION OF POWERS**, the now-increased powers of the federal government were divided among these branches. In addition, each branch was given powers that would limit the power of the other branches in a system called **CHECKS AND BALANCES**. For example:

- The executive branch—via the role of president—has the power to veto (reject) laws passed by the legislature.
- The legislative branch can override the president's veto (with a two-thirds vote) and pass the law anyway.

- The judicial branch can determine the constitutionality of laws (the principle of **JUDICIAL REVIEW**).

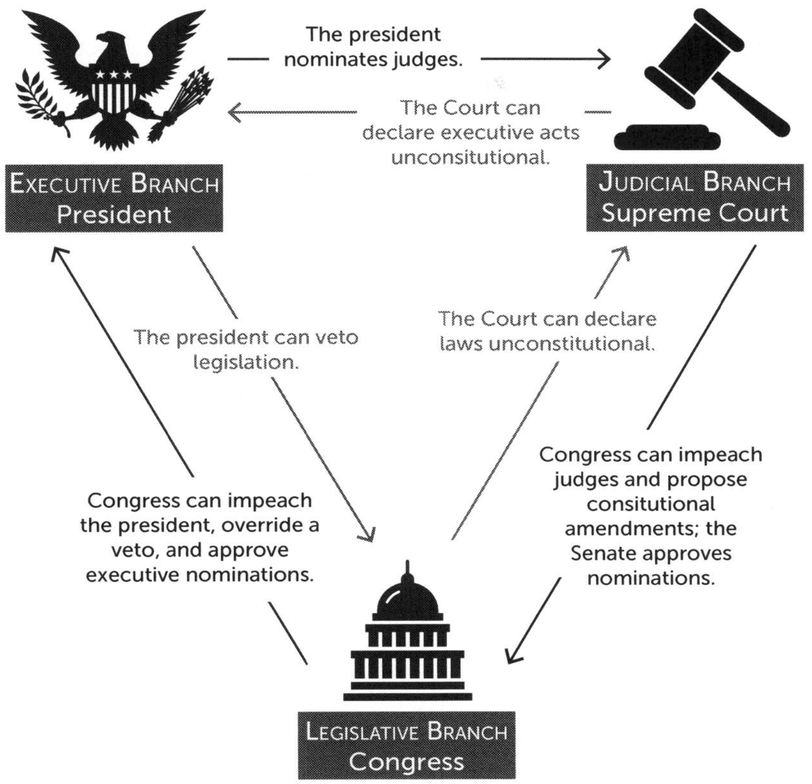

Figure 2.1. Checks and Balances

ENLIGHTENMENT PHILOSOPHY

The founders of the United States were all educated in the philosophy of the **ENLIGHTENMENT.** Several key elements of this philosophy are reflected in the Constitution.

RULE OF LAW: The very desire for a written constitution—a law above all others—reflected Enlightenment thinking, as it ensures a rule of law, rather than a rule of man. In a nation ruled by man, governance is at the whim of an individual or small group of individuals. Decisions are arbitrary based on the interests and needs of those in authority. In a nation ruled by law, governance is based on a body of written, or otherwise codified, law (such as the Constitution). No individual can make a governing decision in conflict with those laws.

REASON: The Constitution is a document based on reason, and is therefore relatively simple and straightforward. It lays out the structure of government without detailing every single function of that government. Rather than simply empowering authority, the Constitution aims to limit government while still allowing it to fulfill its function. It also insists that governing decisions are made outside the scope of religion, by actively separating the two.

Social Contract: The document begins "We the People..." because the founders believed that government was a social contract, legitimized only by the consent of the people. This is also known as **popular sovereignty**. The Constitution protects individual liberty, life, and property, the fundamental natural laws laid out by the Enlightenment philosopher **John Locke**.

Social Progress: Enlightenment thinkers believed strongly that social progress was possible. As a result, the writers of the Constitution built in a means for *amending* the Constitution, allowing it to progress with the nation it governed.

GOVERNMENTAL POWERS

Governmental powers in the Constitution can be divided into six types:

Expressed Powers or **enumerated powers** are powers that are specifically granted to the federal government only. An example of an expressed power is the power to make treaties with foreign nations.

Implied Powers are powers the federal government has that are not in the Constitution. They derive from the elastic clause of the Constitution, Article I, Section 8. The **elastic clause** gives Congress the right to "make all laws necessary and proper" for carrying out other powers. For example, over time as new technologies have emerged, such as radio and television, the commerce clause has been expanded to allow the federal government to regulate them.

The idea of implied powers was supported by the Supreme Court in *McCulloch v. Maryland* (1819). The state of Maryland tried to tax the Maryland branch of the Bank of the United States. When the bank refused to pay the tax, the case landed in the Maryland Court of Appeals; the court ruled that the Bank of the United States was unconstitutional, as the Constitution did not expressly give the federal government the power to operate a bank. Later, the Supreme Court overturned the ruling, citing the elastic clause.

Reserved Powers are powers that are held by the states through the Tenth Amendment, which states that all powers not expressly given to the federal government belong to the states. For example, the management of public education is a reserved power.

Inherent Powers are powers that derive specifically from US sovereignty and are inherent to its existence as a nation. For example, the powers to make treaties and to wage war are both inherent powers.

Concurrent Powers are powers that are shared equally by both the national and state government. The power to tax and the power to establish courts are both concurrent powers.

Prohibited Powers are powers that are denied to both the national government and the state governments. Passing bills of attainder (laws that declare someone guilty without a trial) is a prohibited power.

The separation of powers limited the powers within the federal government, but did not address the power relationship between the federal government and the states. Under the Articles, the federal government was completely beholden to the states for its very existence. However, it was clear that complete state sovereignty did not work. Instead, the Constitution created a **federal** relationship between the two levels of government. **Federalism** is a system in which both the state government and federal government retain sovereignty by dividing up the areas for which they are responsible.

Under the Constitution, the federal government is charged with matters that concern the population at large: for example, handling federal lands, coining money, and maintaining an army and navy. It also handles conflicts between the states via the federal judiciary and by regulating interstate trade. Matters of regional or local concern are handled by state or local governments. This relationship is best codified in the Tenth Amendment, which states that any powers not explicitly given to the federal government are reserved for the states. However, according to the **supremacy clause** (Article VI, Clause 2) the Constitution is the "supreme law of the land." Therefore, in cases of conflict between the states and the federal government, the federal government's authority generally supersedes that of the states.

The division of power has shifted over time with more power going to the federal government as its scope has expanded. The federal government also can exert influence over state governments through **grant-in-aid**, money that is provided for a particular purpose. The federal government can attach stipulations to this funding. For example, grant-in-aid was given to the states in the late 1970s for highway improvement. However, states who accepted the money were required to set the drinking age at twenty-one years old in their state. This was a way for the government to influence law that was technically beyond their purview.

EXAMPLE

1. In the American federal system of government, the power of state governments derives from
   - **A)** the Constitution
   - **B)** the people of the nation
   - **C)** the state legislatures
   - **D)** the people of that state

Organization of the Federal Government

THE LEGISLATIVE BRANCH

At the writing of the Constitution, the branch of the federal government endowed with the most power was the legislative branch. Called **Congress**, this branch is composed of a bicameral legislature (two houses). Based on the British model, most colonies—and then states—had bicameral legislatures with an upper and lower house. While this structure was not originally adopted under the Articles of Confederation, the framers chose it when reorganizing the government. This was in large part due to a dispute at the convention over the structure of the legislative body—specifically the voting power of each state.

DID YOU KNOW?

The bicameral system had other advantages. The House of Representatives would be directly elected by the people, and the Senate by the state legislatures. This supported the federal structure of the government: one house would serve the needs of the people directly, and the other would serve the needs of the states. Also, it curbed federal power by fragmenting it and slowing down the legislative process.

Small states advocated equal representation, with each state having the same number of representatives, each with one vote. Called the **New Jersey Plan,** this plan distributed decision-making power equally among the states, regardless of land mass or population. The more populous states found this system to be unfair. Instead, they argued for a plan called the **Virginia Plan**, based on **proportional representation.** Each state would be assigned a number of representatives based on its population (enslaved people deprived of their rights would even be counted among the population, benefiting those states with large slave populations). In the end, the **Great Compromise** was reached. There would be two houses: the **House of Representatives** (the lower house) would have proportional representation, and the **Senate** (the upper house) would have equal representation.

The structure and powers of Congress are outlined in Article I of the Constitution. As the most representative branch of government, the legislative branch was also designed to be the most powerful. Hence, it has the most expressed powers in the Constitution. Section Eight contains eighteen clauses listing specific powers which can be divided into peacetime powers and war powers:

Table 2.1. Powers of Congress

Clause	Peacetime Powers	Clause	War Powers
1	to establish and collect taxes, duties, and excises	11	to declare war; to make laws regarding people captured on land and water
2	to borrow money	12	to raise and support armies
3	to regulate foreign and inter-state commerce	13	to provide and maintain a navy
4	to create naturalization laws; to create bankruptcy laws	14	to make laws governing land and naval forces

Clause	Peacetime Powers	Clause	War Powers
5	to coin money and regulate its value; regulate weights and measures	15	to provide for summoning the militia to execute federal laws, suppress uprisings, and repel invasions
6	to punish counterfeiters of federal money	16	to provide for organizing, arming, and disciplining the militia and governing it when in the service of the Union
7	to establish post offices and roads		
8	to grant patents and copyrights		
9	to create federal courts below the Supreme Court		
10	to define and punish crimes at sea; define violations of international law		
17	to exercise exclusive jurisdiction over Washington, D.C. and other federal properties		
18	to make all laws necessary and proper to the execution of the other expressed powers (elastic clause)		

The **House of Representatives** is the house which was designed to directly represent the people, and it was originally the only part of the federal government that was directly elected by the citizens. It is the larger of the houses with the number of representatives from each state based on the states' population (**proportional representation**). Every state is guaranteed at least one representative. Apportionment of representatives is based on the census, so seats are reapportioned every ten years with the new census.

At the convention, Southern states argued that their (non-voting) slave population should count towards their overall population, therefore entitling them to more representatives. Northern states with few slaves disagreed. This issue was settled with the **Three-Fifths Compromise** which declared that each slave would be counted as three-fifths of a person for the purpose of the census. (Women, who could not vote until the ratification of the Nineteenth Amendment, were also counted in the census.)

The size of the House grew every ten years along with the population of the United States until 1929, when Congress set the number at 435 voting representatives where it has remained since. Today, each member of Congress represents approximately 700,000 people. Residents of Washington D.C. and territories held by the United States (Guam, American Samoa, and the US Virgin Islands) are represented by non-voting observers; Puerto Rico is represented by a resident commissioner.

Each state legislature divides its state into essentially equally populated congressional districts. This process can become political, with political parties attempting to draw the lines to ensure the maximum number of seats for their party. This is called **GERRYMANDERING.** The Supreme Court has made several rulings to limit gerrymandering, including requiring each district to have equal population and contiguous or connected lines. It is also unconstitutional to draw lines based solely on race.

Members of the House of Representatives are elected for two-year terms in an effort to keep them beholden to the people. The Constitution lays out basic requirements for membership in the House. In order to qualify, candidates must be at least twenty-five years old, have been a US citizen for at least seven years, and live in the state they are representing at the time of the election. The leader of the House is called the **SPEAKER OF THE HOUSE.** He or she is the leader of the majority party in the House.

Although it is technically considered the lower house, there are still powers that belong only to the House of Representatives:

- All revenue bills must start in the house. While the Senate may amend the bills, the framers wanted to keep fiscal power in the hands of the house most beholden to the people.
- The House may bring charges of **IMPEACHMENT** against the president or a Supreme Court justice. Impeachment is the process by which a federal official can be officially charged with a crime. If found guilty, he or she is removed from office. In order to impeach a president or justice, a simple majority is required. Only two presidents have ever been tried for impeachment: Andrew Johnson and Bill Clinton.
- The House must choose the president if there is no majority in the Electoral College. The House has only selected the president once: in 1824, Andrew Jackson, John Quincy Adams, and Henry Clay split the electoral vote. Jackson had the plurality (the greatest percentage), but did not win a majority. The vote went to the House, and, after some backroom politics, they voted for John Quincy Adams.

The **SENATE** was designed to be the house of the states. To signify that no one state is more important than any other, representation in the Senate is apportioned equally, with two senators per state, making a total of 100 senators. The framers designed the Senate so that representatives were chosen by the state legislatures; there was no direct connection between the Senate and the people. However, as the power of the federal government grew, the people increasingly came to think of it as representing themselves rather than their states. Corrupt state legislatures sold Senate seats to the highest bidder rather than electing the most qualified individual. As a result, the Senate seemed disconnected from the democratic process, a corrupt millionaire's club.

The tension between the people's perception of their relationship to the federal government and the mechanism of Senate elections came to a head during the Progressive Era. Political machinations led to deadlocks in state legislatures over appointments, leaving Senate seats vacant for months at time. In 1913, the **Seventeenth Amendment** to the Constitution was ratified; it required the direct election of senators by the people of a state.

As the upper house, the Senate was designed to have greater autonomy with stricter qualifications. Senators are elected for six year terms to allow them time to make decisions that might not be popular but that are best for the nation. They are staggered in three groups; one group is up for election every two years. This ensures that all senators do not face re-election at the same time, allowing for more consistent governance.

To be a senator, candidates must be at least thirty years old, have been a citizen of the United States for nine years, and—at the time of the election—live in the state they will represent. The president of the Senate is the US vice president. However, he or she only has the power to vote in case of a tie. The vice president is often absent from the Senate, in which case the **president pro tempore** presides. He or she is generally the longest-serving member of the Senate.

Much like the House, the Senate has certain unique powers:

- Whereas the House has the power to impeach, the Senate acts as the jury in the impeachment of a president and determines his or her guilt. In order to remove, or oust, a president from office, the Senate must vote two-thirds in favor. Removal has never happened in American history.
- The Senate approves executive appointments and appointments to federal positions in the judicial system. These include, among others, members of the Supreme Court and other federal courts, the attorney general, cabinet members, and ambassadors.
- The Senate ratifies (approves) all treaties signed by the president. The president is in charge of foreign relations and is responsible for negotiating all treaties; however, as part of the system of checks and balances, the president requires the Senate's approval before any treaty becomes a permanent agreement.

The primary function of the legislature is to write and pass laws. Approximately 5,000 bills are introduced in Congress each year, only 2.5 percent of which become laws. There are no restrictions on who can write a bill. In fact, most are not written by Congress, but begin either in the executive branch or are written by special interest groups. A member of Congress is required, however, to introduce the bill. With the exception of revenue bills, bills can start in either house. Since the two houses have parallel processes, the same bill often starts in both houses at the same time.

Once it is placed in the "hopper," the bill is assigned a number and sent to the appropriate committee. Committees and their subcommittees are where most of the hard work of lawmaking is actually done. Here bills are read, debated, and revised. It is also where most bills die, by either being **tabled** (put aside) in subcommittee or committee, or by being voted down. If a bill does get voted out of committee, it goes to the floor for debate. In the House of Representatives, the powerful **Rules Committee** not only determines which bills make it to the floor for debate, but also sets time limits for debate on each bill.

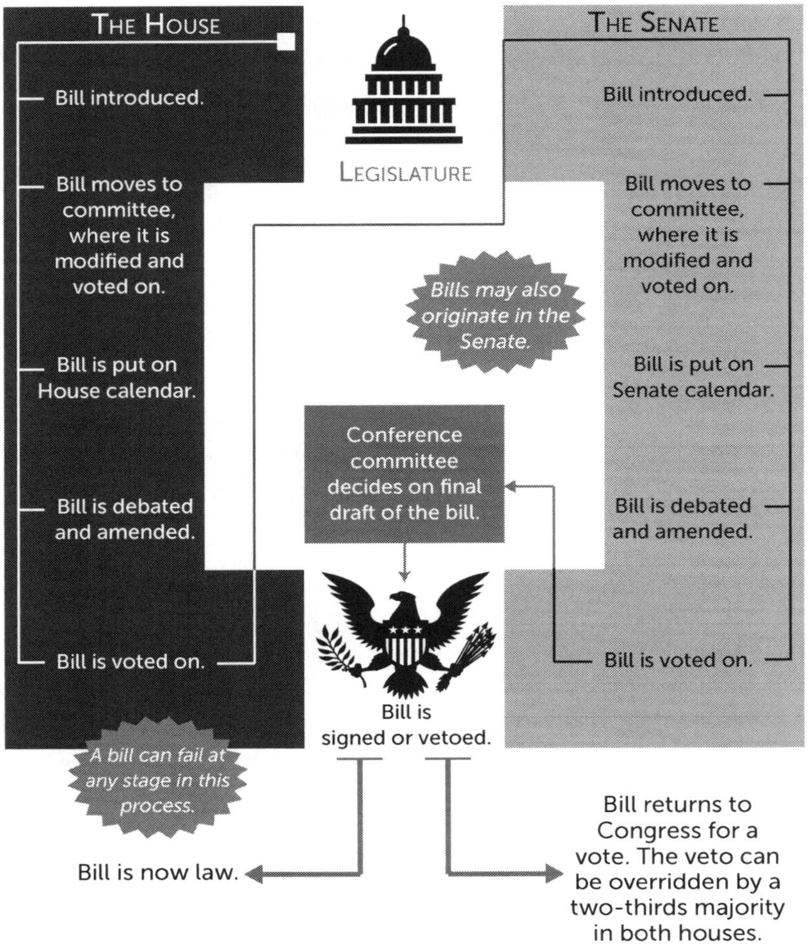

Figure 2.2. Bill to Law

In the Senate, debate is unlimited. This allows for a unique tactic called the **filibuster**, in which a senator or group of senators continues debate indefinitely to delay the passage of a bill. Sixty votes are needed to end a filibuster, so senators often attempt to gather sixty or more votes for a bill before it comes to the floor to ensure it is not filibustered.

After debate has ended, the members of each house vote on the bill. If it passes out of both houses, it moves to the **Conference Committee** which must transform the two very different draft bills (as different revisions and amendments were made as the bill made its way through each house) into one. Once that is done, the unified bill returns to both houses for a final vote. If it passes, it then proceeds to the president for signature or veto. If the president does veto the bill, it returns to Congress where both houses can vote again. If two-thirds of each house vote in favor of the bill, Congress will override the veto and the bill will become law anyway. However, this rarely happens.

Congress is responsible for another significant legislative process: amending the Constitution. The framers understood that they could not possibly foresee every threat to state sovereignty and personal liberty nor every need that would require government management. So they added Article V to the Constitution, which lays out a procedure for amending it. This is one of the most significant aspects of the Constitution as it makes it a "living document."

Amendments to the Constitution can either come from Congress or from the state legislatures. For Congress to propose an amendment to the Constitution, two-thirds of each house must vote in favor of the amendment. Alternatively, an amendment can be proposed if two-thirds of the states call for a national constitutional convention. All amendments to date, however, have been proposed by Congress. Either way, once the amendment has been officially proposed, it is not ratified until three-quarters of state legislatures (or special conventions convened by each state) approve it. There are twenty-seven amendments to the Constitution, the first ten of which were passed immediately in 1791. These first ten amendments, called **THE BILL OF RIGHTS**, were a condition for ratification imposed by those who thought the new government wielded too much power. These **ANTI-FEDERALISTS** argued that individual liberty had to be explicitly protected from federal intervention. According to the amendments, the government may not:

DID YOU KNOW?

The process by which laws are written and passed is intentionally cumbersome and complicated. The framers of the Constitution believed that the longer the process took, the more deliberation there would be, decreasing the risk of abuse of power.

Amendment I: prohibit freedom of religion, speech, press, petition and assembly

Amendment II: prohibit the right to bear arms

Amendment III: quarter troops in citizens' homes

Amendment IV: conduct unlawful search and seizures

Amendment V: force anyone to testify against themselves or be tried for the same crime twice

Amendment VI: prohibit the right to a fair and speedy trial

Amendment VII: prohibit the right to a jury trial in civil cases (remember the original Constitution only guaranteed a jury in criminal cases)

Amendment VIII: force citizens to undergo cruel and unusual punishment

Amendment IX: violate rights that exist but are not explicitly mentioned in the Constitution

Amendment X: usurp any powers from the states not given to them in the Constitution (so all other powers not listed in the Constitution belong to the states)

While the only official way to change the Constitution is through the amendment process, other loopholes for change exist within its framework. These include:

- **Clarifying legislation**: Using the **elastic clause**, much legislation has been passed whose purpose is to clarify or expand the powers of the federal government. For example, the Constitution only provides directly for the Supreme Court, but empowers Congress to create other courts. The Judiciary Act of 1789 created the federal judiciary.
- **Executive actions**: Although Congress holds most lawmaking power, the president is able to issue executive actions which have the force of law without having to involve Congress. The most famous of these is Abraham Lincoln's Emancipation Proclamation.
- **Judicial decisions**: In *Marbury v. Madison* (1803) the Supreme Court established the precedent of **judicial review**, the power of the Supreme Court to determine the constitutionality of laws. *Marbury v. Madison* not only illustrated how judicial decisions can expand federal power in general, but it also broadened the power of the Supreme Court in particular, laying the groundwork for future decisions that would have a similar impact.
- **Political parties**: The rise of political parties changed the political landscape as well. Some aspects of American politics—like how the Speaker of the House is chosen and nomination conventions for presidential candidates—have come from political parties rather than through a formal legislative process.

Although Congress was made much more powerful by the Constitution, a real fear of tyranny existed among the framers. While Section VIII of the Constitution lists the powers of Congress, Section IX lists what Congress cannot do. Most notable are:

1. **No suspension of habeas corpus**: A writ of habeas corpus is a legal demand a prisoner can make to appear in court in order to profess their innocence. Essentially a means of preventing unreasonable imprisonment, habeas corpus was viewed as an essential element of a just government. The Constitution forbids its suspension except in cases of rebellion or invasion. (Abraham Lincoln, during the Civil War, was the first president to suspend habeas corpus.)
2. **No bills of attainder**: A bill of attainder is a law that declares an individual or a group guilty of a crime without holding a trial. Much like with the writ of habeas corpus, this was seen as an essential protection in a fair society.
3. **No ex post facto laws**: An ex post facto law is a law which punishes an individual or group for breaking a law that was not a law when the act was committed. For example, slavery was abolished in 1865. If an ex post facto law was passed at that time, it would have punished anyone who had owned slaves before 1865.

4. **No titles of nobility:** It was important to the framers to provide safeguards against a return to monarchy. Therefore, they prohibited an American nobility of any kind.

EXAMPLE

2. Why did the framers give the House of Representatives the power to start revenue bills?
   - A) Based on their qualifications, members of the House would have more economic knowledge.
   - B) Members of the House would be less influenced by outside forces and political parties than members of the Senate.
   - C) The House was more truly a national legislature; therefore, it should be in charge of the national budget.
   - D) The frequency of elections for House of Representatives would make them more responsive to the will of the people in terms of spending.

THE EXECUTIVE BRANCH

Defined by Article II of the Constitution, the executive branch enforces all federal law. Article II only provides for a president, vice president, and an unspecified number of executive departments. However, the federal government has expanded considerably over the past 225 years, in large part due to the expansion of the executive branch. Today, the executive branch is also responsible for administering a federal bureaucracy that spends $3 trillion a year and employs 2.7 million people.

Of the three mentioned, the president is the only executive role that is specifically defined in the Constitution. The president serves a term of four years and may be re-elected up to two times. While the term length was set in the original Constitution, the term limit was added in the Twenty-Second Amendment in 1951, in response to Franklin Delano Roosevelt's four elections to the presidency. Many felt that allowing unlimited terms opened the door for a de facto dictator and threatened liberty.

In order to qualify for the presidency, candidates must be natural-born American citizens, at least thirty-five years old, and have resided in the United States for at least fourteen years. While the Constitution does not specifically list requirements for the vice presidency, it does state that the vice president becomes the president in case of death, resignation, or impeachment. As a result, the vice president must meet the same qualifications as the president.

The **cabinet** consists of the heads of the executive departments and may advise the president on a variety of matters. It is not directly referred to at all in the Constitution. Instead, it was derived from one line in Section 2: "[the president] may require the opinion, in writing, of the principal officer in each of the executive departments, upon any subject relating to the duties of their respective offices." However, the cabinet as we know it today was established immediately under George Washington. He established four executive departments, so the first cabinet consisted of four positions: the Secretary of State, the Secretary of the Treasury, the Secretary of War (now, the Secretary of Defense) and the Attorney General, or head of the Justice Department. Over time, eleven new executive departments were added, for a total of fifteen cabinet positions.

1. Department of State
2. Department of the Treasury
3. Department of Defense
4. Department of Justice
5. Department of Interior
6. Department of Agriculture
7. Department of Commerce
8. Department of Labor
9. Department of Energy
10. Department of Education
11. Department of Housing and Urban Development
12. Department of Transportation
13. Department of Veterans Affairs
14. Department of Health and Human Services
15. Department of Homeland Security

These fifteen departments employ more than two-thirds of all federal employees.

In addition to managing their departments, the members of the cabinet are also all in the line of presidential succession as established by the Presidential Succession Act (first passed in 1792 but most recently amended in 1947). The line of succession is as follows: following the vice president is the Speaker of the House, then the president pro tempore of the Senate, followed by each cabinet member in the order of the department's creation, beginning with the Secretary of State and ending with the Secretary of Homeland Security.

DID YOU KNOW?

While you do not need to memorize every departmaent for the GED, you should understand they have a wide-ranging effect on American society. How has your life been affected by these departments? For instance, if you pay taxes, your life is affected by the Treasury Department, which controls the Internal Revenue Service (IRS).

Article II is considerably shorter than Article I because the framers intended the role and powers of the president to be more limited than those of Congress. However, the president does have a number of expressed powers.

One of the most significant presidential powers is the power to appoint federal officials. The president's **APPOINTMENT POWER** is far-ranging and includes cabinet members, heads of independent agencies, ambassadors, and federal judges. Through this power, the president not only controls the entirety of the executive branch as well as foreign policy, but also wields significant and long-term influence over the judicial branch. This power, however, is not unlimited. Based on the advise and consent clause of the Constitution, the Senate must approve all presidential appointments. The president does have the power to remove any of his or her appointees from office—with the exception of judges—without Senate approval.

The first line of section 2 of Article II declares the president **COMMANDER-IN-CHIEF** of the army and navy. In this role, the president is the supreme leader of US military forces. He or she can deploy troops and dictate military policy. However, this power is checked as well. While the president controls the military, Congress retains the power to declare war. Presidents have circumvented this check in the past, however, by deploying troops without requesting a formal declaration of war. In the twentieth century, this happened most notably in the Vietnam War, which was never officially declared. In 1964, Congress passed the Gulf of Tonkin Resolution in response to the perceived attack on an American ship in the Gulf of Tonkin. The resolution essentially gave the president a blank check for military action in Vietnam, which led to a rapid and massive escalation of US military spending and troops. Because of this, in 1974 Congress passed the **WAR POWERS RESOLUTION**; this resolution requires the president to inform Congress within forty-eight hours of a troop deployment and restricts deployment unsupported by congressional authorization to sixty days.

The president is also considered the **CHIEF DIPLOMAT** of the United States. In this capacity, the president has the power to recognize other nations, receive ambassadors, and negotiate treaties. However, any treaties negotiated by the president must be approved by the Senate before taking effect.

Many of the president's diplomatic powers are informal. In the twentieth century, the US became a superpower, transforming the role of the president into that of a world leader as well as the leader of the nation. As a result, the president is now expected to manage international crises, negotiate executive agreements with other countries, and monitor and maintain confidential information related to the security of the nation and to the rest of the world.

While the executive and judicial branches are quite separate, the president has powers intended to check the power of the judicial branch. Primarily, this is the power to appoint federal judges. The president may also grant pardons and reprieves for individuals convicted of federal crimes. The purpose of this is to provide a final option for those who have been unfairly convicted. This is one of the president's more controversial powers, as pardons are often seen to be politically motivated or a tool for those with political or personal connections.

Like the judicial branch, the president is constitutionally accorded some **LEGISLATIVE POWERS** in order to limit the powers of the legislative branch. All laws that are passed end up on the president's desk. He or she has the choice to either sign the bill—in which case it becomes a law—or to **VETO** the bill. The president's veto prevents the bill from becoming law (unless Congress overrides the veto). The president is required to either fully accept or fully reject a bill; he or she may not veto only sections of it.

This is called a **LINE-ITEM VETO**, and the Supreme Court declared it unconstitutional in 1996. If the president does not wish to take such a clear stand on a bill, he or she can also simply ignore it. If the president does nothing for ten days, the bill automatically becomes law, even without a signature. If, however, there are less than ten days left in Congress's session, and the president does not sign the bill, it automatically dies. This is called a **POCKET VETO.**

The president also has the power to convene both houses of Congress to force them to consider matters requiring urgent attention.

While this is technically the extent of the president's legislative powers, in reality the position has a much greater legislative impact. The president sets the policy agenda both as the leader of his or her party and through the **STATE OF THE UNION** address. Section 3 of Article II states, "He [or she] shall from time to time give to the Congress information of the state of the union, and recommend to their consideration such measures as he [or she] shall judge necessary and expedient." This has evolved into an annual formalized address to Congress in which the president lays out executive legislative priorities.

Many bills originate in the executive branch, either from the president's office or from one of the executive departments. The president also often uses the power of the veto to influence legislation. By threatening to veto, the president can force changes to bills that align more with her or his political agenda.

Almost half of Article II is dedicated to describing the process of electing the president. The framers wanted to ensure the president represented all of the states and was immune from the mob rule of democracy. As a result, they created the **ELECTORAL COLLEGE.** Over the years, the political parties have expanded the process into a nine-month series of elections by various groups of people.

The first step in choosing a president is selecting the candidates. Originally, this was done in smoke-filled back rooms; it then became the provenance of party caucuses and then conventions, eventually evolving into the current system of primaries and caucuses. In a **PRIMARY** election, members of a political party in a state vote at a polling place for whom they believe is the best candidate for their party. In ten states, a **CAUCUS** system is used, in which members of a party in a state gather together at party meetings and vote for the candidate using raised hands or by gathering in groups.

Then, in July of the election year, the party holds a **NATIONAL NOMINATING CONVENTION.** Historically, this is where the candidate was chosen after days of heated debate and dealings. However, because of the primary and caucus systems, delegates at the convention arrive already knowing whom their state supports. The delegates vote for the candidate who won their primary or caucus. The candidate with the most votes becomes the party's nominee.

Presidential elections are held nationwide every four years on the Tuesday following the first Monday in November. Today, all American citizens over the age of eighteen are allowed to vote, but this was not always the case. The framers viewed the electorate as a small, select segment of the population. However, no voter qualifications are written into the Constitution; those were left to the states. In 1789, in every state, only propertied white men—one in fifteen white men—were allowed to vote. Starting with the removal of property qualifications during the Jacksonian era (1830s), views of democracy began to change, and the electorate expanded. Aside from property requirements, each expansion resulted from a new amendment to the Constitution.

Table 2.2. Constitutional Amendments Expanding Voting Rights

Amendment	Year	Provision
Fifteenth	1870	All male citizens, regardless of race, are allowed to vote.
Nineteenth	1920	Women are allowed to vote.
Twenty-Third	1961	Residents of the District of Columbia are allowed to vote in presidential elections.
Twenty-Fourth	1964	Poll taxes, an indirect restriction of black voting rights, are prohibited.
Twenty-Sixth	1971	All citizens over the age of eighteen are allowed to vote (in most states the voting age had previously been twenty-one years).

While the popular vote is tallied on Election Day, it does not determine the outcome of the presidential election. That is the job of the Electoral College. The **ELECTORAL COLLEGE** is composed of electors from each state who vote for the president. Electors are apportioned based on population; the number of a state's electors is the same as its number of representatives plus its number of senators (so each state has at least three electors).

In the January following the election, electors gather in their states to cast their votes for president. Technically, electors are not bound to vote in line with their state's popular vote. However, rarely has an elector taken advantage of this, and it has never affected the outcome of an election. Today, most states are winner-take-all, meaning the electors are expected to all vote in line with the outcome of the state's popular vote. The president must win a majority—not a plurality—of the Electoral College in order to win. This is 270 votes.

The Electoral College was designed to elect a president for a nation that was scattered and had greater regional than national loyalty. It favors small states and minority groups, giving them greater influence on the election than they would have in a direct election system. Today many people feel that the Electoral College is outdated and ill-fitting. They argue it is undemocratic, and that it gives undue importance to certain states based on their number of electoral votes. Instead, they support a direct election system.

DID YOU KNOW?

A state's number of electors is equal to its number of representatives plus its number of senators (which is two for every state). So, every state (and Washington, DC) has at least three electoral votes. There are a total of 538 votes available.

EXAMPLE

3. The Electoral College represents which of the beliefs of the framers of the Constitution?

A) Government derives its authority from the consent of the people.

B) Concentration of power can lead to tyranny.

C) The federal government derives its authority from the states.

D) The federal government needs greater power to provide stability to the nation.

THE JUDICIAL BRANCH

The Constitution's framework for the judicial branch is the least detailed of the three branches. It is also a passive branch. Where the legislative branch creates laws, and the executive branch takes actions to enforce those laws, the judicial branch can only weigh in when an actual case is presented to it. It may not rule or make decisions based on hypotheticals. Yet this branch has grown to be at least as influential as the other two branches both in setting policy and molding the size and shape of the federal government.

The United States has a complex **DUAL COURT SYSTEM**; each state has its own multi-part judicial system in addition to the federal one. Even though federal district courts handle over 300,000 cases a year, ninety-seven percent of criminal cases are heard in state and local courts. While the federal courts hear more civil cases than criminal, the majority of these are still handled within the states. Because of the federal system, state courts have **JURISDICTION**—or the authority to hear a case—over most cases. Only cases that meet certain criteria (e.g. a dispute between two states, a case involving federal employees or agencies, or a violation of federal law) are heard in federal courts. Most cases also can only be **APPEALED**—or reviewed by a higher court—up to the state supreme court. For the federal Supreme Court to review a state supreme court's decision, there must be an issue involving the interpretation of the federal Constitution.

DID YOU KNOW?

Article III, the article of the Constitution which discusses the judicial branch, only details the Supreme Court. It then empowers Congress to create the rest of the judiciary, which it did beginning with the Judiciary Act of 1789.

The federal court system is composed of three levels of courts. First are the district courts. There are ninety-four district courts in the country, served by 700 judges. They handle 80 percent of all federal cases. The next level of courts are the twelve circuit courts of appeal. These courts review district court decisions and the decisions of federal regulatory agencies.

At the top is the **SUPREME COURT**. Sometimes called the "court of last resort," the Supreme Court reviews cases from the circuit court and from state supreme courts, and is the final arbiter of constitutionality. Decisions made by the Supreme Court establish **PRECEDENTS**, rulings that guide future court decisions at all levels of the judicial system.

While the Constitution delineates which kinds of cases the Supreme Court may hear, its real power was established by the precedent of an early case, *Marbury v. Madison* (1803). In this case, William Marbury—citing the Judiciary Act of 1789—sought relief from the court when James Madison, Secretary of State to the newly inaugurated Thomas Jefferson, did not deliver the federal appointment Marbury was given under the previous president, John Adams. The court, under Chief Justice John Marshall, ruled that while Madison was in the wrong, the section of the Judiciary Act allowing Marbury to petition the Supreme Court was unconstitutional because it extended the jurisdiction of the court beyond the scope established in Article III. This established **JUDICIAL REVIEW**, the Supreme Court's power to determine the constitutionality of laws. This has become the most significant function of the court, and has allowed it to shape public policy.

There are nine justices who serve on the Supreme Court. Appointed by the president and approved by the Senate, Supreme Court justices serve for life. The Constitution does not provide any criteria for serving on the court. However, unofficial requirements do exist: justices must demonstrate competence through high level credentials or through prior experience. Today, all of the justices on the Supreme Court hold law degrees from major universities and first served in federal district or appellate courts. They also generally share policy preferences with the president who appointed them, although judicial inclinations do not always neatly align with political ones.

DID YOU KNOW?

You do not need to memorize all the important Supreme Court cases to do well on the GED. Instead, focus on understanding why they were important and how they affected US government and society.

There are several significant Supreme Court cases to know, some of which are listed in Table 2.3.

Table 2.3. Supreme Court Cases

CASE NAME	RULING
Marbury v. Madison (1803)	This case established judicial review.
McCulloch v. Maryland (1819)	The court ruled that states could not tax the Bank of the United States; this ruling supported the implied powers of Congress.
Dred Scott v. Sandford (1857)	The Supreme Court ruled that enslaved persons were not citizens; it also found the Missouri Compromise unconstitutional, meaning Congress could not forbid expanding slavery to US territories.
Plessy v. Ferguson (1896)	This case established the precedent of separate but equal (segregation).
Korematsu v. US (1945)	This case determined that the internment of Japanese Americans during WWII was lawful.

CASE NAME	RULING
Brown v. Board of Education (1954)	The Supreme Court overturned *Plessy v. Ferguson*; it ruled that separate but equal, or segregation, was unconstitutional.
Gideon v. Wainwright (1963)	The Supreme Court ruled that the court must provide legal counsel to poor defendants in felony cases.
Miranda v. Arizona (1966)	This ruling established that defendants must be read their due process rights before questioning.
Tinker v. Des Moines (1969)	This case established "symbolic speech" as a form of speech protected by the First Amendment.
Roe v. Wade (1973)	This case legalized abortion in the first trimester throughout the United States.
Bakke v. Regents of University of California (1978)	This case ruled that while affirmative action was constitutional, the university's quota system was not.
Citizens United v. Federal Elections Commission (2010)	The court ruled that restricting corporate donations to political campaigns was tantamount to restricting free speech; this ruling allowed the formation of influential super PACs, which can provide unlimited funding to candidates running for office.
Obergefell v. Hodges (2015)	The court ruled that same-sex marriage was legal throughout the United States.

Civil Liberties and Rights

Influenced by the ideas of the Enlightenment and fresh from revolution, the framers of the Constitution valued **CIVIL LIBERTIES**. Civil liberties are rights—provided for either directly by the Constitution or through its historical interpretations—which protect individuals from arbitrary acts of the government. The framers protected some liberties explicitly in the Constitution via the prohibited powers, and expanded on them in the **BILL OF RIGHTS**. Each of these amendments restricts the actions of the federal government rather than actually granting a freedom to the people.

The liberties most central to the American identity are articulated in the **FIRST AMENDMENT**: speech, press, petition, assembly, and religion. The first four are all closely related. No liberty is truly unlimited, however, and the court has imposed restrictions on **FREEDOM OF SPEECH** over time. It has upheld laws banning libel, slander, obscenity, and symbolic speech that intends to incite illegal actions.

The **FREEDOM OF RELIGION** comes from two clauses in the First Amendment: the **ESTABLISHMENT CLAUSE** and the **FREE EXERCISE CLAUSE**. The first prohibits the government from establishing a state religion or favoring one religion over another. The second prohibits the government from restricting religious belief or practice. Again, this is not unlimited. The court has found that religious practice can be banned if it requires engagement in otherwise illegal activity. There are also continuing debates on allowing prayer in schools and granting vouchers to students to attend parochial schools.

Most of the civil liberties written into the body of the Constitution addressed the rights of the accused, including prohibitions on bills of attainder, ex post facto laws, and denials of writs of habeas corpus. Three of the amendments in the Bill of Rights address this as well.

The **FOURTH AMENDMENT** restricts unlawful searches and seizures. In *Mapp v. Ohio* (1961), the Supreme Court ruled that evidence obtained illegally—so in violation of the Fourth Amendment—could not be used in court. This **EXCLUSIONARY RULE** is very controversial, and the courts have struggled since to determine when and how to apply it.

The **FIFTH AMENDMENT** protects the accused from self-incrimination. Drawing on this amendment, the Supreme Court ruled in *Miranda v. Arizona* (1966) that arrestees must be informed of their due process rights before interrogation in order to protect them from self-incrimination. These rights, along with those in the Sixth Amendment, are now colloquially known as **MIRANDA RIGHTS.**

The **SIXTH AMENDMENT** guarantees the accused the right to a fair, speedy, and public trial, as well as the right to counsel in criminal cases. While originally this only applied at the federal level, in *Gideon v. Wainwright* (1963) the Supreme Court ruled that states must provide counsel to those who cannot afford it.

The Court's ruling in *Gideon v. Wainwright* was based on the Fourteenth Amendment's **EQUAL PROTECTION CLAUSE.** Ratified in 1868, the amendment's original purpose was to ensure the equal treatment of African Americans under the law after the abolition of slavery. However, its use has been expanded far beyond that original purpose. The equal protection clause has been used to protect the **CIVIL RIGHTS**—protections against discriminatory treatment by the government—of individuals of a variety of groups.

DID YOU KNOW?

What rights do Americans enjoy under these constitutional amendments and court rulings? To do well on the exam, it is more important to have an understanding of citizens' rights than to memorize each court case and amendment.

The courts have regularly protected political and legal equality, as well as equality of opportunity (like the *Brown v. Board of Education* decision in 1954). However, the courts do not recognize a right to economic equality. The Supreme Court also recognizes the need for reasonable classifications of people, and allows discrimination along those lines. For example, age restrictions on alcohol consumption, driving, and voting are all considered constitutional.

The Supreme Court has also used the **FOURTEENTH AMENDMENT** over time to extend federal civil liberties to the state level. Today, all states are held to the same standard as the federal government in terms of civil liberties.

The second part of the Fourteenth Amendment extends the Fifth Amendment's **DUE PROCESS** guarantees to the state level. "No person shall be deprived of life, liberty or property without the due process of law..." While this typically refers to the processes of the accused, as discussed above, it has also come to represent certain unnamed, or implied, rights. At the heart of most of these **IMPLIED RIGHTS** is the right to privacy, which is not specifically protected in the Constitution. However, the court has ruled that it is implied by the Fourth, Fifth, and Fourteenth Amendments. This was the basis for its decision to legalize abortion in *Roe v. Wade* (1973).

EXAMPLE

4. Which of the following is NOT considered protected speech?

A) burning the American flag

B) writing an article criticizing the government

C) publishing a false list of supposed KKK members

D) protesting outside of an abortion clinic

Political Parties

Although the framers envisioned a political system without political parties, by the election of 1800, two official parties existed. A **POLITICAL PARTY** is a group of citizens who work together in order to win elections, hold public office, operate the government, and determine public policy. Some countries have one-party systems; others have multiple parties.

Although party names and platforms have shifted over the years, the United States has maintained a two-party system. Since 1854, our two major parties have been the **DEMOCRATIC PARTY** and the **REPUBLICAN PARTY.** Democrats generally follow a liberal political ideology, while Republicans have a conservative ideology. The parties operate at every level of government in every state. Although many members of a party serve in elected office, political parties have their own internal organization. Parties are hierarchical: they are comprised of national leaders, followed by state chairpersons, county chairpersons, and local activists.

The parties serve an important role in the American political system, fulfilling functions that aid government operations. These include:

- recruiting and nominating candidates for office
- running political campaigns
- articulating positions on various issues
- connecting individuals and the government

In Congress, parties have become integral to the organization of both houses. The leadership of each house is based on the leadership of whichever party has the majority.

The majority party also holds all of the committee chairs, assigns bills to committees, holds a majority in each committee, controls the important Rules Committee, and sets the legislative agenda.

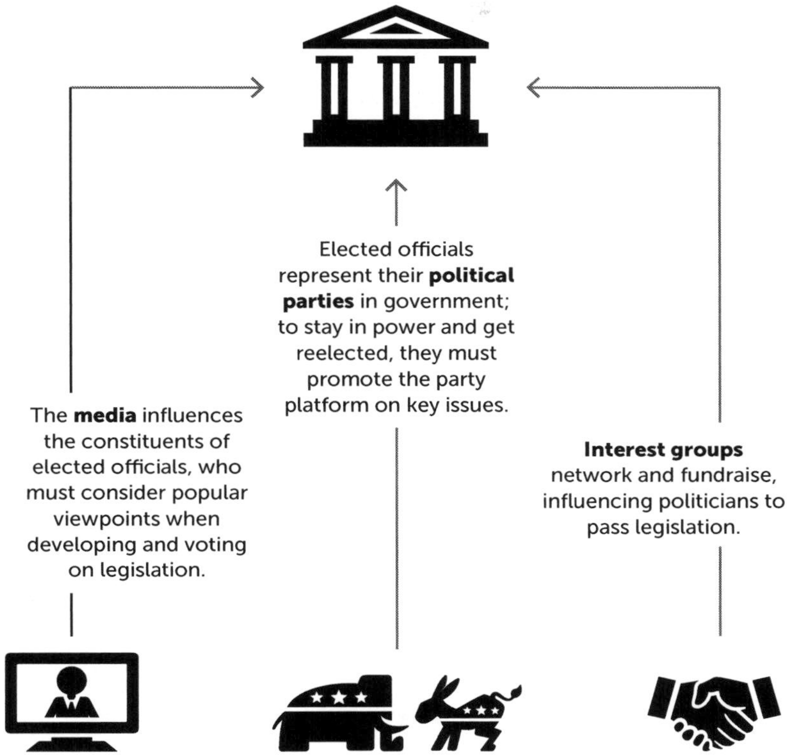

Figure 2.3. Political Influence

While still very important, the power of political parties has declined dramatically since the beginning of the twentieth century. In response to the dominance and corruption of political machines, many states implemented **DIRECT PRIMARIES** to circumvent the parties. Individual politicians can now build power without the party machinery.

Although the United States has a two-party system, third parties still emerge from time to time. These parties are always relatively small and come in three types:

1. **CHARISMATIC LEADERSHIP PARTIES** are dominated by an engaging and forceful leader. Examples include the Bull Moose Party (Teddy Roosevelt, 1912), the American Independent Party (George Wallace, 1972), and the Reform Party (Ross Perot, 1992 and 1996).
2. **SINGLE-ISSUE PARTIES** are organized around one defining issue. Examples include the Free Soil Party and the Know Nothing Party in the 1840s, and the Right to Life Party in the 1970s and 1980s.
3. **IDEOLOGICAL PARTIES** are organized around a particular non-mainstream ideology. Examples include the Green Party and the Libertarian Party.

Although they rarely succeed in gaining major political office, these third parties play an important role in American politics. The two main parties tend toward the middle in an attempt to garner the majority of votes. Third parties, on the other hand, target select populations and are thus able to express strong views on controversial issues. Because their views are usually shared by the most extreme elements of one of the major parties, their stances often push the major parties into more radical positions. They also can affect the outcome of an election, even without winning it. By siphoning off a segment of the vote from one of the dominant parties, they can "spoil" the election for that party. For example, in the 2000 presidential election, Ralph Nader, the Green Party candidate, did not win any electoral votes. However, he drew away votes that most likely otherwise would have gone to Al Gore, contributing to George W. Bush's election.

EXAMPLE

5. Third parties primarily impact presidential elections by

A) increasing voter turnout.

B) preventing either party from winning a majority in the Electoral College.

C) encouraging more voters to officially join a political party.

D) bringing forward issues to be adopted by the major parties later.

Other Groups

Organizations and individuals who are not politicians or employed by the government still have a role to play in politics. Washington, DC and state capitals are home to many interest groups, and the media is key in governance.

INTEREST GROUPS

An **INTEREST GROUP** is a private organization made up of individuals who share policy views on one or more issues. Organized together, the group then tries to influence public opinion to its own benefit. Interest groups play an important role in American politics. Much like political parties (and often even more directly than political parties), they connect citizens to the government. They act as a two-way street, both bringing their members' concerns and perspective to government officials and sharing information with their members about government policy. They wield more influence than the average citizen: they speak for many, and they raise money to influence policymakers, thereby influencing policy.

DID YOU KNOW?

Interest groups play an increasingly dominant role in American political life. The number of groups increased from 6,000 in 1959 to 22,000 in 2010.

Most interest groups focus on one core issue or on a set of issues and draw their membership from people interested in those issues. For example, the National Rifle Association (NRA) focuses on protecting the right to gun ownership. Other organizations focus on a specific group of people, and then determine their interests based on the interests of that group. The AARP (American Association of Retired Persons) is an example of this type of interest group. It determines which issues are most relevant to senior citizens (who make up their membership), and pursues those issues. In addition, large corporations, industry organizations, agricultural groups, professional associations, and unions act as interest groups.

Interest groups **LOBBY** lawmakers to try to effect the change they wish to see. To lobby means to attempt to persuade policymakers to make a certain decision. There are about 30,000 lobbyists in Washington D.C., making $2 billion a year. It is their full-time job to advance the agenda of their interest groups. They do this by testifying before congressional committees, meeting with aides, connecting influential constituents to lawmakers, drafting legislation, and providing relevant technical information to members of Congress.

When all else fails, interest groups will turn to the courts to help them achieve their goals. They write amicus briefs (supporting documents arguing for a side) in Supreme Court cases or initiate court cases to challenge existing laws. They also can play a significant role in determining who is nominated to the federal courts, including the Supreme Court.

Another tool interest groups use to influence policymakers is the **POLITICAL ACTION COMMITTEE**, also known as a PAC. These are committees that interest groups form with the purpose of raising money to support the campaigns of specific candidates who can further their interests. PACs are limited to contributions of $5000 per candidate per election. In 2010, however, the Supreme Court ruled in *Citizens United v. Federal Elections Commission* that limiting corporate donations to candidates was tantamount to limiting free speech. This controversial decision resulted in the creation of super PACs which have no limits on spending.

The role of lobbying, and most specifically PACs and super PACs, in American politics is a hotly debated one. Some political analysts are concerned that politics and money have become too closely tied together. Others argue that the sheer number of special interest groups is a benefit because they each balance each other out. In order to accomplish anything, politicians must bargain and compromise, creating solutions that are ultimately better for more people. Others still argue that rather than creating solutions, the number of competing interests leaves politicians scared to take any action for fear that they will anger one interest group or another.

MASS MEDIA

Any means of communication—newspapers, magazines, radio, television, or blogs—that reaches a broad and far-reaching audience is considered part of the **MASS MEDIA**. Although certainly not a formal part of the political process, the mass media has a significant impact on American politics. It connects people to the government by providing them with inside information on its people and processes, through reports, interviews, and exposés. The media also can help set the political agenda by drawing attention to issues through its coverage. For example, the medical treatment of veterans became a significant political issue after two lengthy exposés in the *Washington Post* on the conditions at Walter Reed Medical Center in 2007.

Mass media has also reshaped American campaigns. Campaigns have become more candidate-centered rather than issue-centered, as candidates now must consider their image on television and other video sources. They also have to be media savvy, making appearances on popular nightly shows and radio programs. The need for a strong media presence is largely responsible for the increase in campaign spending, as candidates work to maintain an up-to-date web presence and spend millions of dollars on television advertising space. Candidates' lives and pasts are also more visible to the public as journalists research their backgrounds to a further extent than ever before. In the 1960 presidential campaign, John F. Kennedy and Richard Nixon engaged in the first televised presidential debate in American history. Those who listened to it on the radio declared Nixon—who was confident in speech, but sweaty and uncomfortable on camera—the winner, while those who watched it on television saw the suave and image-savvy Kennedy as the victor. Many credit this debate for Kennedy's eventual win, demonstrating the new importance of crafting a public image for politicians.

EXAMPLE

6. Throughout the twentieth and twenty-first centuries, changes in politics have coincided with the emergence of new media or a change in the organization of media. This shows that:

A) Politics is responsive to changes in how people communicate.

B) Media has a greater impact on the functioning of government than other political systems.

C) There is no connection between the functioning of media and politics.

D) New media develops in response to political changes.

Test Your Knowledge

Read the question, and then choose the most correct answer.

1. Which of the following illustrated the problems with the Articles of Confederation?

   A) conflict between Federalists and Anti-Federalists

   B) Shays' Rebellion

   C) the Revolutionary War

   D) conflict between slave and free states

2. Which of the following is a safeguard against federal overreach built into the U.S. Constitution?

   A) a system of checks and balances, in which a president can only be elected to two consecutive terms

   B) a system of checks and balances, in which the House, Senate, and president are able to limit each other

   C) a system of checks and balances, in which the president—a civilian leader—controls the military

   D) a system of checks and balances, in which the three branches of government—executive, legislative, and judicial—are able to limit each other

3. Which group insisted on including the Bill of Rights in the Constitution in order to ratify it?

   A) Constitutionalists

   B) Revolutionaries

   C) Federalists

   D) Anti-Federalists

4. John Locke's theory of a social contract is best reflected in which section of the Constitution?

   A) the Bill of Rights

   B) Article V, which refers to amending the Constitution

   C) the Preamble

   D) Article VII, which refers to ratification

5. Which of the following is an accurate example of checks and balances?

   A) The president signs treaties, and the Senate ratifies them.

   B) A bill becomes a law when Congress votes on it and the Supreme Court declares it constitutional.

   C) The Senate appoints justices to the Supreme Court, and the House of Representatives approves them.

   D) Congress has the power to remove the president, and the Supreme Court has the power to remove members of Congress.

6. Which clause of the Constitution best supports the idea of the rule of law?

   A) the Supremacy Clause

   B) the Elastic Clause

   C) the Advise and Consent Clause

   D) the Due Process Clause

7. Which of the following best explains the Three-Fifths Compromise?
   - **A)** Three-fifths of the states would be permitted to own slaves.
   - **B)** Three-fifths of the states needed to ratify amendments before they could go into effect.
   - **C)** To account for a state's population size, a slave would count for three-fifths of a person.
   - **D)** Three-fifths of the states had to ratify the Constitution before it could go into effect.

8. The Bill of Rights was added to the Constitution
   - **A)** in response to the Supreme Court's ruling in *Marbury v. Madison*.
   - **B)** by the first Congress immediately after ratification.
   - **C)** by Congress slowly over the first twenty years of the nation's existence.
   - **D)** through George Washington's signature before he left office.

9. When the president vetoes a bill, he or she is effectively
   - **A)** sending it back to conference committee.
   - **B)** rejecting one part of the bill.
   - **C)** rejecting the whole bill.
   - **D)** declaring the bill unconstitutional.

10. Constitutional amendments have been proposed to make abortion illegal, to ban same-sex marriage, and to prohibit flag burning. What can be deduced from these movements?
   - **A)** It is easy to amend the Constitution.
   - **B)** People sometimes disagree with Supreme Court decisions.
   - **C)** Some people believe that the Constitution is outdated.
   - **D)** Americans tend to avoid complicated social issues.

11. The executive can check the legislative branch by doing which of the following?
   - **A)** The president can remove members of Congress.
   - **B)** The president selects the Speaker of the House.
   - **C)** The president can pocket veto laws passed by Congress.
   - **D)** The president can line-item veto laws passed by Congress.

12. At the Constitutional Convention, what did small states and large states disagree about?
   - **A)** the creation of an executive branch
   - **B)** the federal power to tax
   - **C)** the method of electing Senators
   - **D)** representation in the legislature

13. Which of the following is the most common critique of the Electoral College system?

    A) A president can be elected without winning the majority of the popular vote.

    B) It threatens the two-party system.

    C) It gives too much power to small states.

    D) Electors have too often voted for candidates not listed on the ballot.

14. Which of the following concepts most directly pertains to the relationship between national and state governments?

    A) federalism

    B) separation of powers

    C) checks and balances

    D) proportional representation

15. What lasting impact did *Marbury v. Madison* and *McCulloch v. Maryland* have?

    A) They ensured the Bill of Rights applied to enslaved persons as well as free.

    B) They restricted congressional power.

    C) They expanded the powers of the federal government.

    D) They drew a clear line between the executive and judicial branches.

16. To which of the following does the Supreme Court's power of judicial review NOT apply?

    A) laws passed by Congress

    B) laws passed by state legislatures

    C) executive orders

    D) lower-court decisions

17. The Bill of Rights expressly prohibits all of the following EXCEPT

    A) unlawful searches.

    B) double jeopardy.

    C) poll taxes.

    D) cruel and unusual punishment.

18. Which of the following constitutional rights is fully unrestricted?

    A) the freedom to say anything

    B) the freedom to go anywhere

    C) the freedom to believe anything

    D) the freedom to keep anything private

19. What contributed to the declining power of political parties in the twentieth century?

    A) the rise of third parties

    B) the influence of mass media

    C) increasing alignment of party platforms

    D) more direct primaries

20. What purpose do political parties serve in American politics?

    A) They ensure fair and democratic elections.

    B) They guard against tyranny.

    C) They nominate candidates and run campaigns.

    D) They provide structure for the organization of both houses of Congress.

Answer Key
EXAMPLES

1. **D) is correct.** Each state government is a democratic republic in which authority is derived from the consent of the governed.

2. **D) is correct.** The framers thought it was important that those who spent the money be held most accountable to the people to avoid corruption and misuse.

3. **C) is correct.** The Electoral College is designed to balance the power of the states and to best represent their interests without allowing a single state to dominate.

4. **C) is correct.** Incorrectly alleging that someone is a member of a white supremacist group is considered libel (if written) or slander (if spoken). This is not protected by the Constitution.

5. **D) is correct.** This is by far the most significant role third parties play. They are able to discuss more controversial issues and espouse more radical positions. This often pushes the major parties to discuss the issues as well and take a stand.

6. **A) is correct.** Politicians are always trying to find the best way to connect to their constituencies; therefore they must be adaptable to new media as it emerges. Also, new media changes the way in which politics is reported, which then changes the way it functions.

TEST YOUR KNOWLEDGE

1. A) is incorrect. Federalists and Anti-Federalists disagreed on many points, but their disagreements were political, not military.

B) is correct. Daniel Shays led a rebellion against tax collectors in 1786. Congress could not raise an army and was powerless to intervene. It became clear that the Articles of Confederation needed to be strengthened.

C) is incorrect. The Revolutionary War, or the American Revolution, was fought before the Articles of Confederation were written.

D) is incorrect. Conflict between slave states and free states led to the Civil War later on in American history.

2. A) is incorrect. An individual president was not limited to two terms of service until the twentieth century.

B) is incorrect. The system of checks and balances, as built into the Constitution, includes the judicial branch.

C) is incorrect. While civilian oversight of the military is an important part of the American government, this answer choice does not properly describe the system of checks and balances reinforced by the three branches of government.

D) is correct. The Constitutional system of checks and balances is comprised of the three branches of government, which limit each other, thereby limiting federal power.

3. A) is incorrect. Today, *Constitutionalists* refers to politicians and members of the judiciary who believe in following the Constitution today exactly as it was written; it was not a term used in the late eighteenth century.

B) is incorrect. The Revolution was over by the time of the Constitutional Convention.

C) is incorrect. Federalists were content with the Constitution as it was written.

D) is correct. Anti-Federalists would not accept the Constitution without the Bill of Rights, believing it did not go far enough to protect individual and states' rights.

4. A) is incorrect. The Bill of Rights is an example of Locke's theory of natural rights: it lists rights protected from government interference.

B) is incorrect. Article V is an example of the rule of law: it states that the only way to override the provisions of the Constitution is to legally change it.

C) is correct. The Preamble states, "We the People," supporting the idea that the government exists with the consent of the governed.

D) is incorrect. Article VII is an example of federalism: the federal government could not exist without the approval of the states.

5. **A) is correct.** The Constitution empowers the president to make treaties with the advice and consent of the Senate.

B) is incorrect. For a bill to become a law, Congress votes on it, and the president must sign it. The Supreme Court rules on it only if a relevant case comes before the court.

C) is incorrect. The president appoints justices to the Supreme Court and the Senate approves them.

D) is incorrect. Congress does have the power to impeach and remove the president, but members of Congress can only be removed by the House or the voters.

6. **A) is correct.** The Supremacy Clause declares the Constitution the highest law in the land. The only way to change the Constitution is through the amendment process; no individual has authority higher than the Constitution.

   B) is incorrect. The Elastic Clause, also known as "necessary and proper," provides room for Congress to utilize powers not specifically listed in the Constitution. It does not assert the law's authority over individuals.

   C) is incorrect. The Advise and Consent Clause gives the Senate the power to approve presidential appointees. This is a prime example of a check on executive authority.

   D) is incorrect. The Due Process clause is one of the clauses of the Fourteenth Amendment. It guarantees all citizens fair treatment under the law. While it does deal with the relationship between individuals and the law, it does not explicitly restrict any individual's authority from superseding the law.

7. A) is incorrect. At the time, slavery was legal throughout the United States.

   B) is incorrect. Three-quarters of the states must ratify amendments in order for them to take effect.

   C) is correct. The Three-Fifths Compromise accounted for slaves as part of a state's population (although they could not vote or enjoy the same rights as white citizens).

   D) is incorrect. Nine states needed to ratify the Constitution for it to go into effect.

8. A) is incorrect. *Marbury v. Madison* did not address individual liberties.

   B) is correct. Including the Bill of Rights in the Constitution was a condition of ratification for several states.

   C) is incorrect. The first ten amendments were added to the Constitution collectively and immediately.

   D) is incorrect. The president does not have the authority to add amendments to the Constitution.

9. A) is incorrect. A bill is only in conference committee in order to unify versions of the bill before it goes to the president.

   B) is incorrect. This would be a line-item veto, which the Supreme Court has declared unconstitutional.

   C) is correct. A veto is a formal rejection of a bill by the president. The only way for a vetoed bill to become a law is through a two-thirds vote in both houses of Congress.

   D) is incorrect. The president does not determine the constitutionality of laws; that is the job of the Supreme Court.

10. A) is incorrect. While all of these amendments have been proposed, none of them have ever been ratified. This shows it is actually quite difficult to amend the Constitution.

B) is correct. Each of these amendments was proposed either after a Supreme Court decision or in anticipation of one. For example, in 1973 the Supreme Court determined in *Roe v. Wade* that abortions are legal. Now, the only way to change that would be through a new decision or constitutional amendment.

C) is incorrect. None of the issues listed above are addressed in the Constitution. The desire to add these amendments is not a sign of dissatisfaction with the Constitution itself; instead, support for these amendments is an attempt to override the Supreme Court.

D) is incorrect. These attempts at constitutional amendments demonstrate the ways in which Americans grapple with difficult issues.

11. A) is incorrect. Each house has the authority to remove members for inappropriate or illegal activity. In most cases however, members of Congress lose their seats when their constituencies vote them out.

B) is incorrect. The Speaker of the House is selected by the majority party and is typically the congressional leader of that party.

C) is correct. If a bill arrives at the president's desk within ten days of the end of the term, he or she can cause the bill to fail simply by doing nothing. This is called a pocket veto.

D) is incorrect. The president must either wholly accept or reject a bill. He or she may not reject only certain parts of it.

12. A) is incorrect. Disagreement over the executive was between those who supported a strong central government and those who wanted to safeguard state sovereignty.

B) is incorrect. The inability of the national government to tax was one of the key issues that led to the Convention. All delegates agreed on its importance.

C) is incorrect. The size of a state has no bearing on the method of electing Senators.

D) is correct. Small states wanted equal apportionment of representation in the legislature, while large states wanted proportional representation.

13. **A) is correct.** As the American political system has moved closer to a direct democracy, many people feel that the Electoral College is anachronistic. They believe the president should be the candidate who wins the majority vote of the people.

B) is incorrect. The two-party system is unaffected by the Electoral College. In fact, because it is a winner-takes-all system in most states, it is nearly impossible for a third party to win any electoral votes.

C) is incorrect. States will small populations do have increased representation in the Electoral

College. However, large states still have a much greater impact on the outcomes of elections.

D) is incorrect. While electors have occasionally voted differently than the popular vote in their state, this has been very rare and has never impacted the outcome of an election. Today, most electors are bound by law to follow the state's popular vote.

14. **A) is correct.** Federalism is a political system in which power is shared between the national and state governments.

B) is incorrect. The separation of powers describes how power is distributed throughout the federal government. It does not address the states.

C) is incorrect. Checks and balances refers to the ways branches of government limit each other's power. This term does not address the states.

D) is incorrect. Proportional representation is how representation is determined in the House of Representatives: it is based on the population of each state. However, this term does not address the relationship between the states and the national government.

15. A) is incorrect. Neither *Marbury v. Madison* nor *McCulloch v. Maryland* addressed the status of enslaved persons.

B) is incorrect. While *Marbury v. Madison* did address an act of Congress, it did not restrict congressional power. *McCulloch v. Maryland* interpreted the elastic clause as an expansion of Congress's powers.

C) is correct. *Marbury v. Madison* expanded the power of the judiciary by establishing judicial review (the power to determine the constitutionality of laws). *McCulloch v. Maryland* expanded congressional power by establishing its right to create a national bank.

D) is incorrect. Neither case addressed the relationship between the executive and judicial branches.

16. A) is incorrect. The Supreme Court may determine the constitutionality of laws passed by Congress. In fact, the case that created the power of judicial review, *Marbury v. Madison*, dealt with a law passed by Congress (the Judiciary Act of 1789).

B) is correct. The Supreme Court's power—as well as the rights and powers listed in the Constitution—only apply to the federal government. The states are beholden to their own constitutions, which are interpreted by their own supreme courts.

C) is incorrect. As acts of the federal government, executive orders are subject to judicial review.

D) is incorrect. Using a writ of certiorari, the Supreme Court has the power to demand any case within its jurisdiction be sent up for review.

17. A) is incorrect. The Fourth Amendment prohibits unlawful searches and seizures.

B) is incorrect. The Fifth Amendment prohibits trying

someone twice for the same crime.

C) is correct. The Twenty-Fourth Amendment prohibits poll taxes; however, this amendment is not part of the Bill of Rights.

D) is incorrect. The Eighth Amendment prohibits cruel and unusual punishment.

18. A) is incorrect. Freedom of speech can be restricted if it is obscene, defamatory, or intentionally incites others to violence.

B) is incorrect. The right to travel is an implied right and can be limited if a more important government interest is involved. For example, individuals may not enter a prison whenever they want. The more important government interest is society's safety.

C) is correct. While religious practice can be restricted if it violates pre-existing, neutral laws, religious (or nonreligious) belief can never be.

D) is incorrect. The right to privacy is also an implied right and may be restricted when a more important government interest is involved.

19. A) is incorrect. Third parties have never had a serious impact on American political structure.

B) is incorrect. While mass media has come to play a more significant role in politics, both parties have used that to their advantage.

C) is incorrect. While both parties tend toward the middle, they have maintained opposing viewpoints on many issues throughout the twentieth century and continue to do so today.

D) is correct. The increase in direct primaries allowed candidates to bypass political machines, decreasing their importance in the overall system.

20. A) is incorrect. While each party does monitor the other to an extent during elections, it is simply to increase its own chances of winning.

B) is incorrect. Political parties do act as watchdogs of each other, so they often help to identify abuses of power. However, this is a byproduct of their behavior, not their primary function.

C) is correct. Political parties developed and persist as a means of organizing people with similar political views in order to ensure that public officials who support those views are in office.

D) is incorrect. The parties do play a role in structuring the Senate and House of Representatives, but this is not their primary purpose.

CHAPTER THREE
Economics

Economists study how goods and services are produced and distributed. Economic activity is generally assumed to occur on the market (although there are different economic systems).

The **MARKET** refers to how goods and services are bought and sold. Historically, a market was an actual location where merchants would buy and sell goods; this remains true today. However, the term *market* also refers more abstractly to commercial networks of buying, selling, and production on the local, regional, national, and international scale. There are different types of markets: investors buy and sell stocks and bonds in the financial markets, individuals can find food and clothing in the retail market, and the housing market varies from city to city and region to region as home prices rise and fall.

PRODUCTION is the creation of goods and services that are sold on the market for profit. Producers, or **FIRMS**, **PROFIT** when they sell a product for a higher price than it cost to create the product. Goods and services are **DISTRIBUTED** through the market: that is, they are made available for **CONSUMPTION**, or purchase.

LABOR refers to the work done by humans in an economy to produce goods and services. **CAPITAL** is something that produces income. Capital might be a farmer's tractors, a restaurant's kitchen equipment, or a contractor's tools. Labor turns capital into goods and services that are then sold on the market. The people that do the labor are compensated for it with **WAGES**.

Types of Economic Systems

There are four kinds of economic systems. A **TRADITIONAL ECONOMY** is a pre-industrialized economy, guided by tradition, and often using **BARTERING** rather than currency. For instance, farmers in medieval societies might have traded crops for handmade goods like tools.

A **PURE COMMAND ECONOMY** is usually found in **COMMUNIST** societies. In a pure command economy, the government—rather than the market—determines all aspects of production. Today, they are very rare; North Korea is an example.

A **PURE MARKET ECONOMY**, also known as **CAPITALISM**, is governed by the laws of supply and demand with no outside interference. The economist **ADAM SMITH** theorized that the **"INVISIBLE HAND"** of the market would direct activity to maximize economic efficiency. Government should let the economy behave freely—a concept called ***LAISSEZ-FAIRE***, or "let do" in French. Pure market economies are usually found where there is weak or no government, for instance in parts of Somalia.

A **MIXED ECONOMY** is governed by both the market and the government. The people may decide what is produced by what they are willing to buy, but the government regulates different aspects of the economy with regards to the safety of the population. Most modern economies are mixed economies. The United States economy is based on capitalism, but it is a mixed economy because the government intervenes in some aspects.

EXAMPLE

1. In the 1870s in the United States, Americans favored laissez-faire economics, minimizing government regulations and controls on business. This most closely resembles which type of economy?

A) traditional
B) market
C) command
D) mixed

Functions of the Market

There are several defining principles of a market economy. **PRIVATE PROPERTY:** The market favors private ownership of most economic resources. Private ownership leads to innovation and investment, which in turn lead to growth. It also allows for trade (of services and goods). Economists often point to the inefficiency of the United States Postal Service (USPS) as compared to private carriers like FedEx or UPS to illustrate this point. FedEx and UPS have an incentive to provide better service, in order to stay in business and grow. The better their services, the more likely consumers are to choose them, keeping their businesses alive and thriving. USPS, as a publicly owned entity, is guaranteed survival by the government. So even if the USPS provides bad service, it will not lose government support (though customers may choose to send packages by FedEx or UPS instead).

Freedom of choice: In a market economy, all individuals are free to acquire, use, and sell resources without restriction or regulation. This allows market forces to function properly. Two important elements in the market are supply and demand. If there was a restriction on buying large cars, for example, this would artificially alter demand, and throw off the functioning of the automobile market.

Private property and freedom of choice create the two primary driving forces of the market: self-interest and competition.

Economists assume that people are motivated by **self-interest** as they use their own resources. The seller in the market wants to maximize resources (or profit). The buyer wants to maximize utility (or happiness). As a result, the seller offers goods that will maximize the happiness of buyers in order to attract sales. Self-interest, then, leads to innovation and quality, as it creates a market where the best products are available to buyers. For example, Apple has noted that technological integration brings buyers a great deal of happiness, so the company works to continually innovate new ways of integrating technology (like the Apple watch) in its quest for profit.

Because all individuals are motivated by self-interest, new sellers will enter the market when they determine that there is a possibility for profit. And, because all individuals have freedom of choice, buyers will buy from the sellers whose products maximize their happiness (either through prices or quality). Therefore, sellers compete with each other to attract buyers by appealing to their maximum happiness. **Competition** leads to lower prices and higher quality.

Consequently, the primary communication tool of the market is **price.** Because of competition, prices are set by the market rather than by individuals. As a result, price signals buyers and sellers who, in turn, use it to make decisions about how to use their resources. Prices communicate the relative value of products in the market and deliver to both sellers and buyers what they seek through their own self-interest: profit and happiness, respectively.

ECONOMIC BEHAVIOR

Economists assume that all people have unlimited wants; however, there are limited resources to satisfy those wants. This concept is called **scarcity.** Scarcity forces individuals to make a **choice**, to select one want over another. In making choices, people seek to maximize their **utility**, the point of greatest happiness.

For example, a student wants to go to the movies with her friends, but also wants to do well on her exams the next day. Her resource—in this case, time—is limited, so she must choose between the options. She will weigh the cost, or value lost, of not studying for her exam, against the benefit, or value attained, of seeing the movie, and vice versa. The value of the option *not* selected is called the **opportunity cost.** So, the opportunity cost of staying home to study is the lost fun of seeing the movie and strengthening the bonds with friends.

Resources, also called **FACTORS OF PRODUCTION**, fall into four basic categories:

1. labor
2. land/natural resources
3. physical capacity
4. entrepreneurial ability, or know-how

Each of the four factors of production is necessary for producing anything in the marketplace. They are considered some of the most basic parts of the business equation.

EXAMPLE

2. Which of the following is NOT an example of the principle of scarcity?
   - A) a pharmaceutical company lowers the price of a commonly used drug
   - B) overfishing in key coastal waters
   - C) drought reduces the amount of pumpkins sold in fall farmer's markets
   - D) flu season ramps up and flu vaccines are hard to find

DEMAND AND SUPPLY

The **LAW OF DEMAND** is simple. As the price for a good or service increases, the demand for it will decrease. In other words, if the price goes up, purchases usually go down. For example, a coffee shop sells coffee for $1 a cup and sales skyrocket. The coffee shop then quadruples the price to $4 a cup, and sales plummet.

Whereas demand addresses the behavior of buyers, supply deals with the behavior of sellers. The **LAW OF SUPPLY** states that as the price of a good increases, suppliers will increase the quantity of the good they supply. This is because of **INCREASING MARGINAL COSTS**: as suppliers increase the amount they are supplying, the marginal costs of production (the costs of capital, labor, etc.) increase as well. Therefore, they will only increase supply if price is high enough to offset that cost.

For example, at the holidays, a toy company decides to double its supply of its most popular toy. In order to do this, the company must hire more workers, keep the factory open longer, run the machines longer, pay more in electricity, and pay more in packing materials and shipping costs to get the toys to the stores. If they decided to triple the supply, these costs would only increase. So, the price of the toy would need to be high enough to generate enough revenue to offset these additional costs.

The interplay of supply, demand, and price is used to describe the state of the market. When the quantity demanded equals the quantity supplied at a given price, the market is in a state of **EQUILIBRIUM**. Essentially, this means that both suppliers and buyers are satisfied with the price.

When the quantity demanded exceeds the quantity supplied, a **SHORTAGE**, or **EXCESS DEMAND**, exists. Shortages occur when prices are low because low prices lead to high demand but low supply. For example, if the market price of a television is $20, demand for these inexpensive TVs will be high, but increasing supply would be too expensive for producers because they are not making enough money to offset production costs. Therefore, producers would not make more TVs to meet demand, keeping the supply low.

When the quantity supplied exceeds the quantity demanded, a **SURPLUS**, or **EXCESS SUPPLY**, exists. Again, this is caused by the supply and demand's opposing relationships to price. If the TVs are now $2,000 each, fewer buyers will be willing to purchase one. However, the high price allows the supplier to clearly outstrip the costs of production.

DID YOU KNOW?

When have you been affected by price changes due to demand and supply? For instance, stores heavily discount leftover Valentine's Day candy on February 15 because demand for it drops after the holiday.

The market always tends toward equilibrium. So, in the case of a shortage, buyers will offer to pay more for the television, and suppliers will begin to increase supply. This trend will continue until they reach equilibrium. On the flip side, when a surplus exists, suppliers will lower prices in order to attract buyers, thereby increasing demand until equilibrium is reached.

THE BASIC CATEGORIES of FINANCIAL ASSETS

STOCKS AND BONDS are securities, monetary units that can be exchanged. Public and private interests and individuals may invest in stocks as stockholders, or in bonds as lenders. Stocks and bonds are traded on the **STOCK MARKET**, a venue where private individuals, businesses, government agencies, and even foreign investors and foreign countries can invest.

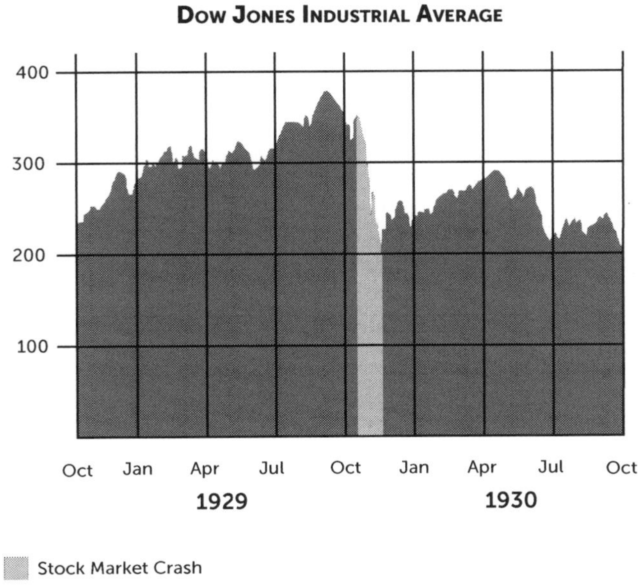

Figure 3.1. Stock Market Crash and Consequences

Stocks are essentially shares of any given company or corporation that has "gone public" or offered its stock for sale to the highest bidder, whomever that may be. In the last century, the value of the stock market has come to reflect the state of the American economy as never before.

In 1929, the stock market was the precursor to an economic downturn that history has called the **Great Depression.** It was not just an American economic downturn. Most of the world was affected by the stock market crash in 1929 and the decade of depression that followed. The graph below shows the pitfalls of more than a decade of questionable buying practices by investors of all economic demographics.

The American economy is still more or less a mirror reflection of the American stock market. Its movement, both up and down, is the fodder of presidential campaigns and Congressional debate. For smaller investors, the risks and rewards can be high. There are fortunes to be made and lost for anyone who wants to take the risk. This graph explores the three different stock measures over a period of several years.

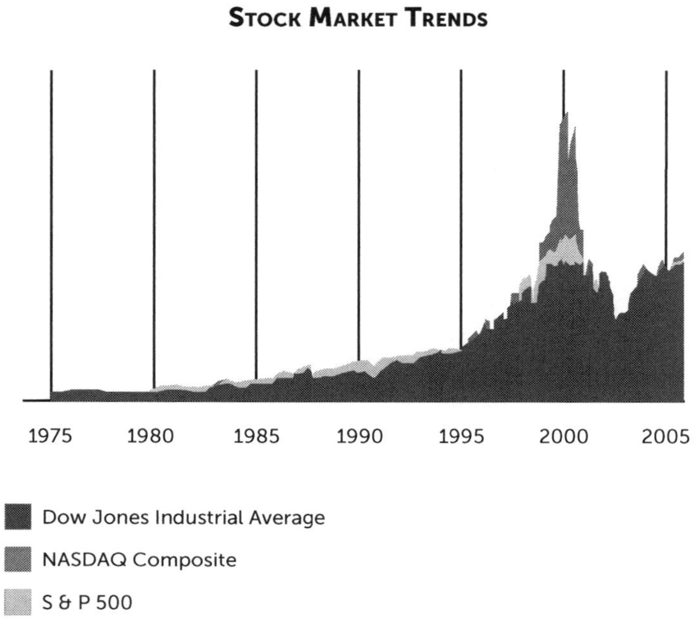

Figure 3.2. Stock Measures

Money market funds invest in short-term investments like treasury bonds. These are considered safe and solid investments much like bank deposits, but encompass a broader scope for large scale investors.

THE ALLOCATION of RESOURCES

Allocation of resources, or how resources are distributed across an economy, can fall to either the government or the market, depending on the type of economy. Within a specific firm, the allocation of resources is determined by profit maximization: how can the resources be used most efficiently?

One of the best ways to explain government control of the allocation of resources is to look at rationing during the Second World War in the United States. Rather than allow the public to hoard goods and create shortages, the federal government decided to control the flow of goods to civilians by allocating only a small amount of goods to the public on a weekly and monthly basis. Most resources are limited. In this case, economists determine the best way to allocate resources that does the least harm to all parties.

PUBLIC GOODS are products that an individual can consume without reducing their availability to other individuals. Public goods are also equally available to all. Basic television, plumbing infrastructure, and sewage systems are all examples of public goods. Some people now argue that internet access should be a public good. In a pure market economy, the market would provide for all public goods. However, in reality, often private markets fail to provide the allocatively efficient level of public goods, and providing them falls to the government.

EXAMPLE

3. Which of the following is NOT an example of a public good?

- **A)** public parks
- **B)** streetlights
- **C)** air travel
- **D)** radio broadcasts

Government Intervention

In the United States, one of the government's most important roles in the economy is to foster **COMPETITION** to guarantee a fair market and help ensure that consumers have choices. **ANTITRUST LAWS** promote a competitive market environment. Antitrust laws exist to protect consumers from illegal mergers and other unfair business practices. Antitrust laws emerged out of the Progressive movement of the nineteenth century in response to the monopolies and trusts dominated by banking and heavy industry in the Second Industrial Revolution.

DID YOU KNOW?
Understanding the US government's basic role in the economy will be an asset on the GED.

The richest businessmen of the nineteenth century were called **ROBBER BARONS** because they controlled vast amounts of money and property. For the robber barons, controlling all aspects of one given industry was simply good business practice. For example, a steel magnate might control the steel industry of a given region of the United States. That means he or she controls the mines where raw ingredients are mined from the earth as well as the miners, even providing company houses and a company store. Furthermore, the magnate controls the railroad that hauls raw ingredients to the steel foundries and the railroads that carry the finished product to its destination.

Competition is key to a market economy and a capitalist system. Establishing a **TRUST**—control over the entire industrial process—defeats that purpose. It was for that reason that the US government set out to break the trusts of the late nineteenth and early twentieth centuries.

THE GOVERNMENT ALSO INTERVENES IN THE FORM OF TAXATION. IN THEORY, PROGRESSIVE TAXES tax the income of the wealthy more than other groups in society. These taxes increase gradually as income rises for an individual, but in a free market economy, taxes are adjusted to account for income losses in business, charitable contributions, and other circumstances. Therefore, in reality, tax rates may vary considerably across income levels.

Other forms of taxation include **PROPORTIONAL** and **REGRESSIVE TAXES. PROPORTIONAL TAXES** are similar to flat rate taxes in that all taxpayers are taxed at the same rate or at the same proportion of their incomes. **REGRESSIVE TAXES** affect everyone at the same rate without a sliding proportional scale, making life more expensive for the lower classes.

EXAMPLE

4. Which of the following statements is true of antitrust laws?
   - **A)** They are designed to modify perfect competition markets.
   - **B)** They are designed to protect controlling firms in trusts.
   - **C)** They are designed to shift markets towards monopolies.
   - **D)** They are designed to decrease the power of monopolists.

THE FEDERAL RESERVE

THE FEDERAL RESERVE behaves as a central bank of the United States and ensures the safety of the American monetary system. In the century since its inception, the role of the Fed has expanded tremendously, but the Fed's primary role at the end of the day is to maximize employment and stabilize prices in the United States.

The Federal Reserve was created in 1913 to help thwart the rising numbers of financial panics that seized the nation every few years. The Fed was created to stabilize the US money supply and to moderate interest rates. As mentioned earlier, the Fed's duties have also expanded to include monitoring and maintaining reserves for US banks. With its own seal and flag, the Federal Reserve is among the most important components of the US federal government.

DID YOU KNOW?

You do not need to memorize every responsibility of the Fed for the GED, but you should know its purpose.

The Federal Reserve is the arbiter of interest rates for mortgages, the stock market, and any other monetary policy involving interest (such as money markets). **EQUILIBRIUM INTEREST RATES**, regulated by the Fed, occur only when interest rates and the money supply are roughly equivalent.

The interest rate set by the Federal Reserve is established by a number of factors, including the federal funds rate, the interest that the Federal Reserve charges banks. Figure 3.4 shows the fluctuating interest rates that banks have paid in recent decades and how they ultimately trickled down to consumers.

The Federal Reserve also monitors **MONETARY STABILIZATION**: efforts to keep prices, unemployment, and the money supply, among other fiscal indicators, relatively stable. Monetary stabilization helps to prevent the economy from oscillating between inflation and recession.

Figure 3.3. The Federal Reserve

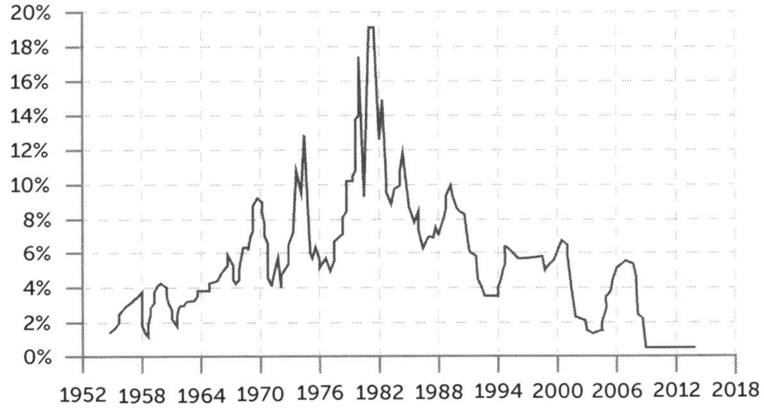

Figure 3.4. Federal Funds Rate

EXAMPLE

5. Which of the following is NOT a responsibility of the Federal Reserve?
   - **A)** to set interest rates
   - **B)** to determine government spending
   - **C)** to maximize employment
   - **D)** to stabilize prices

FISCAL POLICY

FISCAL POLICY is an approach to economic management in which the government is deeply involved in managing the economy. When an individual or firm spends or saves money, those choices impact that individual's or firm's own finances. When the government makes similar choices, the government's decisions impact the economy as a whole. These economic decisions are called **MULTIPLIERS.**

Countries experience business cycles. In a **BUSINESS CYCLE**, businesses tend to expand and grow. Consumer spending and employment increase. Then, the economy experiences a period of contraction and slowdown. The contraction period is known as **RECESSION** and is marked by unemployment, low wages, and low consumer spending. A particularly harsh recession is a **DEPRESSION.** After a period of time, recession is followed by **RECOVERY**, which may be stimulated by government intervention, and growth begins anew.

In **INFLATION**, the price of goods and services in an economy outpaces the ability of the local currency to purchase them. Inflation is not necessarily related to the business cycle.

In **EXPANSIONARY FISCAL POLICY**, the government either increases spending or decreases taxes to counteract a recession. When the economy experiences inflation, government uses **CONTRACTIONARY FISCAL POLICY**: reducing government spending or increasing taxes.

A **TARIFF** is a tax or duty paid on anything imported or exported into or from a given country. Low tariffs encourage foreign goods to enter the market. Countries may do this to stimulate trade or in exchange for other trade agreements. For example, the North American Free Trade Agreement (NAFTA) essentially eliminated tariffs among Canada, the United States, and Mexico. This is also known as **FREE TRADE.**

High tariffs protect domestic industry by making foreign goods more expensive. This is known as **PROTECTIONISM.** However, they also risk slowing trade. For example, between World War I and World War II, the United States passed a very high protectionist tariff. In response, other countries instituted retaliatory tariffs to block American trade as Americans had blocked foreign trade. Consequently, world trade ground to a halt.

When governments make changes to spending and taxes, it affects the government's budget. When revenue (primarily money from taxes) exceeds spending, the government has a **SURPLUS.** When spending exceeds revenues, the government has a **DEFICIT.** A deficit is not the same thing as a debt. A deficit is simply the gap between what the government has spent and what it has earned. In order to cover that deficit, it must borrow money, generating government debt. National debt develops over years of deficits.

Changes in **CURRENCY** are caused by and impact the strength of a nation's economy. **CURRENCY APPRECIATION** occurs when a country's money gains value in national and international markets. This increases foreign investment, as other countries are able to gain more value for their money. However, a strong currency makes that nation's exports more expensive, which can affect trade.

CURRENCY DEPRECIATION occurs when a country's money loses value in national and international markets. Currency depreciation may point to instabilities in the nation's economy (such as high rates of inflation). However, when carried out in an intentional and orderly manner, it can increase a nation's global competiveness by lowering the cost of its exports. For example, China has used intentional currency depreciation to build a strong export-based economy and foster economic growth.

EXAMPLE

6. Which of the following would NOT be an example of contradictory fiscal policy?

A) freezing annual increases on government employees' salaries

B) reducing the operating hours of national parks

C) increasing property taxes

D) financing a new dam

Test Your Knowledge

Read the question, and then choose the most correct answer.

1. Which of the following is NOT a basic factor of production?

A) labor

B) land

C) consumers

D) capital

2. In the production possibility curve below, economic growth would be indicated if the curve moved

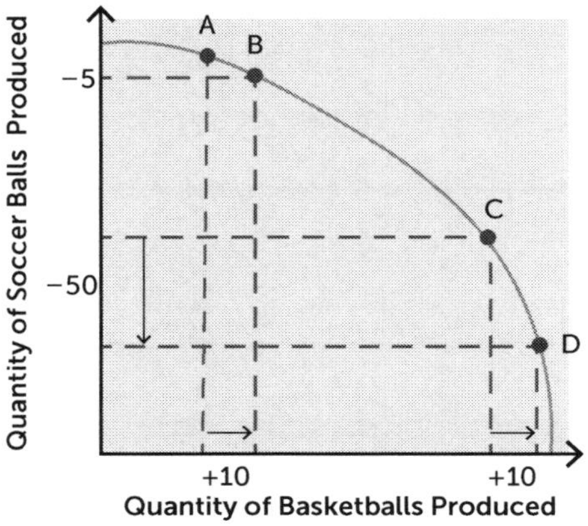

A) from point C to point A.

B) from point A to point B.

C) from point A to point D.

D) from point D to point C.

3. According to the law of demand, when the price of cucumbers increases, which of the following should happen?

A) The quantity of cucumbers demanded increases.

B) The quantity of cucumbers demanded falls.

C) The demand for cucumbers falls.

D) The demand for cucumbers increases.

4. Which of the following is the best example of a public good?

A) tickets to a popular concert

B) electricity

C) an energy bar

D) a newspaper subscription

5. The price of the type of tomatoes used in ketchup drops dramatically. At the same time, the price of mustard, a substitute for ketchup, increases. What impact will these two events have on the supply and price of ketchup?

A) Price falls, but quantity is hard to determine.

B) Price rises, but quantity is hard to determine.

C) Price is hard to determine, but quantity rises.

D) Price is hard to determine, but quantity falls.

6. What is the role of the Federal Reserve?

A) to coin money

B) to control government spending

C) to determine tax policy

D) to stabilize prices

7. If the price of razor blades increases, what will happen to the demand for shaving cream, a complementary good?

A) Demand will increase.

B) Demand will decrease.

C) Demand will stay the same.

D) Demand for shaving cream is unrelated to demand for razor blades.

8. What is the purpose of antitrust laws?

   A) to transition monopolies into oligopolies
   B) to transition monopolies and oligopolies into perfectly competitive markets
   C) to maintain a perfectly competitive market
   D) to transition a perfectly competitive market into an oligopoly

9. Which of the following statements is true about a mixed economy?

   A) The "invisible hand" of the market alone determines allocation.
   B) Government departments determine decisions related to production.
   C) The private sector and the free market work together to determine economic decisions.
   D) Government and the market both solve economic problems.

10. Which of the following is NOT a principle of the pure market?

   A) freedom of choice
   B) self-interest
   C) competition
   D) government safety net

Answer Key

EXAMPLES

1. **B) is correct.** Laissez-faire economics essentially means to leave the market alone to function. The United States came close to having a pure market economy in the 1870s.

2. **A) is correct.** The lowered price by itself does not create scarcity, as the supply of the drug is not impacted.

3. **C) is correct.** Air travel is not available to everyone; it is restricted by price. Also, once one person "consumes" air travel by taking up a seat on a plane, the passenger prevents someone else from "consuming" that good.

4. **D) is correct.** With the rise of the robber barons and the consolidation of market power in several industries (including steel, railroads, and oil), the government took action to reduce that power and restore balance in the market.

5. **B) is correct.** Although the Federal Reserve plays an important role in fiscal policy, it has no control over government spending.

6. **D) is correct.** If the government builds a new dam, it injects new spending into the economy, thereby expanding the economy.

TEST YOUR KNOWLEDGE

1. A) is incorrect. Labor is an essential factor of production, involved in all economic activity.

B) is incorrect. While some industries may no longer require physical land, most do. Land is still considered a basic factor of production.

C) is correct. Consumers provide the demand for products. They do not play a role in production.

D) is incorrect. All businesses require capital to start and to maintain production. This is an essential factor of production.

2. A) is incorrect. Point C represents under-utilization of resources. Movement from C to A simply demonstrates that resources are now being used at their full potential.

B) is incorrect. Movement along the production possibility frontier indicates a shift in the ratio of output for the two products. This is not economic growth but simply a reallocation of resources.

C) is correct. Economic growth is shown by an overall outward shift in the production possibility curve, as would happen if A moved to D.

D) is incorrect. Movement from D to C would indicate an inefficient use of resources, not a shift in overall economic growth.

3. A) is incorrect. Price and quantity demanded have an inverse relationship. When prices rise, consumers are less willing to buy the product.

B) is correct. The law of demand states that, holding all else constant, an increase in price causes a fall in demand.

C) is incorrect. Demand—rather than quantity demanded—is affected by changes in determinants of demand, including consumer income and prices of substitute or complimentary goods.

D) is incorrect. Demand only increases when consumer income increases or there is a change to another determinant of demand. Changes in price impact quantity demanded.

4. A) is incorrect. Use of the tickets prevents others from seeing the concert; therefore, the tickets cannot be a public good.

B) is correct. When one person turns on the lights in their house, it does not prevent anyone else from turning on their own lights.

C) is incorrect. Once eaten, an energy bar cannot be eaten by anyone else, making it a private good.

D) is incorrect. Although a newspaper can be read by many people, once that newspaper is delivered it cannot be delivered to anyone else. Sharing something is not the same as it being available to all regardless of consumption.

5. A) is incorrect. With two opposing forces on the ketchup market, it is impossible to tell the impact on price without knowing which force is stronger. The hypothetical does not give us that information.

B) is incorrect. There are too many factors in this situation to determine the impact on price without more specific information.

C) is correct. Price cannot be determined from the information given; however, the lowered tomato price will increase the supply of ketchup, and the higher mustard price will increase the demand for ketchup. Together, these will increase the overall supply of ketchup.

D) is incorrect. If tomatoes became more expensive or mustard less expensive, the supply of ketchup would fall because both would act as deterrents to ketchup production. However, that is not the case in this situation.

6. A) is incorrect. The US Mint coins money; the Federal Reserve controls the flow of money in the economy.

B) is incorrect. The Federal Reserve has no power over government spending. That is within the purview of Congress.

C) is incorrect. Like government spending, tax policy is controlled by Congress. The Internal Revenue Service is responsible for the collection of taxes.

D) is correct. The Federal Reserve's job is to stabilize prices in order to prevent inflation and keep the economy strong.

7. A) is incorrect. The price of razor blades has an inverse relationship to the demand for both razor blades and the complementary good of shaving cream.

B) is correct. If the price of razor blades increases, the demand for razor blades will decrease. Because shaving cream is a complementary good, the demand for each product is linked. As a result, the demand for shaving cream will decrease as well.

C) is incorrect. Demand for shaving cream and demand for razor blades are linked together. Therefore, changes in the price of one affects the demand of the other.

D) is incorrect. Because shaving cream is required for the use of razor blades, the two are complementary goods and are linked in terms of demand.

8. A) is incorrect. Anti-trust laws target both monopolies and oligopolies equally, and striving to prevent a concentration of market power.

B) is correct. Anti-trust laws break up single firms or several large firms that control an industry in order to return that industry to a perfectly competitive market.

C) is incorrect. Anti-trust laws were created in response to the increasing concentration of power in the hands of a few across industries. When they were written, few perfectly competitive markets existed in the United States.

D) is incorrect. This is the opposite of the goal of anti-trust laws, which break up groups that hold a disproportionate share of market power.

9. A) is incorrect. Only in a pure market does the market operate entirely independently of government.

B) is incorrect. The government makes decisions about production in a command economy.

C) is incorrect. The private sector is a player in the free market and cannot collude with it to guide the economy.

D) is correct. A mixed economy utilizes both market forces and government intervention to ensure the economy benefits the greatest number of people.

10. A) is incorrect. The freedom to choose which products to buy and sell is essential to the functioning of the economy.

B) is incorrect. Self-interest drives the market as buyers seek to maximize utility and sellers seek to maximize profit. The result is the best quality products at the best price.

C) is incorrect. Like self-interest, competition is an important force in the market. Competition leads to innovation and higher quality products.

D) is correct. Market theory states that the market self-corrects, tending towards equilibrium. In this case any government interaction acts only to impede the functioning of the market.

CHAPTER FOUR
Geography and the World

Geography
HUMAN-ENVIRONMENT INTERACTION

Humans have always modified the environment to suit their needs. For example, with the advent of agriculture, humans began loosening the topsoil to make planting easier. A looser topsoil is more susceptible to erosion from wind and rain, allowing greater changes to the physical landscape. Cities are also a prime example. Cities significantly reduce the amount of exposed ground in an area and lead to a concentration of fuel and resource consumption.

The environment has also shaped human activity. For example, the main economic activities of a place—farming, fishing, trade—have historically been determined, in large part, by the physical characteristics of the place. People living in deserts have traditionally been nomadic because restricted access to food and water requires them to continually move around in search of it. Climate impacts clothing, housing, and work and leisure patterns. For example, a period of rest in the middle of the day is common in cultures in hot climates.

One of the most significant ways humans have impacted their environment is through the use of natural resources. Some resources are **RENEWABLE RESOURCES**, meaning they are virtually unlimited or can be grown and regrown. Wind, sun, and plants are all examples of renewable resources. Other resources are **NON-RENEWABLE RESOURCES** because they cannot be replaced once they are consumed. Iron ore, coal, and petroleum are three of the most important nonrenewable resources.

DID YOU KNOW?

Trees can be considered both renewable and nonrenewable. If managed properly, they can be replanted and grown again. However, the rapid consumption of old growth forests uses up a resource that essentially cannot be replaced. Also, the land trees are on is often repurposed for farm land, urbanization, or mining, resulting in a permanent loss of the resource.

Consuming nonrenewable resources—and consuming renewable resources too quickly—is a growing concern as industrialization has greatly increased overall consumption. Many countries are searching for ways to promote **SUSTAINABLE DEVELOPMENT**, the use of natural resources and the growth of new ones at a rate that can be maintained from one generation to the next. The **UNITED NATIONS COMMISSION ON SUSTAINABLE DEVELOPMENT** defines several criteria for global sustainable development: caring for the soil, avoiding overfishing, preserving the forest, protecting species from extinction, and reducing air pollution.

Other sustainability efforts focus on indirect factors impacting the earth's natural resources. For example, efforts to reduce fuel consumption are motivated by both the finite quantity of oil and also by the **GREENHOUSE EFFECT** caused by industrialization. Industrial production unleashes carbon dioxide, methane, and other gases. These create a vapor that transforms radiation into heat, which leads to **GLOBAL WARMING**, an overall rise in the earth's temperature. As a result, the ice caps are melting prematurely, leading to rising sea levels and changes in oceanic patterns.

EXAMPLE

1. Which of the following statements is true about sustainable development?
   - A) Sustainable development requires a prohibition on the use of nonrenewable resources.
   - B) Sustainable development only applies to energy resources like wind, sun, oil, and coal.
   - C) Sustainable development requires the proper management of renewable resources like trees and fish.
   - D) Sustainable development contributes to the greenhouse effect and increases global warming.

HUMAN CHARACTERISTICS of PLACE

The human characteristics of a place make up its **CULTURE**. These characteristics include the shared values, language, and religion of the people living in a location or region. Culture also includes the ways people feed, clothe, and shelter themselves. Cultures can be very specific or regional, like **FOLK CULTURES**, or they can be diffuse and widespread, like **POPULAR CULTURE**.

There are eight locations where formal culture—meaning the development of agriculture, government, and urbanization—began. These locations are known as **CULTURE HEARTHS**.

In the Americas, culture began in Andean America and Mesoamerica. In Africa, the culture hearths were in West Africa and the Nile River Valley. In the Middle East, culture began in Mesopotamia, and in Asia, hearths existed in the Indus River Valley, the Ganges River delta, and along the Wei and Huang Rivers in China. In each of these hearths, similar innovations—the seeds of culture—developed completely independently of one another.

SETTLEMENTS are the cradles of culture. They allow for the development of political structures, the management of resources, and the transfer of information to future generations. While settlements differed greatly, they did all share some commonalities. Settlements all began near natural resources that can support life, namely water and a reliable food source. The success and growth of a settlement was based on its proximity to these natural resources and its ability to collect and move raw materials. As each of these characteristics reached a new level of sophistication, population in that area began to concentrate near the point of resource allocation and production.

The spatial layout of these settlements, then, was determined by the environment and the primary function of the settlement. For example, European villages were clustered on hillsides to more easily protect against invaders and to leave the flat areas for farming. Settlements that rose up around trade, like those on the outskirts of the Saharan desert, concentrated around access to the trade routes and were generally more dispersed.

Later in history, successful settlements also needed an ample work force, and the ability to produce and deliver finished products elsewhere. Once transportation methods were developed, the populations of these settlements became mobile, allowing for a faster diffusion of culture, and—eventually—the development of industrial centers. These industrial centers became cities. A **CITY** is a major hub of human settlement with a high population density and a concentration of resource creation or allocation. Today, more than half of the world's population lives in cities. In more developed regions the percentages are even higher. With the development of cities, three types of areas emerged: **URBAN** (in the city itself), **SUBURBAN** (near the city), and **RURAL** (**AWAY FROM THE CITY**). In some cases, urban and suburban areas or multiple urban areas merge into a **MEGALOPOLIS**, or super-city. The Northeast Corridor from Washington, DC, to Boston is one such example.

EXAMPLE

2. The majority of people in the world today live in

- **A)** urban areas.
- **B)** suburban areas.
- **C)** rural areas.
- **D)** megalopolises.

DEVELOPMENT and GLOBALIZATION

As areas develop and economies grow, manufacturing becomes increasingly important to the functioning of the economy. This phenomenon is called **INDUSTRIALIZATION**. Because industrialization requires a shift in the labor force, it pairs with a decline in subsistence farming: the rural labor force moves to cities.

Industrialization is a relatively recent phenomenon. The **INDUSTRIAL REVOLUTION** began in Great Britain in the 1760s, then diffused to Western Europe and North America by 1825. The discovery of new energy sources like coal (which was later replaced by oil) and technological advancements that allowed machines to replace human labor led to the emergence of manufacturing centers and a shift in the functioning of the economy. As people left rural areas in search of manufacturing jobs, urban areas grew: this phenomenon is called **URBANIZATION**.

Economic growth is strongly connected to **DEVELOPMENT**, the use of technology and knowledge to improve the living conditions of people in a country. While economic in its foundation, development focuses on a range of quality of life issues like access to basic goods and services, education, and healthcare. Countries on the wealthier side of the spectrum are called **MORE DEVELOPED COUNTRIES (MDCs)**, while those on the poorer side are called **LESS DEVELOPED COUNTRIES (LDCs)**. MDCs are concentrated primarily in the Northern Hemisphere. Their primary economic concern is maintaining growth. LDCs, found mostly in the Southern Hemisphere, face the challenge of improving their economic conditions by stimulating significant and sustainable economic growth.

GLOBALIZATION is the trend of increasing interdependence and spatial interaction between disparate areas of the world economically, politically, and culturally. At its core, globalization is an economic trend; however it has significant cultural and political impacts as well. For example, the exportation of American fast food restaurants, like McDonald's, to other parts of the world reflects the capitalist drive to find new markets. Furthermore, the introduction of this type of food has a significant impact on one of the major distinguishing cultural traits of other countries—their cuisine.

The primary driving force of globalization is **MULTINATIONAL CORPORATIONS (MNCs)** or **TRANSNATIONAL CORPORATIONS (TNCs)**. These are companies whose headquarters are located in one country and whose production is located in one or more different countries. The process of moving production to a different country is called **OUTSOURCING**. Outsourcing benefits the MNC because of reduced labor costs, lower tax rates, cheaper land prices, and usually fewer regulations on safety and environmental standards.

DID YOU KNOW?

While much of the world's wealth is concentrated in North America and Western Europe, 80 percent of people live in poor, developing countries in South America, Asia, and Africa. The most populated area in the world is East Asia, which is home to 25 percent of the world's population. In terms of population, East Asia is followed by Southeast Asia, and then Europe, from the Atlantic Ocean to the Ural Mountains.

DEMOGRAPHY is the study of human population. More than half of the world's population today lives in cities. While this is a relatively recent change, the population has always been unevenly distributed based on resources. So, as cities have become better at obtaining and allocating resources, they have attracted more people. Seventy-five percent of all people live on only 5 percent of the earth's land.

Over the last 300 years, the population of Earth has exploded; population has been growing at an exponential rate, meaning the more people are added to the population, the faster it grows. In 1765, the global population was 300 million people. Today it is six billion. This increase has raised concerns for many demographers, particularly in the areas with a higher population concentration. To determine if an area is at risk, demographers determine its **CARRYING CAPACITY**, the number of people the area can support.

The carrying capacity of various areas can differ greatly depending on technology, wealth, climate, available habitable space, access, and **INFRASTRUCTURE**, or institutions that support the needs of the people. When a country exceeds its carrying capacity, it suffers from **OVERPOPULATION**. Countries in danger of overpopulation may attempt to restrict their growth, like China did through its one-child policy.

In spite of the population boom, some countries actually suffer from **UNDERPOPULATION**. They have a much greater carrying capacity—due to their high levels of production, amount of land, or abundance of natural resources—than their population uses.

MIGRATION is the permanent relocation of an individual or group from one home region to another region. As globalization has increased, so has global mobility, both in frequency and length of migrations. Some migration is internal—people moving from one place to another within the same region, like urbanization. Other migration involves people moving from one region of the world to another. Many immigrants have migrated to the United States from other countries around the world.

PUSH FACTORS are the negative aspects of the home region that make someone want to leave it; **PULL FACTORS** are the positive aspects of the new region that make someone want to move there. Push factors include high taxes, high crime rates, resource depletion, and corrupt governments. Migrants who cross international borders fleeing persecution, governmental abuse, war, or natural disaster are called **REFUGEES**. People who migrate intra-nationally by moving from one part of a country to another are called **INTERNALLY DISPLACED PERSONS**.

DID YOU KNOW?

According to the UN, at least 40 percent of Syria's population was internally displaced in 2014, fleeing violence in that country's civil war. In 2015, millions of refugees from Syria and elsewhere in the Middle East, Asia, and North Africa began migrating to Europe, seeking safety from violent conflict.

Not all migration is voluntary. History has many examples of **FORCED MIGRATION**, when a group of people is forcibly removed from their home and brought to a new region. The African slave trade and the removal of Native American tribes from the Southeastern United States are both examples of forced migration.

EXAMPLE

3. Canada produces more resources than its population can consume. This is an example of

A) overpopulation.

B) carrying capacity.

C) underpopulation.

D) graying population.

World History

EARLY CIVILIZATIONS and the GREAT EMPIRES

Around 2500 BCE (or possibly earlier) the **SUMERIANS** emerged in the Near East (eventually expanding into parts of Mesopotamia). Developing irrigation and advanced agriculture, they were able to support settled areas that developed into cities. They also developed **CUNEIFORM**, the earliest known example of writing to use characters to form words.

STUDY TIP
To do well on the GED, focus on understanding historical trends and why they occurred. Don't worry about memorizing dates.

Around the eighteenth century BCE, **BABYLONIA** dominated Southern Mesopotamia and **ASSYRIA** to the north. King Hammurabi in Babylonia had developed courts and an early codified rule of law—**THE CODE OF HAMMURABI**—which meted out justice on an equal basis: "an eye for an eye, a tooth for a tooth."

Meanwhile, development had been under way in the **NILE VALLEY** in ancient **EGYPT.** Despite the surrounding Sahara Desert, the fertile land on the banks of the Nile River lent itself to agriculture, and the early Egyptians were able to develop settled communities thanks to

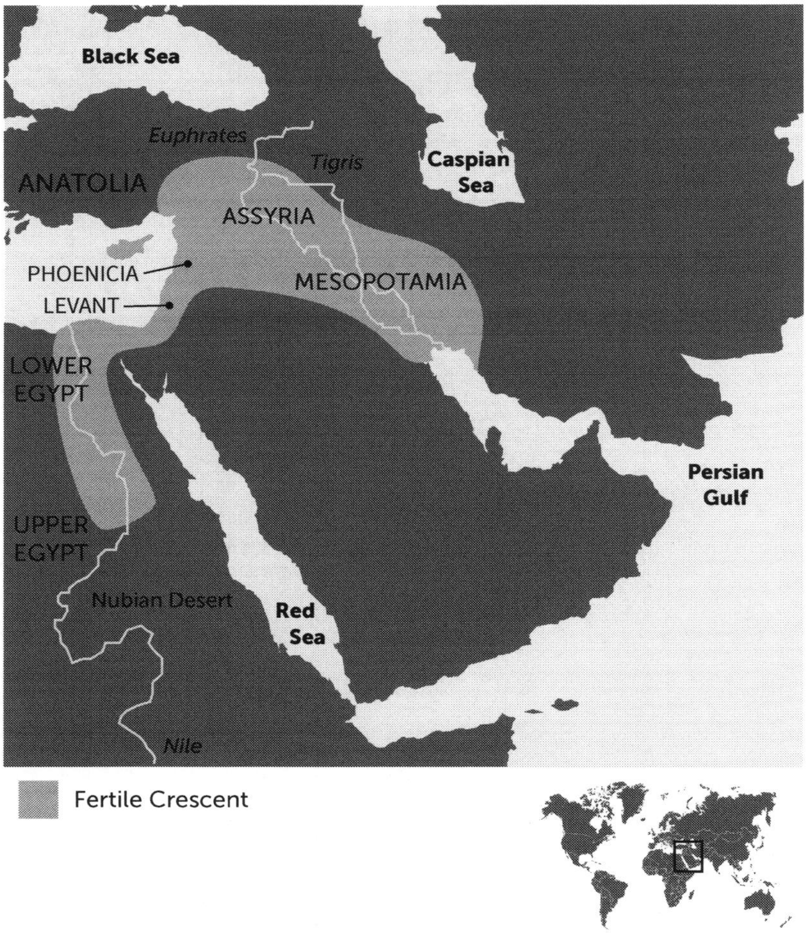

Figure 4.1. Fertile Crescent

agriculture and irrigation. Known for their pyramids, art, and pictorial writing (**HIEROGLYPHS**), the ancient Egyptians emerged as early as 5000 BCE; evidence of Egyptian unity under one monarch, or **PHARAOH**, dates to around 3000 BCE.

Early civilizations also developed farther east. The **INDUS VALLEY CIVILIZATIONS** flourished in the Indian Subcontinent and the Indus and Ganges river basins. The **HARAPPAN** civilization was based in Punjab from around 3000 BCE. Concurrent with the Roman Empire, the **GUPTA EMPIRE** emerged in India. During this period, known as the Golden Age of India, the region was economically strong; there was active trade by sea with China, East Africa, and the Middle East in spices, ivory, silk, cotton, and iron, which was highly profitable as an export.

In China, the **SHANG DYNASTY**, the first known dynasty, ruled the **HUANG HE** or **YELLOW RIVER** area around the second millennium BCE and developed the earliest known Chinese writing, which helped unite Chinese-speaking people throughout the region. The concept of the **MANDATE OF HEAVEN**, in which the emperor had a divine mandate to rule, emerged from the understanding that land was divinely inherited. **CONFUCIUS** taught harmony and respect for hierarchy.

Under the Qin and Han Dynasties, China developed centralized administration, expanded infrastructure, standardization in weights and measures, standardized writing, a standardized currency, and strict imperial control. The administrative **BUREAUCRACY** established by the emperor was the foundation of Chinese administration until the twentieth century. In addition, the Emperor constructed the **GREAT WALL OF CHINA**.

Throughout Mesoamerica, civilizations like the **OLMEC** had developed irrigation as early as 1200 BCE to expand and enrich agriculture, similar to developments in the Fertile Crescent. In South America, artistic evidence remains of the **CHAVIN**, **MOCHE**, and **NAZCA** peoples, who preceded the later Inca civilization and empire.

The **MAYA** came to dominate the Yucatan peninsula around 300. They developed a complex spiritual belief system accompanied by relief art, and built pyramidal temples that still stand today. In addition, they developed a detailed calendar and a written language using pictographs similar to Egyptian hieroglyphs; they studied astronomy and mathematics. Maya political administration was organized under monarchical city-states until around 900, when the civilization began to decline.

PERSIA conquered the Babylonians in the sixth century BCE. Persian rule extended from the Indus Valley to Egypt, and north to **ANATOLIA** by about 400 BCE, where the Persians encountered the ancient **GREEKS**.

Greece was comprised of **CITY-STATES** like **ATHENS**, the first known **DEMOCRACY**, and the military state **SPARTA**. Historically these city-states had been rivals; however, they temporarily united to defeat Persia. Much of Greece became unified under Athens following the war. During this **GOLDEN AGE** of Greek, or Hellenic

DID YOU KNOW?
The term *democracy* comes from the Greek word *demokratia*—"people power." It was participatory rather than representative; officials were chosen by groups rather than elected. Athens was the strongest of the many small political bodies.

Age, civilization, art, architecture, and philosophy emerged that would influence European civilization. **Socrates** began teaching, influencing later philosophers like **Plato** and **Aristotle**, who established the basis for modern western philosophical and political thought.

In Italy, the city of **Rome** was founded as early as the eighth century BCE; it became strong thanks to its importance as a trade route for the Greeks and other Mediterranean peoples.

Originally a kingdom, Rome became a **republic** and elected lawmakers (senators) to the **Senate**. The Romans developed highly advanced infrastructure, including aqueducts and roads, some still in use today. Economically powerful Rome began conquering areas around the Mediterranean with its increasingly powerful military, holding territory thanks to its infrastructure.

However, the Senate became corrupt, and divisions grew throughout the Republic between the wealthy ruling class and the working, poor, and military. The popular military leader **Julius Caesar** forced the corrupt Senate to give him control and began to transition Rome from a republic to an empire. His nephew **Octavian** became the first emperor.

At this time, Rome reached the height of its power, and the Mediterranean region enjoyed a period of stability known as the ***Pax Romana.*** Rome controlled the entire Mediterranean region and lands stretching as far north as Germany and Britain, territory into the Balkans, far into the Middle East, Egypt, North Africa, and Iberia. In this time of relative peace and prosperity, Latin literature flourished, as did art, architecture, philosophy, mathematics, science, and international trade throughout Rome and beyond into Asia and Africa. A series of emperors would follow and Rome

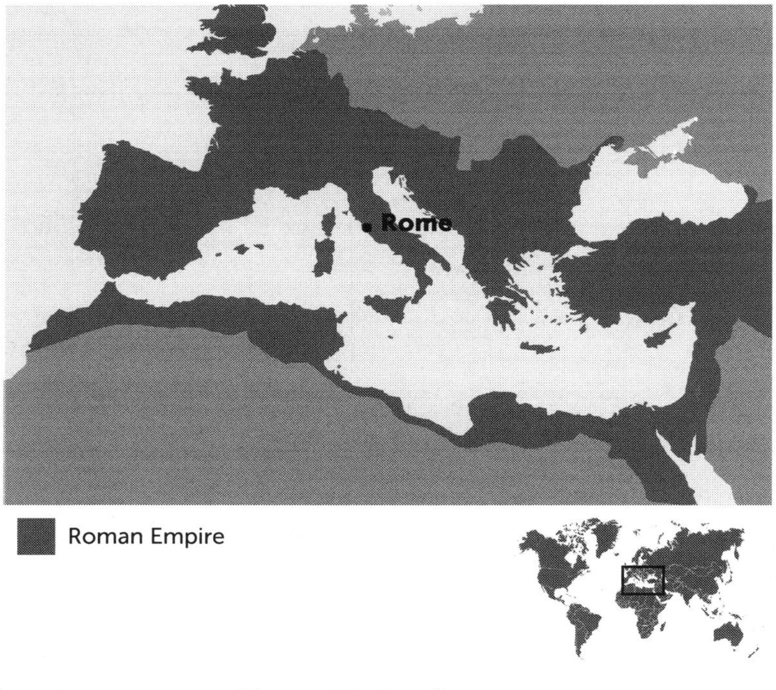

Figure 4.2. Pax Romana

remained a major world power, but it would never again reach the height of prosperity and stability that it did under Augustus.

EXAMPLE

4. Rome was able to maintain imperial control over a vast amount of territory thanks in part to
   - **A)** the idea that the Roman emperor had a divine mandate to rule: the Mandate of Heaven.
   - **B)** a powerful military and strong infrastructure (like roads) throughout the empire.
   - **C)** the concept of one god, and shared religion throughout the empire.
   - **D)** how easy it was to obtain Roman citizenship and all the benefits that came with it.

FEUDALISM THROUGH the ERA of EXPANSION

After the fall of Rome, the Byzantine Empire—formerly the eastern part of the Roman Empire, based in Constantinople—remained a strong civilization and a place of learning. Constantinople was a strategically located commercial center that connected Asian trade routes with Europe. Later, missionaries traveled north to Slav-controlled Russia, spreading Christianity and literacy. Russian Christianity was influenced by the Byzantine doctrine, what would become Greek Orthodox Christianity.

Despite the chaos in Western Europe, the Christian Church in Rome remained strong, becoming a stabilizing influence. However, differences in doctrine between Rome and Constantinople became too wide to overcome. Beginning in 1054, a series of **SCHISMS** developed in the now-widespread Christian religion between the **ROMAN CATHOLIC CHURCH** and the **GREEK ORTHODOX CHURCH** over matters of doctrine and some theological concepts. Eventually the two would become entirely separate churches.

In Europe, the early Middle Ages (or ***DARK AGES***) from the fall of Rome to about the tenth century, were a chaotic, unstable, and unsafe time. What protection and stability existed were represented and maintained by the Catholic Church and the feudal system.

Society and economics were characterized by decentralized, local governance, or **FEUDALISM**, a hierarchy where land and protection were offered in exchange for loyalty. Feudalism was the dominant social, economic, and political hierarchy of the European Middle Ages.

In exchange for protection, **VASSALS** would pledge **FEALTY**, or **PAY HOMAGE TO LORDS**, landowners who would reward their vassals' loyalty with land, or **FIEFS**. Economic and social organization consisted of **MANORS**, self-sustaining areas possessed by lords but worked by peasants. The peasants were **SERFS**, not slaves but not entirely free. Tied to the land, they worked for the lord in exchange for protection; however they were not obligated to fight. Usually they were also granted some land for their own use, but they could not leave the manor. While not true slaves, their lives were effectively controlled by the lord.

Warriors who fought for lords, called **KNIGHTS**, were rewarded with land and could become minor lords in their own right. Lords themselves could be vassals of other lords; that hierarchy extended upward to kings or the Catholic Church. The Catholic Church itself was a major landowner and political power. In a Europe not yet dominated by sovereign states, the **POPE** was not only a religious leader, but also a military and political one.

In what is considered the reemergence of centralized power in Europe, parts of Western and Central Europe were organized under Charlemagne, who was crowned emperor of the Roman Empire by Pope Leo III in **800 CE**. While in retrospect this seems long after the end of Rome, at the time many Europeans still perceived themselves as somehow still part of a Roman Empire.

DID YOU KNOW?

Charlemagne brought stability to Western and Central Europe during a period when two powerful, organized, non-Christian civilizations—the Vikings in the north and the Islamic powers in the south—threatened what was left of western Christendom, and when insecurity was growing to the east with the decline of the Byzantines.

It was also under Charlemagne that the feudal system became truly organized, bringing more stability to Western Europe. The Catholic Church would dominate Europe from Ireland towards Eastern Europe—an area of locally controlled duchies, kingdoms, and alliances. In **962**, the pope crowned the first emperor of the Holy Roman Empire in Central Europe, a confederation of small states which remained an important European power until its dissolution in **1806**.

Meanwhile, in the wake of the decline of the Byzantine Empire, **ARAB-ISLAMIC EMPIRES** characterized by brisk commerce, advancements in technology and learning, and urban development arose in the Middle East.

In Arabia itself, Judaism, Christianity, and animist religions were practiced by the Arab majority. The Prophet **MUHAMMAD** was born in Mecca around 570; he began preaching Islam around 613. Muhammad and his followers established Islam and Arab rule in the region, and the Arabs went on to conquer the Byzantine Empire and Persia in a series of *caliphates*, or empires: first the Umayyad caliphate based in Damascus, and then the Abbasid Caliphate based in Baghdad. By 750, they would control territory from Iberia (Spain) to parts of Central Asia and what is today Pakistan.

Stability permitted open trade routes, economic development, and cultural interaction throughout Asia, the Middle East, North Africa, and parts of Europe. Thanks to the universality of the Arabic language, scientific and medical texts from varying civilizations—Greek, Persian, Indian—could be translated into Arabic and shared throughout the Islamic world. Arab thinkers studied Greek and Persian astronomy and engaged in further research. The Arabs studied mathematics and developed algebra, and fostered literary culture.

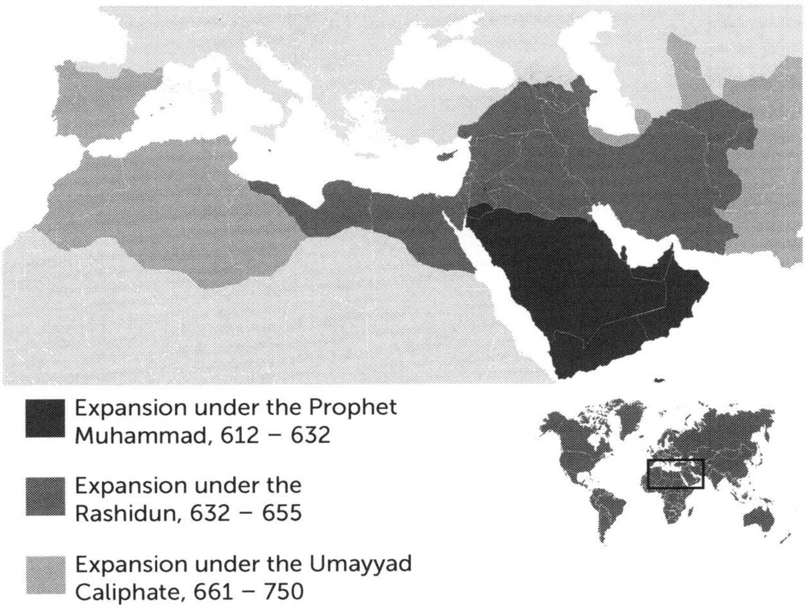

Figure 4.3. Islamic Expansion

Around this time, the **SONG DYNASTY (960 – 1276)** controlled most of China. Under the Song, China experienced tremendous development and economic growth. Characterized by increasing urbanization, the Song featured complex administrative rule, including the difficult competitive written examinations required to obtain prestigious bureaucratic positions in government.

Most traditions recognized as Chinese emerged under the Song, including the consumption of tea and rice and common Chinese architecture. The Song engaged not only in overland trade along the Silk Road, exporting silk, tea, ceramics, jade, and other goods, but also sea trade with Korea, Japan, Southeast Asia, India, Arabia, and even East Africa.

International commerce was vigorous along the **SILK ROAD,** trading routes which stretched from the Arab-controlled Eastern Mediterranean to Song Dynasty China. The Silk Road reflected the transnational nature of Central Asia: the nomadic culture of Central Asia lent itself to trade between the major civilizations of China, Persia, the Near East, and Europe. Buddhism and Islam spread into China. Chinese, Islamic, and European art, pottery, and goods were interchanged between the three civilizations—early globalization. The Islamic tradition of the **HAJJ**, or the pilgrimage to Mecca, also spurred cultural interaction. Islam had spread from Spain throughout North Africa, the Sahel, the Middle East, Persia, Central Asia, India, and China; peoples from all these regions traveled and met in Arabia as part of their religious pilgrimage.

Islam also spread along trans-Saharan trade routes into West Africa and the Sahel. Brisk trade between the gold-rich **KINGDOM OF GHANA** and Muslim traders based in Morocco brought Islam to the region around the eleventh century. The Islamic **MALI**

Empire (1235 – 1500), based farther south in **Timbuktu**, eventually extended beyond the original Ghanaian boundaries all the way to the West African coast, and controlled the valuable gold and salt trades. It became a center of learning and commerce. At the empire's peak, the ruler **Mansa Musa** made a pilgrimage to Mecca in 1324. However, by 1500, the **Songhai Empire** had overcome Mali and eventually dominated the Niger River area.

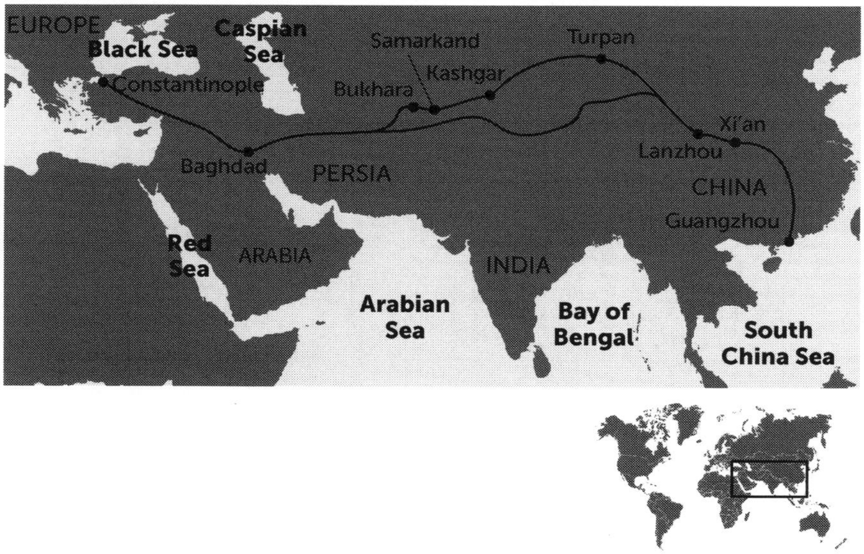

Figure 4.4. The Silk Road

Loss of Byzantine territory to the Islamic empires meant loss of Christian lands in the Levant—including Jerusalem and Bethlehem—to Muslims. In **1095 CE**, the Byzantine emperor asked **the pope** for help to defend Jerusalem and protect Christians. With a history of Muslim incursions into Spain and France, anti-Muslim sentiment was strong in Europe and Christians there were easily inspired to fight them in the Levant, or **Holy Land**; the Pope offered lords and knights the chance to keep lands and bounty they won from conquered Muslims (and Jews) in this *crusade*. He also offered Crusaders **indulgences**—forgiveness for sins committed in war and guarantees they would enter heaven. The **Crusades** continued over several centuries.

Meanwhile, the Abbasid Caliphate went into decline in the tenth century and control in the region splintered. The collapse of the Abbasid Caliphate led to instability and decentralization of power, and production and economic development declined. China closed its borders and trade on the Silk Road declined.

Despite conflict in Europe, Christians found they had more in common with each other than with Muslims, and united to fight in the Middle East. While the ongoing Crusades never resulted in permanent European control over the Holy Land, they did open up trade routes and information exchange between Europe and the Middle East, stretching all the way along the Silk Road to China. This increasing interdependence led to the European Renaissance.

Ongoing interactions between Europeans and Muslims exposed Europeans, who could now afford them thanks to international trade, to improved education and goods. However, the **Bubonic (Black) Plague** also spread to Europe as a result of global exchange, killing off a third of its population from 1347–1351. The plague had a worldwide impact: empires fell in its wake.

Back in Europe, instability reached its height throughout the thirteenth and fourteenth centuries known as the **Hundred Years' War** (1337 – 1453), a chaotic time of conflict between France and England. In Islamic Spain, Christian raids and conflict were ongoing during the lengthy period of the **Reconquista**, which did not end until 1492 when Christian powers led by Ferdinand and Isabella united Spain as one Christian kingdom.

In Southwest Asia, the **Mongol invasions** destroyed agriculture, city life and planning, economic patterns and trade routes, and social stability for some time. The **Mongol Empire** was based in Central Asia; led by **Genghis Khan**, the Mongols expanded thanks to their abilities in horsemanship and archery. The continent was vulnerable: Central Asia lacked one dominant culture or imperial power; Southwest Asia was fragmented following the decline of the Abbasids. These weaknesses allowed the Mongols to take over most of Eurasia. In China, they did maintain infrastructure, but they established their own dynasty, the Yuan Dynasty, in 1271, with Mongols at the top of the social and political hierarchy.

DID YOU KNOW?

The GED will not test you on dates or names directly. Instead, you will be asked to analyze reading passages and images. However, you will need to be familiar with historical events and major figures to do well on the test.

Eventually in China, the Ming Dynasty reasserted Chinese control and continued traditional methods of administration; the construction of the **Forbidden City**, the home of the Emperor in Beijing, helped consolidate imperial rule. The Ming also emphasized international trade; demand for ceramics in particular, in addition to silk and tea, was high abroad, and contact with seafaring traders like the Portuguese and Dutch in the sixteenth century was strong. The Ming also encouraged trade and exploration by sea.

In Russia, **Ivan the Great** brought Moscow from Mongol to Slavic Russian control. In the late fifteenth century, Ivan had consolidated Russian power over neighboring Slavic regions. Through both military force and diplomacy, Ivan achieved Moscow's independence in 1480. Turning Russian attention toward Europe, he set out to bring other neighboring lands under Russian rule. Ivan achieved a centralized, consolidated Russia that was the foundation for an empire and a sovereign nation that sought diplomatic status with Europe.

A century later, **Ivan the Terrible** set out to expand Russia further, to integrate it into Europe, and to strengthen Russian Orthodox Christianity. Named the first **tsar**, or emperor, Ivan reformed government, strengthening centralization and administrative bureaucracy and disempowering the nobility. He led the affirmation of orthodox Christianity and reorganized the military. However, overextension of resources and oppression depopulated the state and gave him the reputation as a despotic ruler.

Despite the instability inland, Indian Ocean trade routes had continued to function since at least the seventh century. These oceanic routes connected the Horn of Africa, the East African Coast, the Arabian Peninsula, Southern Persia, India, Southeast Asia, and China. The ocean acted as a unifying force throughout the region, and the **MONSOON WINDS** permitted Arab, Persian, Indian, and Chinese merchants to travel to East Africa in search of goods such as ivory and gold—and slaves.

Many civilizational advances were achieved on the backs of enslaved persons. The **EAST AFRICAN SLAVE TRADE** remained vigorous until the nineteenth century. Arabs, Asians, and other Africans kidnapped African people and sent them to lives of slavery throughout the Arab world and South Asia. Later, Europeans would take part in the trade, forcing Africans into slavery in colonies throughout South and Southeast Asia, and on plantations in Indian Ocean islands such as Madagascar.

The major East African port was **ZANZIBAR**, from which gold, coconut oil, ivory, other African exports, and enslaved people made their way to Asia and the Middle East. However, enslaved persons from Sub-Saharan Africa were also forced north overland to markets in **CAIRO**, where they were sold and dispersed throughout the Arab-Islamic empires and later, the Ottoman Empire.

Islam also spread throughout the African coast and inland; given the cosmopolitan nature of the coastline, the **SWAHILI** language adopted aspects of Arabic and other Asian languages.

Further north, the Ottoman Turks represented a threat to Central Europe. Controlling most of Anatolia from the late thirteenth century, the Ottomans spread west into the Balkans. In 1453 they captured Istanbul, from which the **OTTOMAN EMPIRE** would come to rule much of the Mediterranean world and eventually the Middle East and North Africa until the nineteenth century. Christians left Constantinople and Greece for Italy, bringing Greek, Middle Eastern, and Asian learning with them and enriching the emerging European Renaissance.

RENAISSANCE and EXPLORATION

The **EUROPEAN RENAISSANCE**, or *rebirth*, included the revival of ancient Greek and Roman learning, art, and architecture. However, the roots of the Renaissance stretched farther back to earlier interactions between Christendom, the Islamic World, and China during the Crusades and through Silk Road trade. Not only did the Renaissance inspire new learning and prosperity in Europe, enabling exploration, colonization, profit, and later imperialism, but it also led to scientific and religious questioning and rebellion against the Catholic Church and, later, monarchical governments.

The fall of Constantinople precipitated the development of **HUMANISM** in Europe, a mode of thought emphasizing human nature, creativity, and an overarching concept of truth in philosophy. Humanism represented a threat to religious, especially Catholic, orthodoxy, as it allowed for the questioning of religious teaching. Ultimately humanism would be at the root of the **Reformation** of the sixteenth century.

Art, considered not just a form of expression but also a science in itself, flourished in fifteenth century Italy, particularly in **Florence**. Major figures who explored anatomy in sculpture, design and perspective, and innovation in architecture included Leonardo da Vinci, Bramante, Michelangelo, Rafael, and Donatello. Leonardo is particularly known for his scientific pursuits in addition to his artistic achievement. Interest in classical (ancient Greek and Roman) artistic work enjoyed a resurgence.

Meanwhile, scholars like Galileo, Isaac Newton, and Copernicus made discoveries in what became known as the **Scientific Revolution**, rooted in the scientific knowledge of the Islamic empires, which had been imported through economic and social contact initiated centuries prior in the Crusades. Scientific study and discovery threatened the power of the Church.

Also in the mid-fifteenth century, **Johann Gutenberg** invented the **printing press**; the first book to be published would be the Bible. With the advent of printing, texts could be more widely and rapidly distributed, and people had more access to information. Here lay the roots of the **Enlightenment**, the basis for reinvigorated European culture and political thought that would drive its development for the next several centuries—and inspire revolution.

DID YOU KNOW?

How might an illiterate European peasant whose only education was from the local church react to news of scientific discoveries?

Transnational cultural exchange had also resulted in the transmission of technology to Europe. During the sixteenth century, European seafaring knowledge, navigation, and technology benefitted from Islamic and Asian expertise; European explorers and traders could now venture beyond the Mediterranean. Portuguese and Dutch sailors eventually reached India and China, where they established ties with the Ming Dynasty. Trade was no longer dependent on the Silk Road. Improved technology also empowered Europeans to explore overseas, eventually landing in the Western Hemisphere.

Interest in exploration grew in Europe during the Renaissance period. Technological advancements made complex navigation and long-term sea voyages possible, and economic growth resulting from international trade drove interest in market expansion. Global interdependence got a big push from Spain when King Ferdinand and Queen Isabella agreed to sponsor **Christopher Columbus'** exploratory voyage in 1492 to find a sea route to Asia, in order to speed up commercial trade there. Instead, he stumbled upon the Western Hemisphere, which was unknown to Europeans, Asians, and Africans to this point.

Columbus landed in the Caribbean; he and later explorers would claim the Caribbean islands and eventually Central and South America for Spain and Portugal. However, those areas were already populated by the major American civilizations.

By around 1400, two major empires dominated Central and South America: the Incas and the Aztecs. These two empires would be the last indigenous civilizations to dominate the Americas before European colonization of the Western Hemisphere.

Their military power and militaristic culture allowed the **Aztecs** to dominate Mexico and Mesoamerica and regional trade in precious objects. The main city of the Aztec empire, **Tenochtitlan**, was founded in 1325 and, at its height, home to several million people. Aztec civilization was militaristic in nature and divided on a class basis: it included slaves, indentured servants, serfs, an independent priestly class, military, and ruling classes. The Aztecs shared many beliefs with the preceding Mayan civilization.

Meanwhile, in the Andes, the **Incas** had emerged. Based in **Cuzco**, the Incas had consolidated their power around 1300. Domesticated llamas and alpacas allowed the military to transport supplies through the mountains. Inca engineers built the citadel of **Machu Picchu** and imperial infrastructure, including roads throughout the Andes. They grew crops at high altitudes. To subdue local peoples, they moved conquered groups elsewhere in the empire and repopulated conquered areas with Incas.

With its weapons and technological superiority, Spain took over the silver- and gold-rich Mesoamerican and Andean territories. The Spanish *conquistador* Hernán Cortés conquered the Aztecs, and Francisco Pizarro the Incas. In the Caribbean islands, sugar became an important cash crop.

The economic system of **mercantilism** developed, in which the colonizing or ***mother country*** took raw materials from the territories they controlled for the colonizers' own benefit. Governments amassed wealth through protectionism and increasing exports at the expense of other rising colonial powers. This eventually involved developing goods and then selling them back to those colonized lands at an inflated price. The ***encomienda*** system granted European landowners the "right" to hold lands in the Americas and demand labor from the local inhabitants. Spreading Christianity was another important reason for European expansion. Local civilizations and resources were exploited and destroyed.

The **Columbian Exchange** enabled mercantilism to flourish. Conflict and illness brought by the Europeans—especially **smallpox**—decimated the Native Americans, and the Europeans were left without labor to mine the silver and gold or to work the land. **African slavery** was their solution.

Slavery was an ancient institution in many societies worldwide; however, with the Columbian Exchange slavery came to be practiced on a mass scale the likes of which the world had never seen. Throughout Africa and especially on the West African coast, Europeans traded for slaves with some African kingdoms and also raided the land, kidnapping people. Europeans took captured Africans in horrific conditions to the

Americas; those who survived were enslaved and forced to work in mining or agriculture for the benefit of expanding European imperial powers.

The Columbian Exchange described the **TRIANGULAR TRADE** across the Atlantic: Europeans took kidnapped African people from Africa to the Americas along the "Middle Passage," sold them at auction and exchanged them for sugar and raw materials; these materials were traded in Europe for consumer goods, which were then exchanged in Africa, and so on.

DID YOU KNOW?

The Haitian Revolution nearly bankrupted France, and was one reason for the sale of its territory in Louisiana to the early United States. Haiti was the first independent state in Latin America.

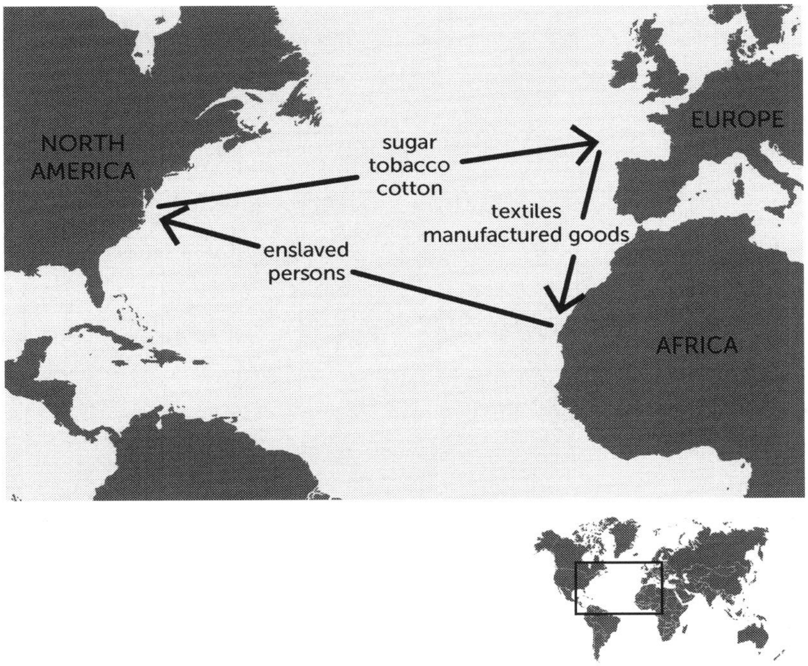

Figure 4.5. Triangular Trade

Throughout this period, Africans did resist both on ships and later, in the Americas; **MAROON COMMUNITIES** of escaped slaves formed throughout the Western Hemisphere, the **UNDERGROUND RAILROAD** in the nineteenth-century United States helped enslaved persons escape the South, and **TOUSSAINT L'OUVERTURE** led a successful slave rebellion in Haiti, winning independence from the French for that country in 1803. However, the slave trade continued for centuries.

During the eighteenth century, Spain and Portugal were preeminent powers in global trade thanks to colonization and **IMPERIALISM**, the possession and exploitation of land overseas. However, Great Britain became an important presence on the seas; it would later dominate the oceans throughout the nineteenth century.

EXAMPLE

5. Major influences on the European Renaissance included

A) cultural discoveries in North America.

B) African music and culture.

C) Greek Orthodox Christianity and learning brought by Byzantine missionaries.

D) scientific knowledge from the Islamic empires and Greco-Roman philosophy and art.

REFORMATION and REVOLUTION

While Spain and Portugal consolidated their hold over territories in the Americas, conflict ensued in Europe. The power of the Catholic Church was threatened; new scientific discoveries and secular Renaissance thought were at odds with many teachings of the Church. The Catholic monk **Martin Luther** wrote a letter of protest to the Pope in 1517 known as the **Ninety-Five Theses**, outlining ways he believed the Church should reform. His ideas gained support, especially among rulers who wanted more power from the Church. Triggering the **Reformation**, or movement for reform of the Church, Luther's ideas led to offshoots of new versions of Christianity in Western Europe. Protestant thinkers like Luther and **John Calvin** addressed particular grievances, condemning the **infallibility** of the Pope (its teaching that the Pope was without fault) and the selling of **indulgences**, or guarantees of entry into heaven.

Conflict between Protestants and Catholics was fierce on the Continent as well. The **Thirty Years' War** (1618 – 1648) began in Central Europe between Protestant nobles in the Holy Roman Empire who disagreed with the strict Catholic **Ferdinand II**, who ruled parts of Central Europe. Elected Holy Roman Emperor in 1619, Ferdinand II was a leader of the **Counter-Reformation**, attempts at reinforcing Catholic dominance throughout Europe during and after the Reformation in the wake of the Renaissance and related social change. Ferdinand was also closely allied with the Catholic **Habsburg** Dynasty, which ruled Austria and Spain.

At the same time, France came into conflict with its Catholic neighbors—Habsburg-ruled Spain and Austria—despite their shared faith. Threatened by a strengthened Spain and Holy Roman Empire, France declared war. European politics began emphasizing state sovereignty over religious solidarity.

The tangled alliances between European powers resulted in widespread conflict. In the 1648 **Treaty of Westphalia**, European powers agreed to recognize **state sovereignty** and practice **non-interference** in each other's matters—at the expense of family and religious allegiance. 1648 marked a transition into modern international relations when politics and religion would no longer be inexorably intertwined.

DID YOU KNOW?
International relations today are based on the principles of the Treaty of Westphalia.

The end of the Thirty Years' War represented the end of the notion of the domination of the Catholic Church over Europe and the concept of religious regional dominance, rather than ethnic state divisions. Over the next several centuries, the Church and religious empires would eventually lose control over ethnic groups and their lands, later giving way to smaller **NATION-STATES**.

Peace did not last, and in 1756, the **SEVEN YEARS' WAR** began between Prussia and Austria, drawing in other allied countries. In Europe, this war further cemented concepts of state sovereignty and delineated rivalries between European powers engaged in colonial adventure and overseas imperialism—especially Britain and France. It would kick-start British dominance in Asia. In North America, it was known as the French and Indian War; France lost its territory there to Britain.

This time of change in Europe would affect Asia. European concepts of social and political organization became constructed around national sovereignty and nation-states. European economies had become dependent upon colonies and were starting to industrialize, enriching Europe at the expense of the Americas, Africa, and increasingly Asia.

Industrialization and political organization allowed improved militaries, which put Asian governments at a disadvantage. The major Asian powers—India, China, the Ottoman Empire, and Persia—would eventually succumb to European influence or come under direct European control.

Monarchies in Europe had been weakened by the conflicts between Catholicism and Protestant faiths; despite European presence and increasing power overseas, as well as its dominance in the Americas, instability on the continent and in the British Isles made the old order vulnerable. Enlightenment ideals like democracy and republicanism, coupled with political instability, would trigger revolution against **ABSOLUTE MONARCHY**. Revolutionary actors drew on the philosophies of Enlightenment thinkers like **JOHN LOCKE**, **JEAN-JACQUES ROUSSEAU**, and **MONTESQUIEU**, whose beliefs, such as **REPUBLICANISM**, the **SOCIAL CONTRACT**, the **SEPARATION OF POWERS**, and the **RIGHTS OF MAN** would drive a series of revolutions.

In the seventeenth century, conflict following the **ENGLISH CIVIL WAR** between the **ROYALISTS**, who supported the monarchy, and the **PARLIAMENTARIANS**, who wanted a republic, eventually resulted in a constitutional monarchy.

The **AMERICAN REVOLUTION**, heavily influenced by Locke, broke out a century later. Chapter One, *US History*, contains details.

The **FRENCH REVOLUTION** was the precursor to the end of the feudal order in most of Europe. **KING LOUIS XIV**, the *Sun King* (1643 – 1715), had consolidated the monarchy in France, taking true political and military power from the nobility. Meanwhile, French Enlightenment thinkers like **JEAN-JACQUES ROUSSEAU, MONTESQUIEU,** and **VOLTAIRE** criticized absolute monarchy and the repression of freedom of speech and thought. In 1789, the French Revolution broke out.

The power of the Catholic Church had weakened and the Scientific Revolution and the Enlightenment had fostered social and intellectual change. Colonialism and mercantilism were fueling the growth of an early middle class: people who were not traditionally nobility or landowners under the feudal system were becoming wealthier and more powerful thanks to early capitalism. This class, the **BOURGEOISIE**, chafed under the rule of the nobility, which had generally inherited land and wealth (while the bourgeoisie earned their wealth in business).

In France, the problem was most acute as France had the largest population in Europe at the time. At the same time, France had one of the most centralized monarchies in Europe and entrenched nobilities. With a growing bourgeoisie and peasant class paying increasingly higher taxes to the nobility, resentment was brewing.

Louis XIV had strengthened the monarchy by weakening the nobility's control over the land and centralizing power under the king. However, his successors had failed to govern effectively or win the loyalty of the people; both the nobility and the monarch were widely resented. Furthermore, the bourgeoisie resented their lack of standing in government and society. Moreover, advances in medicine had permitted unprecedented population growth, further empowering the peasantry and bourgeoisie.

DID YOU KNOW?

The Congress of Vienna was the first real international peace conference and set the precedent for European political organization.

The French government was struggling financially, having supported the American Revolution, and needed to increase taxes. The burden of taxation traditionally fell on the Third Estate, the middle class and the poor peasants, not the wealthier nobility, who were unwilling to contribute. In fact, peasants had to **TITHE**, paying ten percent of their earnings to the nobles.

After a poor harvest in 1788, unrest spread throughout the country. On July 14 the people stormed the **BASTILLE** prison. The peasantry then revolted in the countryside. The National Constituent Assembly was formed and took control. While unrest continued in France, the French Revolution is noteworthy for having inspired revolutionary movements throughout Europe and beyond.

In 1804 **NAPOLEON BONAPARTE** emerged as emperor of France and proceeded to conquer much of Europe. French occupation of Spain weakened that country enough that revolutionary movements in its colonies strengthened. Latin American countries led by **SIMÓN BOLIVAR** joined Haiti and the United States in revolution against colonial European powers. By 1815, other European powers had managed to halt France; at the **CONGRESS OF VIENNA** in 1815, European powers agreed on a **BALANCE OF POWER** in Europe.

EXAMPLE

6. Which of the following best describes the motivation for Protestant reformers?
   - **A)** Protestants, including Martin Luther, originally sought to develop a new form of Christianity separate from the Catholic Church.
   - **B)** Protestants like Martin Luther were unhappy with the teachings of the Church, including papal indulgences and corruption in the Church, and originally sought reform.
   - **C)** Protestants were initially influenced by European political leaders, who used them to limit the power of the Church.
   - **D)** Protestants such as Martin Luther wanted to topple the Catholic Church, believing it to have become too corrupt.

NATIONALISM, INDUSTRY, and IMPERIALISM

The nineteenth century was a period of change and conflict, and the roots of the major twentieth century conflicts—world war and decolonization—are found in it. Modern European social and political structures and norms, including **NATIONALISM** and the **NATION-STATE**, would begin to emerge. Economic theories based in the Industrial Revolution like **SOCIALISM** and eventually **COMMUNISM** gained traction with the stark class divisions brought on by **URBANIZATION** and industry.

Following the Napoleonic Wars, Prussia had come to dominate the German-speaking states that had composed the Holy Roman Empire. **OTTO VON BISMARCK** unified the linguistically and culturally German states of Central Europe. Prussian power had been growing, fueled by **NATIONALISM** and the **NATION-STATE,** or the idea that individuals with shared experience (including ethnicity, language, religion, and cultural practices) should be unified under one government. In 1871, the **GERMAN EMPIRE** became a unified state. Bismarck encouraged economic cooperation, instituted army reforms, and cultivated an image of Prussia as a defender of German culture and nationhood.

In the Balkans, Southwest Asia and North Africa, the Ottoman Empire was in decline. The Ottoman Empire had long been a major force in Europe, controlling the bulk of the Balkans. However, the empire had lost land in Europe to the Austrians and in Africa to British and French imperialists. In the Balkans, rebellion among small nations supported by larger European powers would put an end to Ottoman power in Europe for good.

DID YOU KNOW?
World War I was rooted in complex alliances among countries going back to the mid-nineteenth century.

Eventually tension between Russia and Austria-Hungary—which was supported by Germany—led to the breakdown of Russian relationships with those countries. At the same time, Russian relations with Great Britain and France improved. In 1894, Russia and France became allies. This alliance would culminate in the 1907 **Triple Entente**, setting the stage for the system of alliances at the heart of the First World War.

Continued European involvement in the Balkans accelerated the ongoing loss of Ottoman influence there due to phenomena like nationalism, **Pan-Slavism** (by which Balkan nations like Serbia and Bulgaria were empowered to rebel against the Ottoman Empire by identifying with Russia), military and political power, and religious influence. The Balkan nations continued rebellion against Ottoman rule, and European powers proceeded into the area.

Eventually, instability in the region would lead to the First World War which was triggered by the assassination of the Austro-Hungarian **Archduke Franz Ferdinand** by the Serbian nationalist **Gavrilo Princip** in Bosnia-Herzegovina in 1914.

Meanwhile, European powers were expanding their reach overseas. As colonialism in the fifteenth and sixteenth centuries had been driven by mercantilism, conquest, and Christian conversion, so was seventeenth, eighteenth and nineteenth century imperialism driven by capitalism, European competition, and conceptions of racial superiority.

In 1837, **Queen Victoria** ascended to the English throne. During her reign (1837 – 1901) the British Empire would expand enormously, controlling much of Sub-Saharan Africa, South Asia, and the Pacific. The concept of the ***white man's burden***, wherein white Europeans were "obligated" to bring their "superior" culture to other civilizations around the globe, also drove imperialism, popularizing it at home in Britain and elsewhere in Europe.

The European powers were immersed in what became known as the ***Scramble for Africa***; the industrial economies of Europe would profit from the natural resources abundant in that continent, and the "white man's burden" continued to fuel colonization. At the **1884 Berlin Conference**, control over Africa was divided among European powers without regard for or consultation with existing civilizations on the continent.

To gain access to closed **Chinese** markets, Britain forced China to buy Indian opium; the **Opium Wars** ended with the **Treaty of Nanking (1842)**. As a consequence, China lost great power to Britain and later, other European countries, which gained **spheres of influence**, or areas of China they effectively controlled, and **extraterritoriality**, or privileges in which their citizens were not subject to Chinese law.

However, not all non-European countries fell to European imperialism. **Ethiopia** was never colonized, having repelled Italian forces. In Asia, the Emperor Meiji promoted modernization of technology, especially the military, during the **Meiji Restoration** of 1868. Japan proved itself a world power when it defeated Russia in the **Russo-Japanese War** in 1905, and would play a central role in twentieth century conflict.

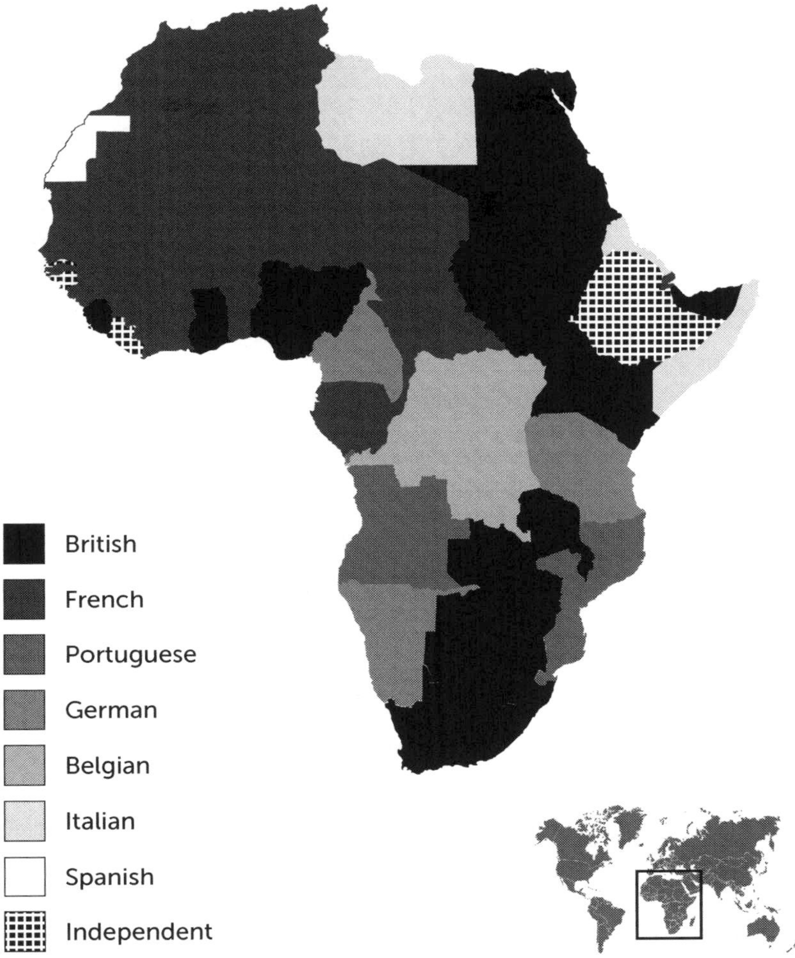

Figure 4.6. Imperial Africa

Raw goods from colonies fueled European economic growth and development, leading to the **Industrial Revolution** in the nineteenth century. Industrialization began in Manchester, where factories produced textiles using cotton from the colonies. Poor people moved from rural areas to cities for higher-paying jobs in factories, beginning **urbanization.**

Early industrial technology sped up the harvesting and transport of crops and their conversion to textiles. This accelerated manufacturing was based on **capitalism**, the ***laissez-faire*** (or **free market**) theory developed by **Adam Smith**, who believed that an ***invisible hand*** should guide the marketplace—that government should stay out of the economy regardless of abuses, as the economy would eventually automatically correct for inequalities, price problems, and any other problematic issues.

To access the raw materials needed to produce manufactured goods, Britain and other industrializing countries in Western Europe needed resources—hence the drive for imperialism. Cotton was harvested in India and Egypt for textile mills; minerals were mined in South Africa and the Congo for industry. Furthermore, as industrialization and urbanization led to the development of early middle classes in Europe and North America, imports of luxury goods from Asia increased to meet consumer demand. Colonial powers also profited by selling manufactured goods back to the colonies.

Largely unbridled capitalism had led to the dangerous conditions of the early Industrial Revolution; workers suffered from poor treatment and unsafe working environments. The German philosophers **Karl Marx** and **Friedrich Engels** were appalled by these injustices. They developed **socialism**, the philosophy that workers, or the **proletariat**, should own the means of production and reap the benefits, rather than the **bourgeoisie**, who were only concerned with profit. Later, Marx and Engels wrote the ***Communist Manifesto***, a pamphlet laying out their ideas and calling for revolution.

Communism inspired the Russian intellectuals **Vladimir Lenin** and **Leon Trotsky**, paving the way for the political and economic organization of the Soviet Union. In Russia, Tsar Nicholas faced dissent at home due to a humiliating defeat by Japan in the 1905 Russo-Japanese War; discontent was fueled by longer-term economic hardship compared to industrial Europe and limited freedoms. Workers began striking, and peasants rebelled against oppressive taxation. Following a period of revolution and instability, Lenin's party, the **Bolsheviks**, would gain power and eventually take over the country. Installing a communist government, they established the Soviet Union in 1921.

EXAMPLE

7. The Meiji Restoration was

A) an attempt to restore traditional Japan as it had been before Western incursions into the country.

B) a period of modernization and westernization in Japan.

C) the early stage of Japanese imperialism in Asia, when it invaded Korea.

D) a cultural movement in Japan to reinvigorate Shintoism and traditional poetry.

Twentieth Century

GLOBAL CONFLICTS

The assassination of the Austro-Hungarian Archduke **Franz Ferdinand** in Sarajevo on June 28, 1914, kicked off the **system of alliances** that had been in place among European powers, setting off the First World War.

Austria-Hungary declared war on Serbia, and Russia came to Serbia's aid. An ally of Austria-Hungary as part of the **Triple Alliance**, Germany declared war on Russia.

Russia's ally France prepared for war; as Germany traversed Belgium to invade France, Belgium pleaded for aid from other European countries and so the United Kingdom declared war on Germany. After several provocations, in 1917 the United States would join the war on the side of the **Triple Entente** (France, Russia, and the United Kingdom), helping defeat Germany.

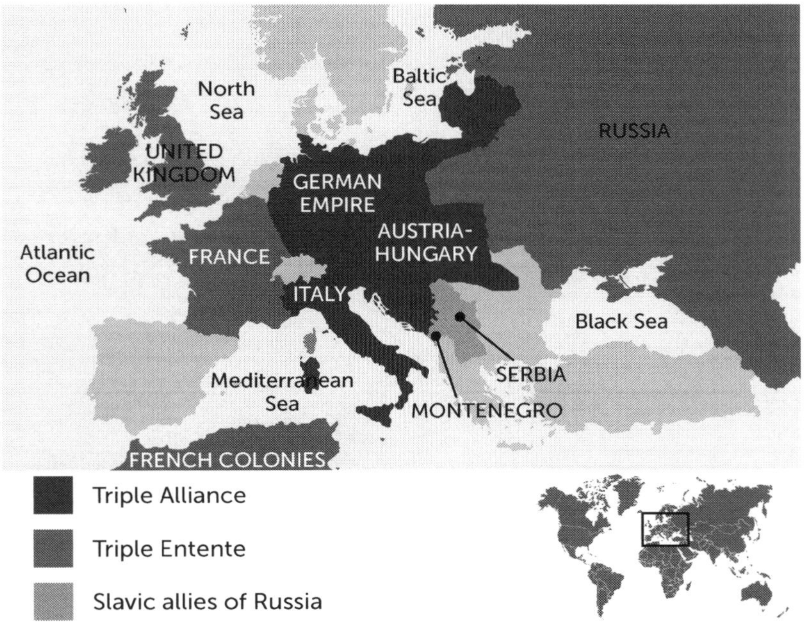

Figure 4.7. WWI Alliances

Germany had been emphasizing military growth since the consolidation of the empire under Bismarck. Now, under **Kaiser Wilhelm II**, who sought expanded territories in Europe and overseas for Germany, it was a militarized state and an important European power.

According to the **Schlieffen Plan**, Germany had planned to fight a war on two fronts against both Russia and France. However, Russia's unexpectedly rapid mobilization stretched the German army too thin on the Eastern Front, while it became bogged down in **trench warfare** on the Western Front against the British, French, and later the Americans. Germany lost the war and was punished with the harsh **Treaty of Versailles**. The treaty brought economic hardship on the country by forcing it to pay **reparations** for the war. German military failure and consequent economic collapse set the stage for the rise of fascism and Adolf Hitler.

DID YOU KNOW?

The treaty also created the **League of Nations**, an international organization designed to prevent conflict; however, it was largely powerless, especially because the United States did not join.

The end of WWI also marked the end of the Ottoman Empire, which was officially dissolved in 1923. From the end of the nineteenth century, the British had been increasing their influence throughout Ottoman territory in Egypt and the Persian Gulf, seeking control over the Suez Canal and petroleum resources in the Gulf. The Ottomans had already lost their North African provinces to France in the mid-nineteenth century.

In 1916, France and Britain concluded the **Sykes-Picot Agreement**, which secretly planned for the Middle East following the defeat of the Ottoman Empire. The agreement divided up the region into spheres of influence to be controlled by each power; Palestine would be governed internationally. In 1917, the secret **Balfour Declaration** promised the Jewish people an independent state in Palestine, but Western powers did not honor this agreement. The state of Israel was not established until 1948.

At the end of the war the area was indeed divided into **mandates** controlled by Britain and France. Most of those borders remain today dividing the modern Middle East. After the First World War, the nationalist Turkish leader **Mustafa Ataturk** kept European powers out of Anatolia and abolished the Caliphate in 1924, establishing modern Turkey.

DID YOU KNOW?
The first international war to use industrialized weaponry, WWI was called "the Great War" because battle on such a scale had never before been seen.

After the dissolution of the Ottoman Empire, the future of the Middle East was uncertain. Despite its weaknesses, the Ottoman Empire had been the symbolic center of Islam, controlling Mecca and Medina. The Ottoman sultan held the title of Caliph, or the one entrusted with the leadership of those two cities holy in Islam. With the region broken up into European-controlled protectorates and an independent, nationalist, secular Turkey turned toward Europe, the social and political fabric of the region was becoming undone.

The roots of two competing ideologies, **Pan-Arabism** and **Islamism**, developed in this context. According to **Pan-Arabism**, Arabs and Arabic speakers should be aligned regardless of international borders. Similar to Pan-Slavism, Pan-Arabism eventually became an international movement espousing Arab unity in response to European and US influence and presence later in the twentieth century. **Islamism** or political Islam began as a social and political movement, where Islam, rather than Arabic and Arab culture, was a unifying factor. It influenced political thinkers and groups, including violent extremists, into the twenty-first century.

In the Soviet Union, following Lenin's death in 1924, the Secretary of the Communist Party, **Josef Stalin**, took power. The USSR became socially and politically repressive; the Communist Party and the military underwent **purges** where any persons who were a potential threat to Stalin's power were imprisoned or executed.

DID YOU KNOW?
In the 1920s, around twenty million Russians were sent to the gulags, usually hundreds or thousands of miles from their homes. Millions died.

The general population suffered under the **Great Terror** throughout the 1920s. Any hint of dissent was to be reported to the secret police and usually resulted in imprisonment in ***gulags***, forced labor camps. Stalin also enforced **Russification** policies, persecuting ethnic and religious minorities.

In 1931, Stalin enforced the **collectivization** of land and agriculture in an attempt to consolidate control over the countryside and improve food security. The government confiscated land and imprisoned landowners; by 1939, most farming and land was controlled by the government, and most peasants lived on collective land. Collectivizing the farms encouraged more peasants to become industrial workers. However, systemic disorganization in the 1920s and early 1930s resulted in famine and food shortages.

As part of modernizing Russia, Stalin focused on accelerating industrial development. Targeting heavy industry, these **Five Year Plans** increased production of industrial materials and developed major infrastructure. The USSR quickly became an industrial power, but at the expense of millions who lost their lives in purges, forced labor camps, and famine.

Similar rapid modernization occurred in East Asia. Japan had undergone rapid modernization as part of the Meiji Restoration in the nineteenth century. After the Russo-Japanese War, Japan turned towards imperialism throughout Asia, gaining control of parts of China, Korea, and the Pacific Islands in the early twentieth century, which Japan considered its ***sphere of influence***.

While Japan was building its global reputation and military and economic strength in Asia, China was undergoing political change. Dynastic Chinese rule ended in 1911 with a revolution. After a short-lived republic, China came under the control of two rival factions: the **Kuomintang (KMT)**, or Nationalist Party led by **Jiang Jieshi** (**Chiang**

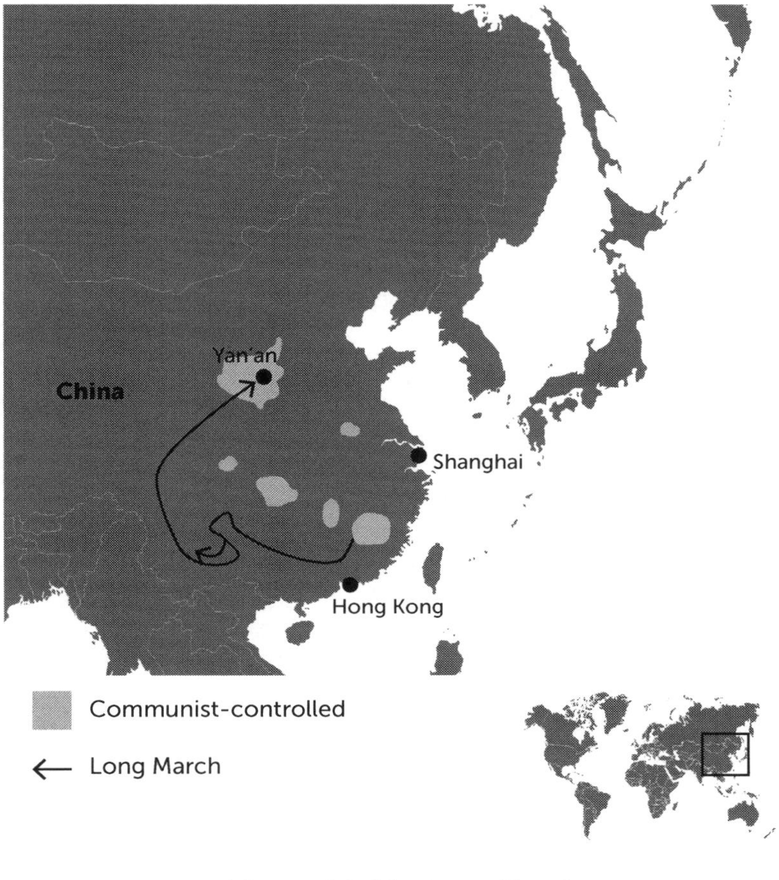

Figure 4.8. The Long March

Kai-shek), and the **Chinese Communist Party (CCP)** led by **Mao Zedong**. In the 1920s and 1930s, parts of coastal and northern China were controlled by Japan; the KMT controlled much of the south, although peasants there supported the communists, and the CCP had been driven north by the KMT in the arduous **Long March**.

Meanwhile, Germany suffered under the provisions of the Treaty of Versailles. In 1919, a democratic government was established—the **Weimar Republic**. But debt from **reparations** owed for WWI set off **hyperinflation**, impoverishing the country and its people. Economic crisis was amplified by the stock market crash in 1929 and the Great Depression. In this climate, the National Socialist Party, or **Nazi Party**, led by **Adolf Hitler**, became powerful as an alternative to the ineffective Weimar government.

Hitler's charisma and popular platform—to cancel the Treaty of Versailles—allowed him to become chancellor and then ***Führer***, or *leader*, by 1934. Nazi ideals and effective propaganda appealed strongly to both industrial interests and workers in the face of global economic depression. Hitler and the Nazis consolidated total control by banning political parties and trade unions and establishing the violent **Gestapo**, or secret police. They also set into motion their agenda of racism and genocide against Jewish people, Roma, Slavic people, homosexuals, disabled people, people of color, communists, and others. So-called "undesirables," particularly the Jews in Germany and eventually other European countries, were discriminated against, forced into ghettoes, and later imprisoned and murdered in **concentration camps**. At least six million European Jews were murdered by the Nazis in the **Holocaust**.

Hitler sought to restore Germany's power and expand its reach by annexing **Austria** and part of what is today the Czech Republic. He invaded the rest of **Czechoslovakia** and formed an alliance with **Italy**. In 1939, Germany invaded **Poland** in what is commonly considered the beginning of the **Second World War (WWII)**. Europe descended into conflict again. Despite staying out of combat, in 1941 the **United States** enforced the **Lend-Lease Act** which provided support and military aid to Britain. The two also released the **Atlantic Charter**, outlining common goals.

Japan joined the **Axis** powers of Germany and Italy, bringing conflict in Asia into the Second World War. Japan had invaded and occupied parts of China and other parts of East and Southeast Asia controlled by Europe, threatening European imperial and economic interests. In December of 1941, Japan attacked the United States at Pearl Harbor. Consequently, the US joined the war in Europe and in the Pacific, deploying thousands of troops in both theaters. In 1944, the Allies invaded France on **D-Day**; as the US led forces from the west and the USSR pushed from the east, Germany surrendered in the spring of 1945.

The war in the Pacific would continue until the summer of 1945, when the US used atomic bombs against the Japanese cities of **Hiroshima** and **Nagasaki**. The tremendous civilian casualties forced the Emperor to surrender; the Second World War came to an end.

DID YOU KNOW?

The Atlantic Charter described values shared by the US and Britain, including restoring self-governance in occupied Europe and liberalizing international trade.

The **Chinese Civil War** between Mao Zedong's CCP and Jiang Jieshi's KMT had halted as Chinese forces united against Japanese invasion. By the end of the war, the CCP was stronger than ever, with widespread support from many sectors of Chinese society. By 1949 the communists had emerged victorious and China became a communist country.

Allied forces took the lead in rebuilding efforts: the US occupied areas in East Asia and Germany, while the Soviet Union remained in Eastern Europe. The Allies had planned to rebuild Europe according to the **Marshall Plan**; however, Stalin broke his promise made at the 1945 **Yalta Conference** held by the Allies to allow Eastern European countries to hold free elections after the war. Instead, the USSR occupied these countries and they came under communist control. The **Cold War** had begun.

Stalin ensured that communists came to power in Eastern Europe, setting up satellite states at the Soviet perimeter. The Soviet rationale was to establish a buffer zone following its extraordinarily heavy casualties in WWII. Germany was divided into east and west, and eventually a wall built dividing the city of Berlin. An ***iron curtain*** had come down across Europe, dividing east from west.

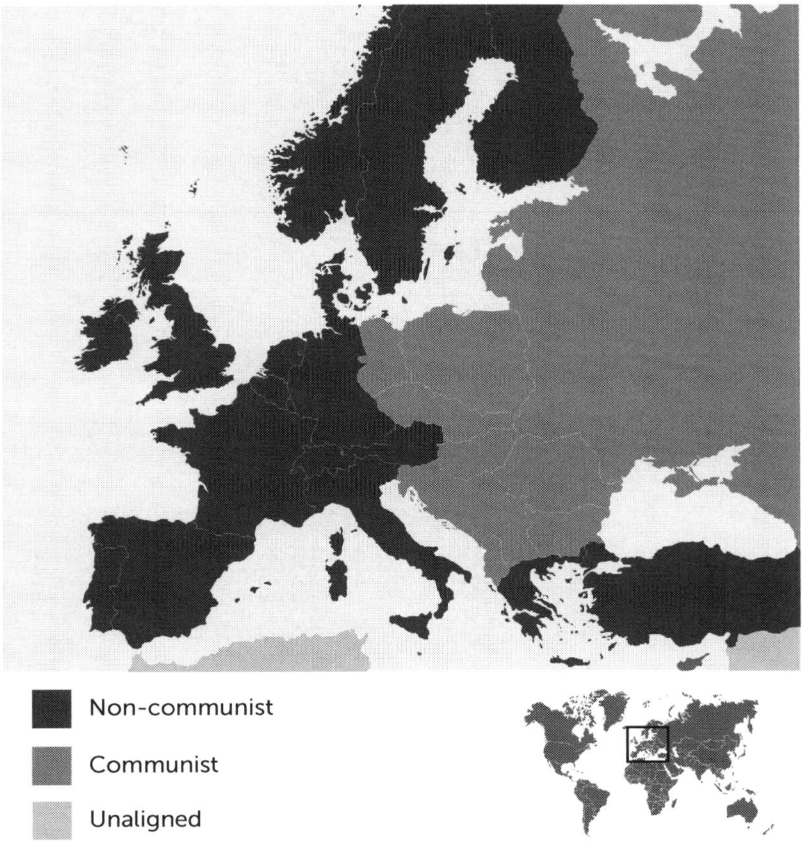

Figure 4.9. Cold War Europe

Consequently, western states organized the North Atlantic Treaty Organization or **NATO**, a **collective security** agreement in the face of the Soviet expansionist threat.

The United States adopted a policy of **CONTAINMENT**, the idea that communism should be *contained*, as part of the **TRUMAN DOCTRINE** of foreign policy.

In response, the Soviet Union created the **WARSAW PACT**, a similar organization consisting of Eastern European communist countries. **ATOMIC WEAPONS**, especially the development of the extremely powerful **HYDROGEN BOMB**, raised the stakes of the conflict. During the **CUBAN MISSILE CRISIS** in 1962, the world came closer than ever to nuclear war when the US found out the Soviet Union was building missile bases in communist Cuba. Diplomacy averted disaster.

QUICK REVIEW

What factors caused the Cold War to erupt between the Allies and the Soviet Union?

According to the Truman Doctrine, communism needed to be contained. Furthermore, according to **DOMINO THEORY**, if one country became communist, then more would, too, like a row of dominoes falling. Therefore, the United States, by way of the United Nations, became involved in the **KOREAN WAR** (1950 – 1953) which divided the country into North and South Korea.

United States pursued conflict in **VIETNAM** for almost a decade beginning in the early 1960s. Supporting anti-communist fighters, the US battled North Vietnamese forces, including the guerrilla fighters called **VIET CONG**, in a war for Vietnamese sovereignty throughout the 1960s. Despite being outnumbered, the Viet Cong's familiarity with the difficult terrain, support from Russia and China, and determination eventually resulted in victory. Extreme objection to the war within the United States, high casualties, and demoralization resulted in US withdrawal in 1973.

Toward the end of the 1960s and into the 1970s, the Cold War reached a period of **DÉTENTE**, or a warming of relations. The US and USSR signed the **NUCLEAR NON-PROLIFERATION TREATY**, in which they and other nuclear powers agreed not to further spread nuclear weapons technology. Later, the USSR and the US signed the **SALT I** (Strategic Arms Limitation Treaty), limiting strategic weaponry. Some cultural exchanges and partnerships in outer space took place also.

At the same time, the United States began making diplomatic overtures toward communist China. Despite its status as a communist country, China and the USSR had difficult relations due to their differing views on the nature of communism. Nikita Khrushchev, Soviet leader from Stalin's death until the 1970s, took a moderate approach to world communism, while Mao supported active revolution. Following the **SINO-SOVIET SPLIT** of the 1960s, China had lost much Soviet support for its modernization programs. Despite advances in agriculture and some industrialization, Mao's programs like the **GREAT LEAP FORWARD** and the **CULTURAL REVOLUTION** had taken a toll on the people. In 1972, President Nixon visited China, establishing relations between the communist government and the United States.

The climate would change again, however, in the 1970s and 1980s. The US and USSR found themselves supporting opposing sides in regional conflicts throughout the world. **PRESIDENT RONALD REAGAN** pursued a militaristic policy, prioritizing weapons development with the goal of outspending the USSR on weapons technology. The **ARMS RACE** was underway.

Meanwhile, the former colonies of the fallen European colonial powers had won or were in the process of gaining their independence through **DECOLONIZATION**. These newly formed countries constituted the ***THIRD WORLD***, an alternative to the countries directly dominated by the democratic-capitalist and communist spheres of the US and USSR. However, the global superpowers fought for dominance worldwide by arming different sides in smaller regional conflicts (fighting *proxy wars*) and influencing regional and global politics.

Already, the leader **MOHANDAS GANDHI** had led a peaceful independence movement in **INDIA** against the British, winning Indian independence in 1949. His assassination by Hindu radicals led to conflict between **HINDUS** and **MUSLIMS** in the **SUBCONTINENT**, resulting in **PARTITION**, the violent division of India into India, Pakistan and later, Bangladesh.

African countries became independent through both revolution and thanks to strong leadership by African nationalist leaders and thinkers. The **APARTHEID** regime in South Africa, where segregation between races was enforced and people of color lived in oppressive conditions, was not lifted until the 1990s; **NELSON MANDELA** led the country in a peaceful transition process.

In the Middle East, post-Ottoman ***PROTECTORATES*** became independent states with arbitrary borders drawn and rulers installed by the Europeans. The creation of the state of **ISRAEL** was especially contentious: in the 1917 **BALFOUR DECLARATION**, the British had promised the **ZIONIST** movement that the Jews would be given a homeland in the British-controlled protectorate of Palestine. However, the US assured the Arabs in 1945 that a Jewish state would not be founded there. Israel emerged from diplomatic confusion, chaos, and tragedy after the murder of millions of Jewish people in Europe, and violence on the ground in Palestine carried out by both Jews and Arabs. This legacy of conflict persists in the Middle East.

In Egypt, **GAMAL ABDUL NASSER** led the Pan-Arabist movement in the region, which included creating an Arab alliance against Israel. Arab allies fought Israel in the 1967 Six-Day War and again in the 1973 Yom Kippur War, but Israel held on to and even gained territory. In 1978, the US brokered a peace agreement between Egypt and Israel—the **CAMP DAVID ACCORDS**. By the 1970s, Pan-Arabism was no longer the popular, unifying movement it had once been.

QUICK REVIEW

What is a proxy war? Why were proxy wars important in the context of the Cold War?

PROXY WARS between the US and the USSR were fought around the world. In 1979, the USSR invaded **AFGHANISTAN**, an event which would contribute to the Soviet collapse; in response, the US began supporting anti-Soviet ***MUJAHIDEEN*** forces there. Other examples include the Nicaraguan Revolution, the **ANGOLAN CIVIL WAR**, the **MOZAMBICAN CIVIL WAR**, and conflict in the Horn of Africa.

While never officially colonized, **Iran** had been under the oppressive regime of the western-supported **Shah** for decades. By the 1970s, the Shah's corrupt, oppressive regime was extremely unpopular in Iran, but it was propped up by the West. Following the 1979 **Iranian Revolution**, Islamist revolutionaries took over the country. The new theocracy was led by the **Ayatollah Khomeini**, who instituted political and social reforms, including stricter interpretations of Islamic laws and traditions. Later that year, radical students stormed the US embassy and held a number of staff hostage for over a year; the **Iran Hostage Crisis** would humiliate the United States.

Following the Iranian Revolution, the Iraqi leader **Saddam Hussein** declared war against Iran. Saddam feared Iran would trigger a similar revolution there. Iraq also sought control over strategic territories. The Iran-Iraq war raged from 1980 – 1990.

EXAMPLE

8. The Warsaw Pact was a supranational organization created in response to

A) NATO.

B) the United Nations.

C) the European Union.

D) the League of Nations.

POST-COLD WAR WORLD

In 1991, the Soviet Union fell when Soviet Premier **Mikhail Gorbachev**, who had implemented reforms like ***glasnost*** and ***perestroika*** (or *openness* and *transparency*), was nearly overthrown in a coup. A movement led by **Boris Yeltsin**, who had been elected president of Russia, stopped the coup. The USSR was dissolved later that year and Yeltsin became president of the Russian Federation. The war in Afghanistan and military overspending in an effort to keep up with American military spending had weakened the USSR to the point of collapse, and the Cold War ended.

In 1990, Saddam Hussein, the leader of Iraq, invaded Kuwait and took over its oil reserves and production facilities. In response, an international coalition led by the United States expelled Iraq from Kuwait and protected Saudi Arabia, regaining control of the world's petroleum reserves in the **Gulf War**. This event cemented the US status as the sole world superpower.

Despite stability throughout most of Europe, the changes following the fall of the Iron Curtain led to instability in the Balkans. The **Bosnian War** raged from 1992 to 1995, resulting in the deaths of thousands of civilians and another European genocide—this time, of Bosnian Muslims. Also following the Cold War, instability in the developing world continued as a result of colonialism and proxy wars. In 1994, conflict in Central Africa resulted in the **Rwandan Genocide**. In the 1980s, drought in the Horn of Africa led to widespread famine; humanitarian affairs and issues came into the public eye and the general public became more concerned about providing foreign aid.

The balance of economic and political power began to change. The **G-20**, the world's twenty most important economic and political powers, includes many former colonies and non-European countries. The **BRICS**—Brazil, Russia, India, China, and South Africa—are recognized as world economic and political leaders.

Steps toward European unification had begun as early as the 1950s; the **European Union**, as it is known today, was formed after the **Maastricht Treaty** was signed in 1992. As the former Soviet satellite states moved from communism to more democratic societies and capitalistic economies, more countries partnered with the EU and eventually joined it; as of 2015, twenty-eight countries are members, with more on the path to membership.

Continental integration exists beyond Europe. In Africa, the **African Union**, originally the Organization of African Unity, has become a stronger political force in its own right, organizing peacekeeping missions throughout the continent. An organization similar to the EU, the AU is a forum for African countries to organize and align political, military, economic, and other policies.

In this era of **globalization**, international markets became increasingly open through free-trade agreements like **NAFTA** (the North American Free Trade Agreement) and **Mercosur** (the South American free-trade zone). The **World Trade Organization** oversees international trade. Technological advances like improvements in transportation infrastructure and the **internet** made international communication faster, easier, and cheaper.

However, more reliable international transportation and faster, easier worldwide communication brought risks, too. In the early twenty-first century, the United States was attacked by terrorists on **September 11, 2001**, resulting in thousands of civilian casualties. Consequently, the US launched a major land war in Afghanistan and another later in Iraq.

Following the attacks on 9/11, the United States attacked Afghanistan as part of the **War on Terror**. Afghanistan's radical Islamist **Taliban** government was providing shelter to the group that took responsibility for the attacks, **al Qaeda**. Led by **Osama bin Laden**, al Qaeda was inspired by radical Islamism. Bin Laden had fought the Soviets with the US-supported Afghan *mujahideen* during the 1980s; despite that alliance, bin Laden and his followers were angered by US involvement in the Middle East throughout the 1990s and its support of Israel. While bin Laden was killed by the United States in 2011, and while control of Afghan security was turned over from the US to the US-backed government in 2014, the US still maintains a strong military presence in the country.

DID YOU KNOW?
While benefits of international trade include lower prices and more consumer choice, unemployment often increases in more developed countries and labor and environmental violations are more likely in developing countries. How do you feel about international trade?

The **Iraq War** began in 2003 when the US invaded that country under the faulty premises that Saddam Hussein's regime was involved with al Qaeda, supported international terrorism, and illegally possessed weapons of mass destruction. Iraq descended into chaos, with thousands of civilian and military casualties, Iraqi and American alike. While the country technically and legally remains intact under a US-supported government, the ethnically and religiously diverse country is de facto divided as a result of the disintegration of central power.

Elsewhere in the Middle East, reform movements began via the 2011 **Arab Spring** in Tunisia, Egypt, Bahrain, and Syria. Some dictatorial regimes have been replaced with democratic governments; other countries still enjoy limited freedoms or even civil unrest. In Syria, unrest erupted into civil war. One consequence has been enormous movements of **refugees** into Europe. Uprisings in Israeli-occupied West Bank and Gaza have continued sporadically. Long-term peace efforts have failed and conflict continues.

EXAMPLE

9. In the twenty-first century, which phenomenon has so far characterized global governance?

A) international terrorism

B) globalized political and economic organization

C) worldwide war and conflict

D) the European Union and the African Union

Test Your Knowledge

Read the question, and then choose the most correct answer.

1. Boston, New York, Philadelphia, Baltimore, and Washington DC, as geographically close urban areas, form a(n)

A) urban realm

B) world city

C) megalopolis

D) transition zone

2. According to the map below, which city is located at approximately 39°N, 126°E?

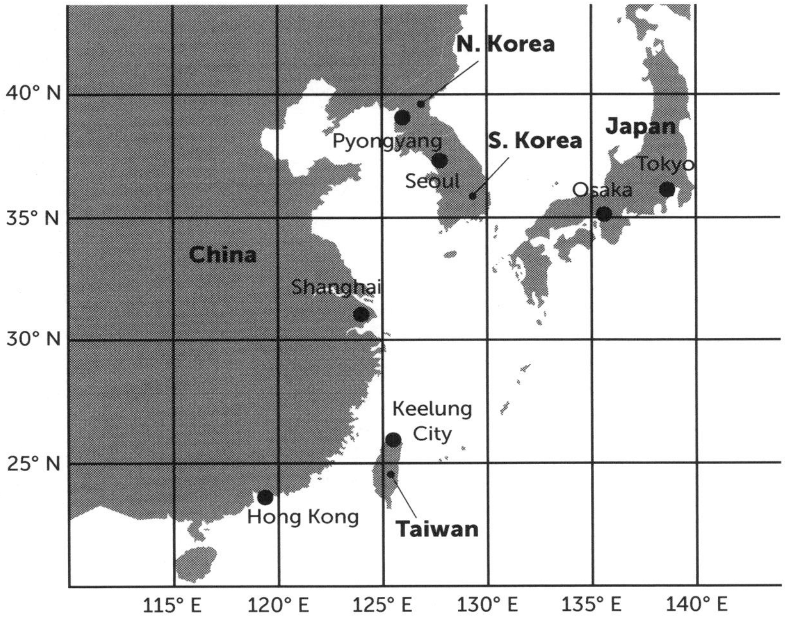

A) Tokyo

B) Keelung

C) Pyongyang

D) Pusan

3. Which of the following is a nonrenewable resource?

A) coal

B) wind

C) plants

D) fish

4. Which of the following would be considered a push factor for migration?
   - **A)** a peace treaty being signed, ending civil war in a country
   - **B)** a new law in the home country requiring a religious practice
   - **C)** the discovery of oil in a certain region
   - **D)** the relocation of a major company to its home region

5. Ancient Egypt was able to develop into a civilizational power due to which of the following?
   - **A)** the Indus River valley
   - **B)** the agricultural yield of Mesopotamia
   - **C)** the Yellow River valley
   - **D)** the Nile Valley

6. Why did Rome evolve into an empire from a republic?
   - **A)** It was able to conquer so much land that it would have been impossible to maintain the Republic in its original form.
   - **B)** The patricians of Rome amassed so much wealth that they were able to take over the Senate and establish an empire.
   - **C)** Hannibal was able to overthrow the Senate and establish an empire in its place.
   - **D)** The wealthy patricians of the Senate became corrupt, disregarding the interests of the plebeians who then supported Julius Caesar's coup.

7. How was the Mandate of Heaven an important concept in early Chinese history?
   - **A)** It taught that the people in the area that became China were divinely fated to unite as one culture.
   - **B)** It taught that the emperor had a divine mandate to rule the people in what would become China.
   - **C)** It taught that China was a divinely important world power, meant to become a global leader.
   - **D)** It taught that the emperor was a divine servant of the people of in the area that would become China.

8. How did political stability or instability impact trade along the Silk Road?
   - **A)** Stable imperial rule allowed for easier trade and travel, as roads were safe.
   - **B)** Political instability made trading more profitable, since demand for scarce goods would rise.
   - **C)** Political stability led traders to use sea routes, even when navigation technology was limited.
   - **D)** Since trade was so profitable, political conditions did not impact the trade routes.

9. Following the collapse of the Western Roman Empire, what was the status of serfs in Europe?

   A) Serfs, while bound to the land on the manors where they lived and forced to farm for the lords, were not enslaved, nor were they forced to fight for lords. Rather, they were to be protected.

   B) Serfs were agricultural slaves expected to farm the land on manors in order to support lords.

   C) Serfs were peasants on manors, expected to farm the land for lords but also able to farm their own land; they were free to leave manors if they wished but rarely did due to unsafe conditions.

   D) Serfs were agricultural slaves who were also expected to fight for lords when called upon for defense.

10. Despite never making significant land gains in the Levant, Europe benefitted from the Crusades through which of the following ways?

    A) Many knights returned from the Middle East with Middle Eastern, Muslim wives, bringing religious and ethnic diversity to Europe.

    B) Many knights returned to Europe with new language skills, helping reinvigorate trade on the Silk Road through Asia and Muslim-held lands into China.

    C) Crusaders returned to Europe with knowledge of Arab-Islamic technology, navigation, and science, eventually contributing to the Renaissance, the Scientific Revolution, and the colonial era.

    D) Crusaders returned to Europe with more knowledge of Eastern Orthodox Christianity, contributing to the rites and teachings of the Catholic Church after centuries of stagnation following the fall of the Roman Empire.

11. What was mercantilism?

    A) A political-economic system that enriched Spain by providing it with valuable raw materials, especially gold and silver.

    B) A financial system that placed particular value on merchants, allowing them to trade without taxes or duties.

    C) A colonial strategy established to counter the African slave trade by focusing on a marketplace of goods, not persons.

    D) A market strategy to enhance trade between indigenous populations in the Americas and Spain's European competitors like the Netherlands and Britain.

12. Which of the following led to the French Revolution?

    A) food shortages, heavy taxation, and Enlightenment thought

    B) the rise of Napoleon and militarization of French culture

    C) the Congress of Vienna and shifting diplomatic alliances in Europe

    D) the reign of Louis XIV

13. During the colonization of the Americas, the triangular trade across the Atlantic developed, and Africans suffered greatly; however, Africans still developed forms of resistance. Which of the following events or phenomena is an example of African resistance to slavery during this period?

A) the Maroon communities

B) the Seminole Wars

C) the Underground Railroad

D) the Ghost Dance movement

14. Which of the following best describes the motivation for Protestant reformers?

A) Protestants, including Martin Luther, originally sought to develop a new form of Christianity separate from the Catholic Church.

B) Protestants like Martin Luther were unhappy with the teachings of the Church, including papal indulgences and corruption in the Church, and originally sought reform.

C) Protestants were initially influenced by European political leaders, who used them to limit the power of the Church.

D) Protestants, including Martin Luther, originally sought to topple the Catholic Church, believing it to have become too corrupt.

15. How were European empires affected by nationalism in the eighteenth and nineteenth centuries?

A) European empires like the Austro-Hungarian Empire benefitted from nationalism, as Austrians and Hungarians were more loyal to the imperial government.

B) The Austro-Hungarian Empire lost its Balkan territories to the Ottoman Empire, which was perceived to be more tolerant of Muslim minorities.

C) Given the nature of empire—consolidated rule over an extended region home to diverse peoples—nationalism threatened empire as ethnic groups began to advocate for representation in imperial government.

D) Given the nature of empire—consolidated rule over an extended region home to diverse peoples—nationalism threatened empire as ethnic groups began to advocate for their own independent states.

16. Which of the following best explains the economic impact on Germany following the First World War?

A) Overspeculation on German farmland caused the market to crash.

B) The Great Depression and wartime reparations mandated by the Treaty of Versailles caused inflation to skyrocket, plunging the German economy into crisis.

C) Germans were forced to pay extra taxes to cover reparations, and due to high prices, many could not afford to do so.

D) The Reichsmark was removed from circulation and replaced with the dollar as a means of punishment, forcing many Germans into poverty.

17. Following the collapse of the Ottoman Empire after the First World War, European countries took control of the Middle East, establishing protectorates according to arbitrary boundaries and installing rulers in accordance with European strategic interests. What effect has this had on the Middle East in the twentieth and twenty-first centuries?

A) The Middle East has not been greatly affected.

B) Illegitimate national borders and rulers have led to instability in the region.

C) Better governance, thanks to the protectorates, improved stability following the decline of the Ottoman Empire in the region.

D) European investment in strategic resources supported long-term political stability in the Middle East.

18. What was one reason for the Sino-Soviet Split?

A) the Chinese alliance with the United States

B) the Soviet alliance with the United States

C) the absence of the People's Republic of China from the United Nations

D) the differences between the communist philosophies of China and the USSR

19. What was Apartheid?

A) strict racial segregation associated with South Africa

B) a type of slavery in South Africa

C) a form of colonial government in South Africa

D) rebellion against colonial South African government

20. After the Soviet invasion of Afghanistan and its subsequent withdrawal, what happened in Afghanistan?

A) Afghanistan came under Indian influence, making it vulnerable to extremist movements like the Taliban.

B) Afghanistan descended into a period of instability and civil war, making it vulnerable to extremist movements like the Taliban.

C) Afghanistan temporarily united with Pakistan in an effort to regain stability.

D) Afghanistan temporarily came under NATO administration in an effort to regain stability and prevent the development of extremist groups.

Answer Key

EXAMPLES

1. **C) is correct.** The goal of sustainable development is to ensure resources are available to the next generation. Therefore, renewable resources must be managed to make sure consumption does not outpace the rate of replacement.

2. **A) is correct.** More than half of the world's population lives in cities.

3. **C) is correct.** When a country does not have enough people to utilize its resources, it is underpopulated.

4. **B) is correct.** Strong infrastructure facilitated trade, communication, and military movement throughout the empire, ensuring unity and security.

5. **D) is correct.** Science and technology imported from the Middle East during the Crusades, coupled with a resurgence of Classical philosophy, art, and scholarship imported by Byzantine refugees, inspired the Renaissance.

6. **B) is correct.** Martin Luther and his followers opposed corruption in the Church and wanted changes.

7. **B) is correct.** The Meiji Restoration was a period of industrialization and westernization in Japan.

8. **A) is correct.** Following the creation of NATO, a military alliance formed to counter the Soviet Union, the USSR and the countries of the Eastern Bloc came to an agreement on collective defense—the Warsaw Pact.

9. **B) is correct.** While the United States remains a leading world power, the emergence of international organizations like the BRICS, the EU, the G-20, and the AU has empowered other countries; furthermore, international trade agreements are helping mold the balance of power. However, the AU, EU, and other organizations do not dominate the world in their own right, so they do not characterize global governance. Nor has the world descended into total chaos, so conflict and terrorism do not characterize global governance, either.

TEST YOUR KNOWLEDGE

1. A) is incorrect. An "urban realm" is not a geographic term. A realm is the largest unit the world can be divided into, and it includes multiple regions.

   B) is incorrect. A world city is a locus of global economic, cultural, or political power. While New York City is a world city, these five cities do not make up one.

   C) is correct. A megalopolis is a large urban area formed by the close proximity of multiple urban centers. These five cities are sometimes called the "BosWash megalopolis."

   D) is incorrect. A transition zone is an area between culture regions where traits from both regions exist. It does not relate to urban zones.

2. A) is incorrect. Tokyo is located at approximately 35°N, 140°E.

   B) is incorrect. Keelung is located at approximately 25°N, 122°E.

   C) is correct. Pyongyang is located at approximately 39°N, 126°E.

   D) is incorrect. Pusan is located at approximately 35°N, 129°E.

3. **A) is correct.** Coal is a finite resource. It is an organic rock formed over millions of years.

   B) is incorrect. Wind is essentially infinite, as it is harnessed and not consumed.

   C) is incorrect. While plants are consumed, they can be regrown relatively quickly.

   D) is incorrect. Like plants, when properly managed, fish populations are self-sustaining.

4. A) is incorrect. Ending conflict and bringing peace to an area would stabilize that area, making it more likely that the inhabitants would stay there. A peace treaty and resulting stability might even be a pull factor, attracting migrants from other places.

   B) is correct. This new law would push out any individuals who did not wish to practice the religion.

   C) is incorrect. The discovery of oil would lead to new job opportunities, acting as a pull factor in migration.

   D) is incorrect. Relocating a company to its home region would likely provide new job opportunities in the home region, discouraging migration out.

5. A) is incorrect. The Indus River is located in South Asia.

   B) is incorrect. Mesopotamia is located in Southwest Asia.

   C) is incorrect. The Yellow River is located in China.

   D) is correct. The Nile River is located in North Africa.

6. A) is incorrect. The Senate did not chose to dissolve itself and form an empire in order to better control land.

   B) is incorrect. The patricians already controlled the Senate and most Roman wealth when the Republic fell.

   C) is incorrect. Hannibal never overthrew the Senate.

   D) is correct. Caesar, with the support of dissatisfied Romans, took over the weak and corrupt Senate.

7. A) is incorrect. The Mandate of Heaven did not enforce cultural unity.

   B) is correct. The Mandate of Heaven legitimized imperial governance.

   C) is incorrect. The Mandate of Heaven did not dictate China's view of itself in the world.

   D) is incorrect. According to the Mandate of Heaven, the emperor was a ruler, not a servant.

8. **A) is correct.** Stability allowed safer travel and a stronger international economy, with demand for international products.

   B) is incorrect. Instability halted trade as it became unsafe to travel long distances in Asia.

   C) is incorrect. Oceanic routes were not widely used until the fifteenth century because navigation improved during the European Renaissance and Scientific Revolution.

   D) is incorrect. Despite the potential for profit, international commerce was impossible without security.

9. **A) is correct.** Serfs were not slaves, but they were not entirely free as they were bound to the lord's land and had to farm it. However, the lord was obligated to protect them, and they were not expected to fight.

   B) is incorrect. Serfs were not slaves and could not be individually bought or sold (although since they were tied to the land, they worked for whoever owned the land).

   C) is incorrect. Serfs could not leave the manor.

   D) is incorrect. Serfs were not slaves, nor were they expected to fight.

10. A) is incorrect. Fighters did not return with Middle Eastern wives and diversity in Europe did not increase.

    B) is incorrect. While some returning Europeans had learned a new language, this alone was not enough of a widespread phenomenon to impact international trade.

    C) is correct. Crusaders had gained knowledge of navigation, technology, medicine, and science, helping spark the Scientific Revolution and the Renaissance. This knowledge transfer also helped bring about the colonial era.

    D) is incorrect. In fact, at times the Orthodox Church and the Catholic Church worked together against Muslims.

11. **A) is correct.** Mercantilism enriched colonial powers at the expense of colonies, increasing their power relative to other European countries.

    B) is incorrect. Mercantilism was advanced by the government; it was not market based.

    C) is incorrect. The slave trade was an important element of mercantilism, enabling the cheap exploitation of labor and raw materials.

    D) is incorrect. In a mercantilist economy, the government promoted protectionism and increasing exports.

12. **A) is correct.** The peasants and bourgeoisie were dissatisfied with

bearing the brunt of the heavy tax burden; meanwhile, poor harvests led to food shortages and panic in rural areas. These factors, along with Enlightenment thought and recent revolutions elsewhere, spurred the French Revolution.

B) is incorrect. Napoleon came to power after the French Revolution.

C) is incorrect. The Congress of Vienna occurred after the French Revolution.

D) is incorrect. The reign of Louis XIV weakened the nobility and centralized power under the king. In the long term, weakening the nobility and isolating them at Versailles contributed to the circumstances that enabled the French Revolution. However, his reign alone did not cause it, and he was long dead by the time the Revolution began.

13. **A) is correct.** Maroon communities were communities of escaped slaves throughout the Americas.

B) is incorrect. The Seminole Wars were fought between the Seminole tribe and United States forces in Florida in the nineteenth century.

C) is incorrect. The Underground Railroad took place in the nineteenth century, after colonization of the Americas and the trans-Atlantic slave trade.

D) is incorrect. The Ghost Dance movement is an example of Native American resistance to westward expansion of the United States.

14. A) is incorrect. Martin Luther was a Catholic monk; he originally sought reform within the Catholic Church.

B) is correct. Martin Luther and his followers opposed corruption in the Church and wanted changes.

C) is incorrect. The Reformation was not originally a political movement.

D) is incorrect. Again, Martin Luther originally wanted reform, not to overthrow the papacy or the Church.

15. A) is incorrect. Nationalism did not benefit the Austro-Hungarian Empire: smaller ethnic groups living in territory controlled by the empire wanted their independence due to nationalism.

B) is incorrect. The Austro-Hungarian Empire began losing control over its Balkan territories due to nationalism and interference from Russia, which supported Slavic minorities in the Balkans.

C) is incorrect. Nationalism drove ethnic groups to seek self-rule and independence, not representation in imperial government.

D) is correct. Nationalism triggered independence movements and advocacy.

16. A) is incorrect. This explanation is insufficient.

B) is correct. The main factors in post-WWI German economic collapse are all addressed here.

C) is incorrect. This explanation does not account for global economic depression.

D) is incorrect. This is untrue.

17. A) is incorrect. Many of the boundaries are the modern borders of Middle Eastern countries today, so the region has been greatly affected.

B) is correct. Borders did not take into account history or ethnic groups; installed rulers did not necessarily have legitimacy in the eyes of the people, leading to political instability and violence.

C) is incorrect. The protectorates did not improve governance or stabilize the region following the decline of the Ottoman Empire.

D) is incorrect. Outside investment in strategic resources (like oil) has contributed to instability in the region by providing support to illegitimate rulers and contributing to income inequality and conflict.

18. A) is incorrect. China was not a US ally.

B) is incorrect. The Soviet Union was certainly not a US ally.

C) is incorrect. While the People's Republic of China was not represented at the UN, this was not the reason for the Sino-Soviet Split; the USSR recognized the PRC.

D) is correct. The Soviet establishment became increasingly alarmed at Maoist interpretations of communism, which differed from Marxism-Leninism.

19. **A) is correct.** Apartheid was a policy of racial segregation and unequal treatment in South Africa.

B) is incorrect. While Apartheid was a system of oppression against blacks and other people of color, it was not legalized slavery.

C) is incorrect. Apartheid was a policy under independent South Africa.

D) is incorrect. Apartheid was a social policy, not a revolutionary philosophy.

20. A) is incorrect. Afghanistan did not come under Indian influence, although it did become vulnerable to extremist influences.

B) is correct. Afghanistan became unstable and entered a period of civil war that ended only with the rise of the extremist Taliban. While the Taliban did stabilize much of the country, they also introduced an extremist, tribal ideology that oppressed women and minority groups and allowed terrorist groups to take hold.

C) is incorrect. While greatly influenced by Pakistan, Afghanistan did not unite with that country.

D) is incorrect. Technically, neither NATO nor any other international organization has governed Afghanistan, though a US-led international presence strongly influenced Afghan politics during the United States' war in Afghanistan in the early twenty-first century.

Click the link below for your second Social Studies GED practice test:
www.acceptedinc.com/ged-2018-online-resources

CHAPTER FIVE
Practice Test

Question 1 is based on a political cartoon entitled "The Temptation," which was written in response to the "Zimmerman Telegram" in 1917. The political cartoon shows two figures from different countries having a conversation about territory in the southeastern United States.

THE TEMPTATION

1. This political cartoon about the "Zimmerman Telegram," which was sent during World War I, signifies that the telegram was mostly focused on which proposal?

   A) Mexico wanted to propose a military alliance with Germany that would give a portion of the southwestern United States to Germany.

   B) Germany wanted to propose a military alliance with Mexico that would return a portion of the southwestern United States to Mexico.

   C) Germany wanted to bribe the United States and purchase the southwestern United States.

   D) Germany wanted to propose a strategic military alliance with the United States in the war against Mexico.

Questions 2, 3, and 4 are based on Section Three of the US Constitution. This section of the Constitution focuses on the Senate and includes directions about the methods and parameters for selecting a senator. Additionally, it provides an analysis of some of the leadership roles and duties of the US Senate.

Section Three

The Senate of the United States shall be composed of two Senators from each State, chosen by the Legislature thereof, for six Years; and each Senator shall have one Vote.

Immediately after they shall be assembled in Consequence of the first Election, they shall be divided as equally as may be into three Classes. The Seats of the Senators of the first Class shall be vacated at the Expiration of the second Year, of the second Class at the Expiration of the fourth Year, and of the third Class at the Expiration of the sixth Year, so that one third may be chosen every second Year; and if Vacancies happen by Resignation, or otherwise, during the Recess of the Legislature of any State, the Executive thereof may make temporary Appointments until the next Meeting of the Legislature, which shall then fill such Vacancies.

No Person shall be a Senator who shall not have attained to the Age of thirty Years, and been nine Years a Citizen of the United States, and who shall not, when elected, be an Inhabitant of that State for which he shall be chosen.

The Vice President of the United States shall be President of the Senate, but shall have no Vote, unless they be equally divided.

The Senate shall [choose] their other Officers, and also a President pro tempore, in the Absence of the Vice President, or when he shall exercise the Office of President of the United States.

The Senate shall have the sole Power to try all Impeachments. When sitting for that Purpose, they shall be on Oath or Affirmation. When the President of the United States is tried, the Chief Justice shall preside: And no Person shall be convicted without the Concurrence of two thirds of the Members present.

Judgment in Cases of Impeachment shall not extend further than to removal from Office, and disqualification to hold and enjoy any Office of honor, Trust or Profit under the United States: but the Party convicted shall nevertheless be liable and subject to Indictment, Trial, Judgment and Punishment, according to Law.

2. According to this document, the original selection process for US senators differed from the current process in which way?

A) Senators were appointed by the vice president and president.

B) Senators were chosen by the US Supreme Court justices.

C) Senators were chosen by the state legislature rather than being voted in by the citizenry.

D) Senators were selected by a process known as impeachment.

3. According to Section Three of the US Constitution, how long was the term for US senators?

A) Senators served six-year terms.

B) Senators served lifelong terms.

C) Senators served four-year terms.

D) Senators served two-year terms.

4. According to this excerpt of the US Constitution, who was designated the "President of the Senate"?

A) vice president of the United States

B) president of the United States

C) attorney general of the United States

D) secretary of state of the United States

Questions 5 and 6 are based on a photograph of a domestic standoff between protesters and military police in Arlington, Virginia, in the late 1960s. A female protester extends a flower to a military police officer who is armed and holding his baton. Another protester holds a sign that states: "Free...Leaders Jailed For Aiding Anti-War GIs." Other military police officers hold their batons tightly as they stand like a barrier in front of the young protesters.

5. This photo likely depicts what domestic conflict during the 1960s?

- **A)** student protests over the Vietnam War
- **B)** civil rights protests in the streets of the South
- **C)** feminist marches on Washington, DC
- **D)** the Black Power movement

6. The photo likely indicates that this event was

- **A)** violent in character, with a call for peace.
- **B)** peaceful in character, with the threat of military force.
- **C)** violent in character, with the threat of military force.
- **D)** generally peaceful in nature, with a few noticeable acts of violence.

Question 7 is based on an 1872 painting called the Spirit of the Frontier *by John Gast. The painting depicts settlers moving into the frontier. They are protected and led by a woman named Columbia, who is dressed in a classical toga. Columbia brings light and technology with her; the right side of the screen is brighter than the left side of the screen (the side Columbia is facing and leaning toward).*

7. *The Spirit of the Frontier* is best summarized as

A) a painting that depicts westward expansion into Native American frontiers by pioneers who are carrying the "manifest destiny" of the United States with them.

B) a painting that depicts the expansion of Native Americans into the eastern coasts of North America as the "manifest destiny" of the United States.

C) a painting that depicts the Revolutionary War and its "manifest destiny" to overthrow the British Crown.

D) a painting that depicts the disastrous "manifest destiny" of the conflict between North and South during the Civil War.

Questions 8 and 9 are based on an editorial cartoon published in the Philadelphia Press *in 1898. It is entitled "Ten Thousand Miles from Tip to Tip." It depicts an American eagle hovering over the globe with its wings extended from Puerto Rico to the Philippines. Below this larger eagle is a smaller eagle with a wingspan that extends from the East Coast to the Mississippi River. This smaller illustration is labeled with a different date: 1798.*

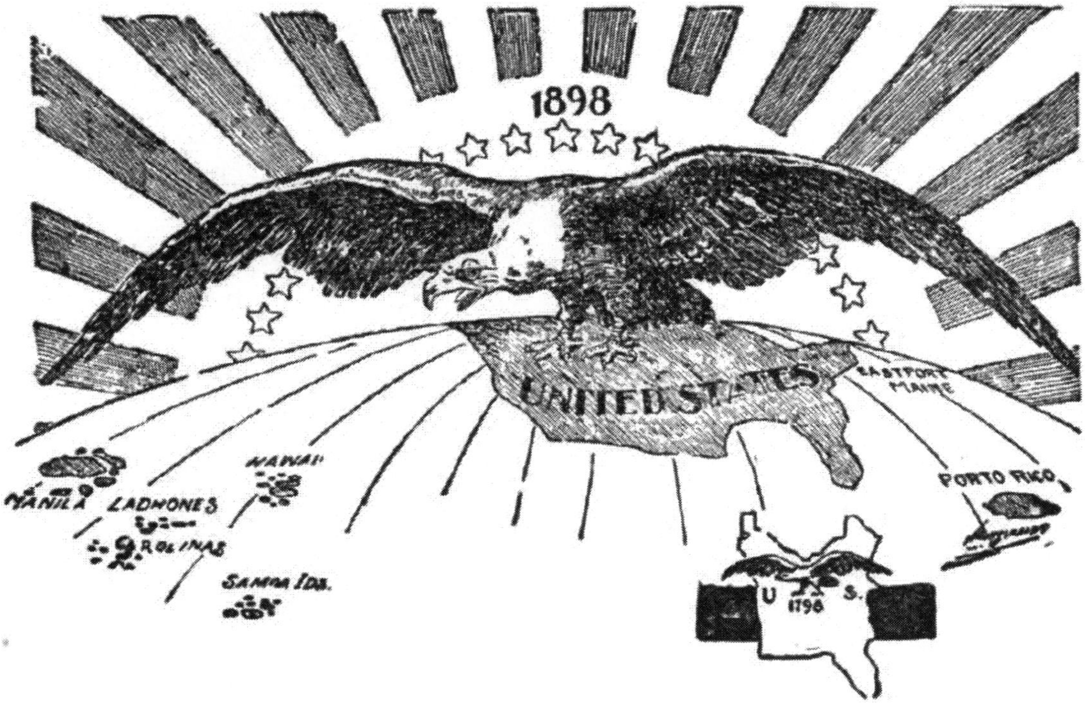

Ten thousand miles from tip to tip.—Philadelphia Press.

8. The widespread wings of the American eagle in this cartoon best represent

A) the wide reach of American imperialism at the turn of the century.

B) the threat of the German military's reach during World War I.

C) the unstable nature of the United States' land claims following the Spanish-American War.

D) the failure of the United States in its display of manifest destiny.

9. Why did the cartoonist juxtapose the larger eagle (labeled 1898) with a smaller eagle (labeled 1798)?

A) to illustrate how much the United States has declined in 100 years

B) to illustrate how far the United States has expanded in 100 years

C) to illustrate that the United States was much better off in 1798

D) to illustrate that the United States is much less powerful in 1898

Questions 10 and 11 are based on a political cartoon published in 1904. It shows President Theodore Roosevelt tiptoeing barefoot through the Caribbean Sea, dragging the US Navy along with him. He carries a "big stick," and the title reads "The Big Stick in the Caribbean Sea." Additionally, the naval boats boast names such as "The Sheriff," "The Debt Collector," and "The Receiver."

THE BIG STICK IN THE CARIBBEAN SEA

10. This political cartoon best represents what aspect of Theodore Roosevelt's presidential policies?

- **A)** his reputation as a "trust buster" in his battle against Big Business
- **B)** his goal to "speak softly and carry a big stick" in enforcing the Monroe Doctrine in Latin America
- **C)** his belief in national conservation efforts and a National Parks system
- **D)** his declaration that he felt as "fit as bull moose" after an assassination attempt on his life

11. What does the political cartoon imply about Theodore Roosevelt and the US Navy's involvement in Latin America at that time?

- **A)** Roosevelt and the US Navy tried to police Latin America while diplomatically tiptoeing there.
- **B)** Roosevelt and the US Navy felt smaller and/or more inferior to the Latin American governments.
- **C)** Roosevelt and the US Navy believed they had no role as leaders in Latin American diplomacy.
- **D)** Roosevelt and the US Navy did not care about the entire region.

Question 12 is based on an excerpt of President Abraham Lincoln's famous "House Divided" speech, which he delivered during a debate in Springfield, Illinois, against Stephen Douglas during his campaign for the US Senate in 1858. Lincoln eventually lost the race to Douglas, but his speech lives on as a prelude to sectional tensions that precipitated the American Civil War.

I believe this government cannot endure, permanently half *slave* and half *free*.

I do not expect the Union to be *dissolved*—I do not expect the house to *fall*—but I *do* expect it will cease to be divided.

It will become *all* one thing or *all* the other.

Either the *opponents* of slavery, will arrest the further spread of it, and place it where the public mind shall rest in the belief that it is in the course of ultimate extinction; or its *advocates* will push it forward, till it shall become alike lawful in *all* the States, *old* as well as *new*—*North* as well as *South*.

12. When Abraham Lincoln talks about a "house divided," he is really talking about

- **A)** the divisions between North and South over slavery.
- **B)** the divisions between the United States and Great Britain.
- **C)** the divisions between the United States and Mexico over the Texas Revolution.
- **D)** the divisions between the United States and the Native Americans in the Old West.

Questions 13, 14, and 15 are based on the following text from the Bill of Rights. The Bill of Rights was added to the Constitution in 1789 as a political compromise. Proponents of the Bill of Rights wanted to ensure that the Constitution is a living document that could be amended. The Bill of Rights offers the first ten amendments to the Constitution, the foundational governing document of the United States of America.

THE BILL OF RIGHTS (full text)

Amendment I

Congress shall make no law respecting an establishment of religion, or prohibiting the free exercise thereof; or abridging the freedom of speech, or of the press; or the right of the people peaceably to assemble, and to petition the government for a redress of grievances.

Amendment II

A well regulated militia, being necessary to the security of a free state, the right of the people to keep and bear arms, shall not be infringed.

Amendment III

No soldier shall, in time of peace be quartered in any house, without the consent of the owner, nor in time of war, but in a manner to be prescribed by law.

Amendment IV

The right of the people to be secure in their persons, houses, papers, and effects, against unreasonable searches and seizures, shall not be violated, and no warrants shall issue, but upon probable cause, supported by oath or affirmation, and particularly describing the place to be searched, and the persons or things to be seized.

Amendment V

No person shall be held to answer for a capital, or otherwise infamous crime, unless on a presentment or indictment of a grand jury, except in cases arising in the land or naval forces, or in the militia, when in actual service in time of war or public danger; nor shall any person be subject for the same offense to be twice put in jeopardy of life or limb; nor shall be compelled in any criminal case to be a witness against himself, nor be deprived of life, liberty, or property, without due process of law; nor shall private property be taken for public use, without just compensation.

Amendment VI

In all criminal prosecutions, the accused shall enjoy the right to a speedy and public trial, by an impartial jury of the state and district wherein the crime shall have been committed, which district shall have been previously ascertained by law, and to be informed of the nature and cause of the accusation; to be confronted with the witnesses against him; to have compulsory process for obtaining witnesses in his favor, and to have the assistance of counsel for his defense.

Amendment VII

In suits at common law, where the value in controversy shall exceed twenty dollars, the right of trial by jury shall be preserved, and no fact tried by a jury, shall be otherwise reexamined in any court of the United States, than according to the rules of the common law.

Amendment VIII

Excessive bail shall not be required, nor excessive fines imposed, nor cruel and unusual punishments inflicted.

Amendment IX

The enumeration in the Constitution, of certain rights, shall not be construed to deny or disparage others retained by the people.

Amendment X

The powers not delegated to the United States by the Constitution, nor prohibited by it to the states, are reserved to the states respectively, or to the people.

13. Which of the following is NOT an amendment discussed in the Bill of Rights?

A) an amendment banning the quartering of soldiers

B) an amendment abolishing slavery

C) an amendment that disallows unlawful search and seizures

D) an amendment that ensures the right to a speedy and public trial

14. The text indicates that the Second Amendment is sometimes colloquially referred to as what?

A) the right to a trial by jury

B) the right to freedom of speech

C) the right to protection from unreasonable searches and seizures

D) the right to bear arms

15. Freedom of religion is protected by the

A) First Amendment.

B) Second Amendment.

C) Eighth Amendment.

D) Tenth Amendment.

Question 16 is based on a painting adapted by a photograph taken in Tiananmen Square (Beijing, China) in 1989. The painting (and original photo) show a man protesting the encroachment of Chinese communist tanks on a crowd of protesters. The man has become famously known as "Tank Man," though his true identity remains a mystery.

16. What historical sentiment does this portrait illustrate?

A) the cowardice of humanity in the wake of modernity

B) the bravery of humanity when confronted by military force

C) the weakness of military power in Cold War China

D) the anxiety associated with a lack of military strength

Questions 17, 18, and 19 are based on a World War I propaganda poster for enlistment in the US Army. The poster was published around 1917. In the poster, a drooling, armored monkey with a club carries a half-naked damsel in distress. The monkey wears a traditional German helmet and mustache. The helmet is labeled with the word militarism. *The club is labeled with the word* kultur *(the German word for culture). The monkey walks on a coast that is labeled* America.

17. Created as propaganda during World War I, this poster sends what kind of message about Germany?

A) The German nation will heroically save Americans.

B) The German nation possesses a civilized culture with peaceful values.

C) The German nation is a barbaric beast that should be stopped.

D) The German nation is a dignified leader in global relations.

18. The inclusion of the word *militarism* on the monkey's military gear is meant to illustrate that

A) militarism is a threat to women.

B) militarism is a rising threat in the US.

C) the US Army is too militaristic.

D) German culture is too militaristic.

19. Why did the artist place the beast on the American coast?

A) to instill hope that Germany and the United States will harmoniously resolve their problems

B) to instill hope that German culture will land upon the shores of America

C) to stir fear that German culture will spread its militarism upon the shores of America

D) to stir fear that women will be attacked by the militarism of the US Army

Questions 20 and 21 are based on an editorial cartoon, which was first published in 1912 and is now in the archives of the National Child Labor Committee. The cartoon depicts a giant hand—labeled "Child Labor Employer"—squashing a crowd of child laborers. The child laborers struggle to resist the diamond-studded hand of "Big Business."

20. Analyzing this political cartoon, what can be assumed about the artist?

A) The artist created the cartoon at a time when child labor laws were not in effect.

B) The artist created the cartoon at a time when child labor laws were in effect.

C) The artist supported the exploitative nature of child labor.

D) The artist supported child labor employers.

21. Which idea does the diamond-studded ring in the cartoon most likely symbolize?

A) Child laborers are destroying the wealth of Big Business.

B) Child laborers are earning money from Big Business.

C) Big Business is getting rich on the backbreaking work of child laborers.

D) Big Business has no vested interest in the labor of children.

Question 22 is based on a piece of propaganda that was sent out to the colonies in the years leading up to the French and Indian War and the Albany Plan. It was originally published in 1754; it shows a snake chopped into pieces that are labeled according to each colony (or colonial region in the case of New England). It reads: "JOIN, or DIE."

22. This poster, which was first created for the Albany Plan leading up to the French and Indian War, is likely sending what message?

   A) The colonies should be loosely organized for security in the face of conflict.

   B) The colonies should not work together in the coming war.

   C) The colonies should not form an alliance against the French and their Native American allies.

   D) The colonies should unite, or they will perish in separation.

Questions 23, 24, and 25 are based on a photo of a sign that was created during the apartheid in South Africa. The sign reads: "FOR USE BY WHITE PERSONS: THESE PUBLIC PREMISES AND THE AMENITIES HAVE BEEN RESERVED FOR THE EXCLUSIVE USE OF WHITE PERSONS." The statement is by order of the Provincial Secretary. The sign includes the same message in Afrikaans, a derived form of Dutch used in South Africa.

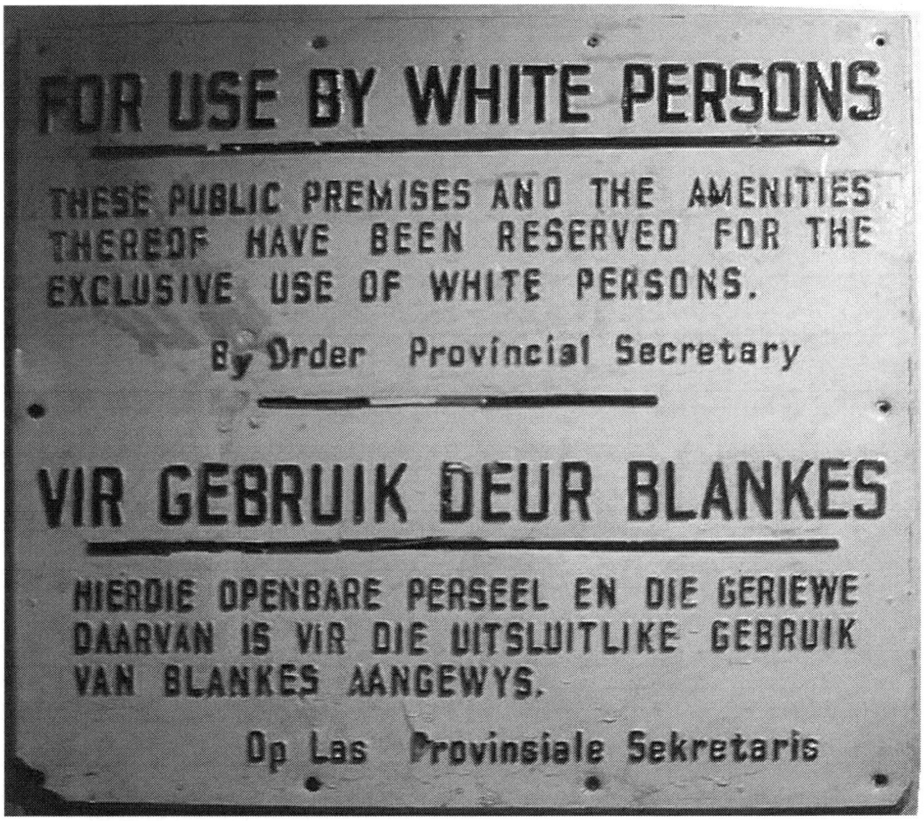

23. The statement tells us what about apartheid in South Africa?

   A) It promoted racial integration.

   B) It promoted social stability.

   C) It promoted racial diversity.

   D) It promoted racial segregation.

24. What can be inferred from the inclusion of two languages on the sign?

A) Most South Africans spoke English, and it was probably the official language of South Africa.

B) Only Afrikaans and English were recognized as major languages in South Africa at the time.

C) The provincial secretary did not want the message to be disseminated to more than one group.

D) People of color were the only intended audience of this sign.

25. The content of the sign sheds light on the fact that apartheid in South Africa was similar to Jim Crow segregation in the American South in what way?

A) Both separated public premises according to race.

B) Both separated public premises according to first language.

C) Both separated public premises according to class.

D) Both separated public premises according to gender.

Questions 26, 27, and 28 are based on an 1874 political cartoon entitled "Woman's Holy War. Grand Charge on the Enemy's Works." In the cartoon, militaristic women, who ride horses and wield axes, destroy barrels of beer, whiskey, gin, brandy, rum, wine, and liquors. They champion banners that say "Temperance League" and "In the Name of God and Humanity." The central woman in the cartoon carries a shield that boasts the American flag.

26. What does the political cartoon indicate about the relationship between the women's rights movement and the temperance movement?

A) Religious leaders headed both nineteenth-century movements.

B) These movements likely worked together in the late nineteenth century.

C) Both the temperance and women's rights movements were violent.

D) The temperance movement forced women to participate.

27. If one did not know the meaning of *temperance* prior to viewing this political cartoon, then the scenes in the cartoon might lead them to understand that *temperance* means

A) anti-alcohol.

B) alcohol consumption.

C) drunkenness.

D) anti-American.

28. The incorporation of the phrase "In the Name of God and Humanity" might indicate that the temperance movement was

A) mostly about civil rights.

B) xenophobic.

C) anti-feminist.

D) religiously motivated.

Questions 29, 30, and 31 are based on a map of the Santa Fe Trail, which was published in 1962, nearly 100 years after the trail's greatest era of pioneer travel. The map depicts the original landmarks of the Santa Fe Trail, according to earlier maps charted in 1860.

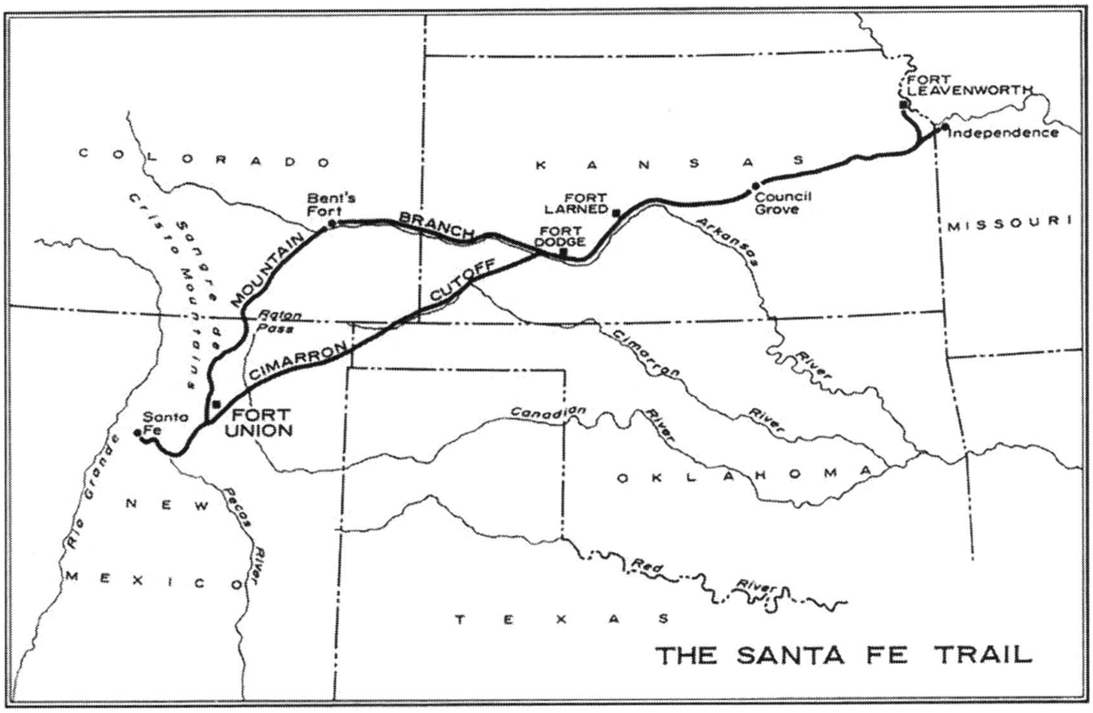

29. According to the map, from east to west, the entire trail runs from

A) Fort Larned to Fort Dodge.

B) Independence to Santa Fe.

C) Council Grove to Santa Fe.

D) Independence to Fort Union.

30. From east to west, the trail splits off into the Mountain Branch and Cimarron Cutoff right around

A) Council Grove.

B) Fort Leavenworth.

C) Bent's Fort.

D) Fort Dodge.

31. The map shows the Santa Fe Trail crossing which states?

A) Texas, Kansas, and Colorado

B) Missouri, Kansas, Texas, and Oklahoma

C) Missouri, Kansas, Colorado, Oklahoma, and New Mexico

D) Texas, Kansas, Colorado, Oklahoma, and New Mexico

Questions 32, 33, and 34 are based on a map published in 1970 in the National Atlas of the United States. *The map shows the breakdown of allegiances between the Union and Confederacy in the Civil War. The black states represent Union states. The solid gray states represent Union territories that did not permit slavery. The states in horizontal stripes represent the "border states" of the Union that permitted slavery but did not join the Confederacy. The light gray state is Kansas, known at the time as "Bleeding Kansas" for its bloodshed over slavery and abolition. Kansas eventually entered the Union. The states in gray with diagonal stripes represent Union territories that permitted slavery. And the states in light gray with stars represent the Confederacy, which permitted slavery.*

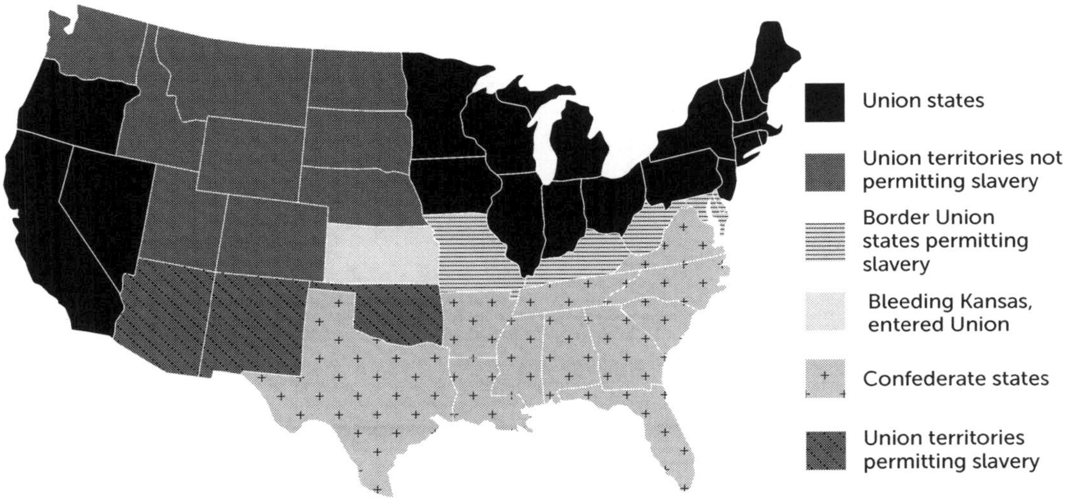

32. According to this map, Texas was a

A) Union territory that did not permit slavery.

B) Union territory that did permit slavery.

C) Confederate state that permitted slavery.

D) Confederate state that did not permit slavery.

33. Which of the following was a Union state that did NOT permit slavery?

A) Florida

B) Kentucky

C) Oklahoma

D) California

34. According to this map, Arizona is best classified as

A) a Union territory that permitted slavery.

B) a Union territory that did not permit slavery.

C) a Confederate state.

D) a Union state.

Questions 35, 36, and 37 are based on the following graph, which was published in 2009, but charts the number of slaves and cotton bales accounted for in the United States from 1790 to 1860.

Growth of Slavery and Cotton in the US

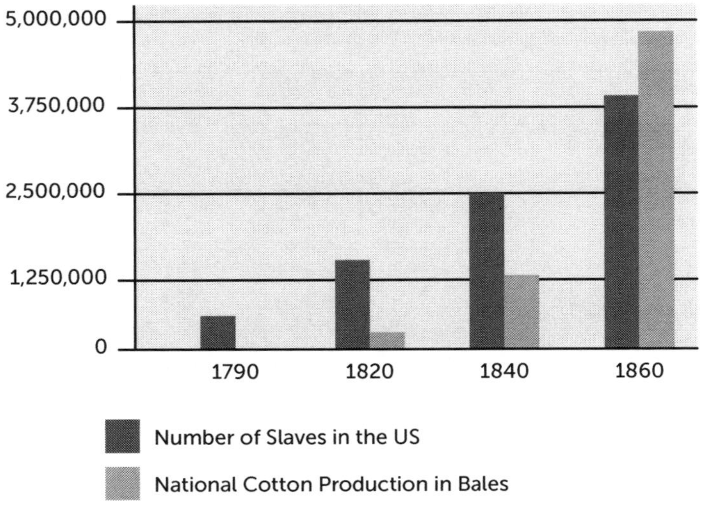

35. This graph shows that the number of slaves working in the United States ________ between 1790 and 1860.

A) decreased

B) plateaued

C) increased

D) fluctuated

36. On the graph, the year ______ is the only time period when the "National Cotton Production in Bales" amounted to more than the "Number of Slaves in the US."

A) 1860

B) 1840

C) 1820

D) 1810

37. In 1840, there were roughly _____ slaves in the US and roughly ____ cotton bales produced.

A) 0 and 5,000,000

B) 1,250,000 and 2,500,000

C) 2,500,000 and 1,250,000

D) 5,000,000 and 5,000,000

Questions 38, 39, and 40 are based on a map of US Territorial Acquisitions that was originally published in the National Atlas of the United States in 1970. *This map notes territorial acquisitions, beginning with the British cessions to the thirteen colonies in 1783 (the end of the American Revolution). The last territorial acquisitions noted are the annexation of Hawaii in 1898 and the purchase of the Virgin Islands in 1917.*

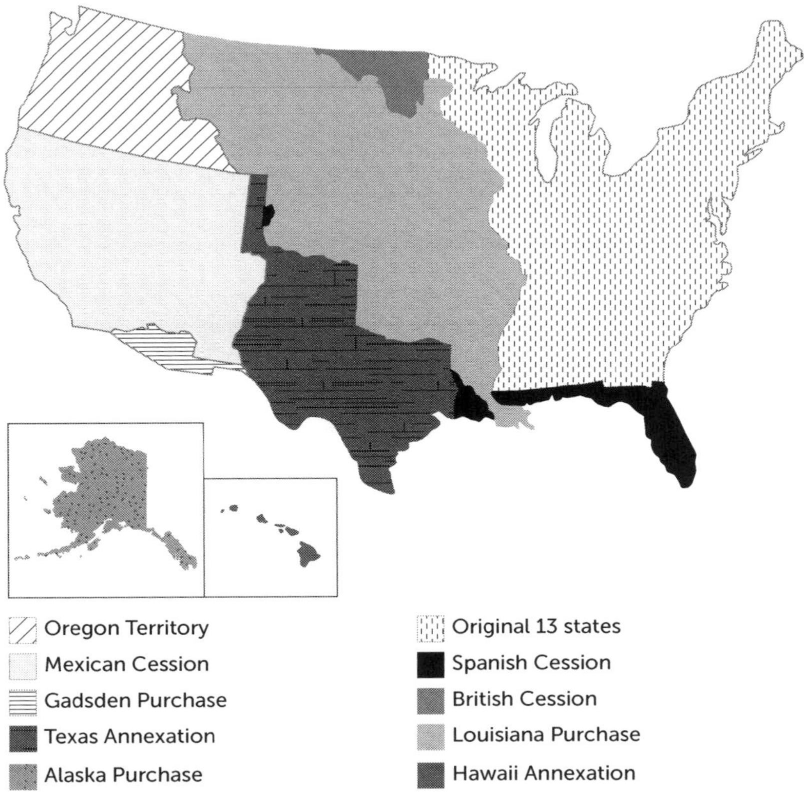

38. What territories did the United States obtain through the Spanish Cession of 1819?

A) the Louisiana Purchase

B) Oregon Territory

C) Alaska

D) East and West Florida

39. According to the map, the Louisiana Purchase occurred in what year?

A) 1803

B) 1845

C) 1848

D) 1867

40. In the years prior to the annexation of Texas in 1845, the territory of Texas was

A) within the jurisdiction of the Republic of Texas.

B) within the jurisdiction of Mexico.

C) within the jurisdiction of Russia.

D) within the jurisdiction of the Spanish Empire.

Question 41 is based on the following picture of a Ghost Dance ceremony in 1890. The caption reads, "The Ghost Dance by the Ogallala Sioux at Pine Ridge Agency, Dakota," and the image is an illustration from a periodical.

41. Which of the following conclusions is supported by the image?

A) By and large, the American public was not aware of the Ghost Dance movement.

B) In general, Ghost Dances were opportunities for men and military leaders to organize.

C) The Ghost Dance movement was violent and a direct threat to the US government.

D) Ghost Dances were usually large public affairs with high rates of attendance.

The following questions are based on the map of OPEC, the Organization of Petroleum Exporting Countries.

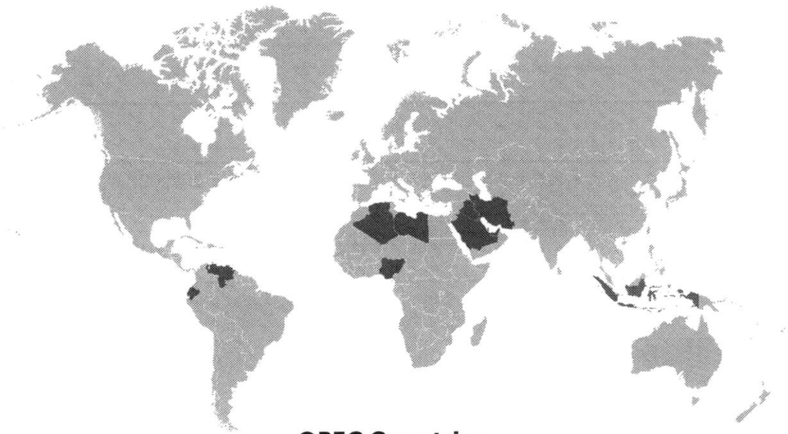

OPEC Countries

Algeria	Iran	Libya	Saudi Arabia
Ecuador	Iraq	Nigeria	United Arab Emirates
Indonesia	Kuwait	Quatar	Venezuela

42. The United States is one of the world's biggest oil consumers. Looking at the map, and knowing that the United States is a top consumer of oil, what might readers conclude about the United States' relationship with OPEC and its gas prices?

A) The United States—like many other oil-consuming nations—likely depends on OPEC to set global oil prices even though it is not part of OPEC or the price-setting process.

B) The United States is part of OPEC, so it likely controls the price-setting process for oil.

C) The United States is not part of OPEC, so it likely does need to worry about OPEC's price-setting process.

D) The United States and OPEC must be enemies.

43. What conclusion can be drawn from the information and map above?

A) OPEC only includes a few countries, so it is probably not very powerful.

B) The Middle East and North Africa are important to world gasoline prices.

C) Most OPEC countries are poor because they are in the developing world.

D) There is less petroleum in South America than there is in Africa.

Questions 44, 45, and 46 are based on the diagram of the "separation of powers" of the three branches of US government: the legislative branch, executive branch, and judicial branch.

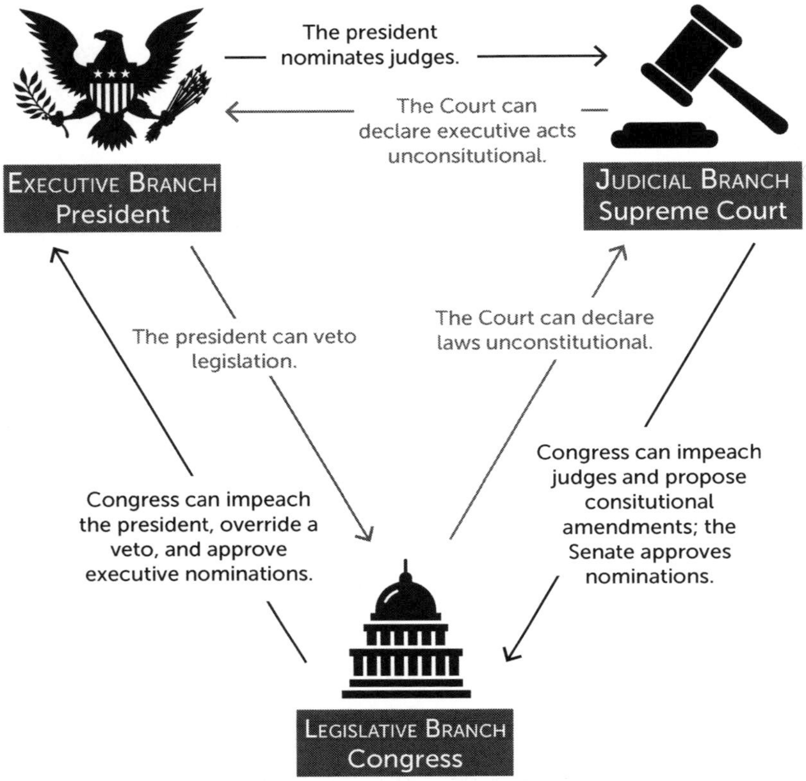

44. According to the diagram, what are the responsibilities of the judicial branch?

A) create the laws

B) veto the laws

C) interpret the laws

D) enforce the laws

45. Who has impeachment power over the president?

A) district courts

B) courts of appeals

C) Supreme Court

D) Congress

46. Which entity has the power to nominate judges?

A) the president

B) Congress

C) the Supreme Court

D) the courts of appeals

Questions 47 and 48 refer to the following passage:

Throughout the 1760s and early 1770s, the North American colonists found themselves increasingly at odds with British imperial policies regarding taxation and frontier policy. When repeated protests failed to influence British policies, and instead resulted in the closing of the port of Boston and the declaration of martial law in Massachusetts, the colonial governments sent delegates to a Continental Congress to coordinate a colonial boycott of British goods. When fighting broke out between American colonists and British forces in Massachusetts, the Continental Congress worked with local groups, originally intended to enforce the boycott, to coordinate resistance against the British. British officials throughout the colonies increasingly found their authority challenged by informal local governments, although loyalist sentiment remained strong in some areas.

47. According to the passage above, what did colonial delegates at the First Continental Congress intend to do?

A) boycott British goods and formally declare independence from the British Empire

B) boycott British goods and threaten to declare independence by drawing up a draft declaration of independence in order to force reform

C) write and sign the Declaration of Independence

D) protest measures taken by the Crown in the colonies and advocate for reform

48. What does the passage convey about the relationship between the boycott and military uprisings in the British colonies?

A) Boycotts helped the British quell American-led military uprisings.

B) Boycotts paved the way to more intentional American-led military uprisings.

C) Boycotts were welcomed by the British.

D) Boycotts helped the Americans create peaceful agreements with the British, ending all military uprisings.

Questions 49, 50, and 51 are based on a 2018 Electoral College map of the current breakdown of Electoral College votes per state. Each state has a certain number of votes based on the number of members it has in Congress. Every state has two senators. Each state also has a certain number of US representatives in the House of Representatives that is based on the total population (not territorial size) of the state.

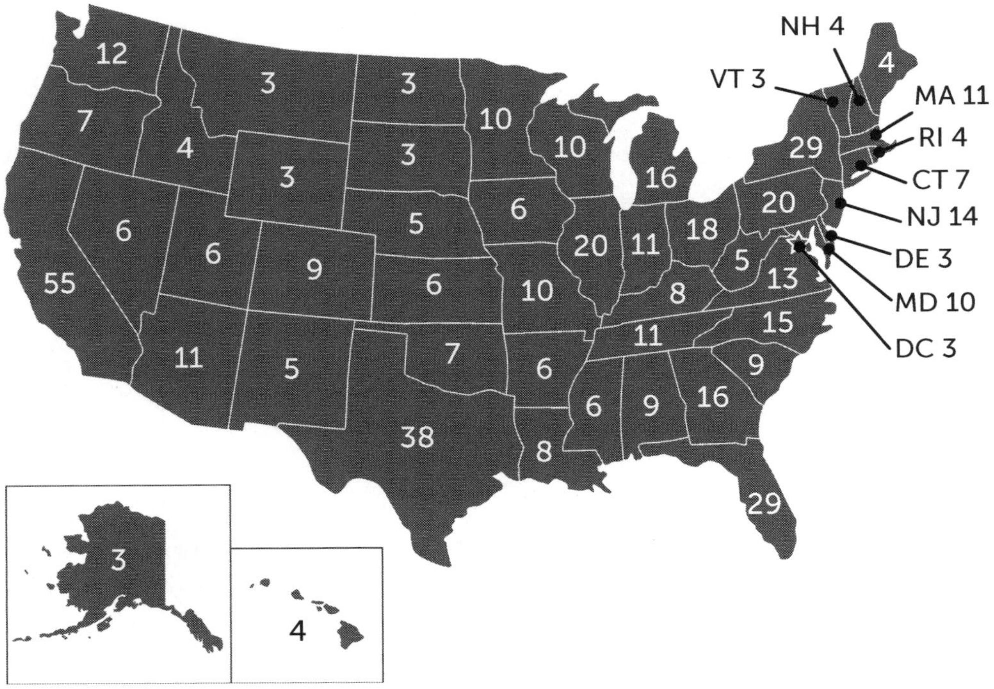

49. Since the electoral map shows that Montana only has three electoral votes, it can be assumed that Montana is a state with

A) a small amount of territory with a small population to match it.

B) a large amount of territory with a large population to match it.

C) a large amount of territory but a small population.

D) a small amount of territory but a large population.

50. How many US representatives does Texas have?

A) 29

B) 36

C) 38

D) 55

51. Since the electoral map shows that New Jersey has a total of fourteen electoral votes, it can be assumed that New Jersey is a state with

A) a large amount of territory with a large population to match it.

B) a small amount of territory with a small population to match it.

C) a large amount of territory but a small population.

D) a small amount of territory but a large population.

Answer Key

1. A) is incorrect. The clear agent in this proposal, as the image indicates, is Germany, not Mexico. The German figure stands with his arm extended to the American Southwest, propositioning the Mexicans to join his cause.

   B) is correct. Again, as mentioned, Germany is the focal point of this political cartoon, which illustrates the "Zimmerman Telegram's" proposal for an alliance between Germany and Mexico. The German figure is offering the Mexican soldier the American Southwest in exchange for a military alliance.

   C) is incorrect. Germany and the United States were at political odds during this era. Moreover, the German figure has his back turned on the United States in this cartoon.

   D) is incorrect. The war was between Germany and the United States. Although Mexico and the United States did not have the best diplomatic relations following the Mexican-American War, they were not in direct conflict during World War I. The political cartoon shows a German figure trying to coax Mexico into an alliance against the United States.

2. A) is incorrect. The vice president was determined to be the president of the Senate in this section. However, this section does not give the vice president the power to appoint senators.

   B) is incorrect. Senators have never been chosen by Supreme Court justices in US history, and it is not mentioned in the text.

   C) is correct. Today we elect senators by direct voting, but in the immediate years following the US Constitution, senators were chosen by state legislatures. The Seventeenth Amendment, which was ratified in 1788, changed the process to a direct election by citizens.

   D) Incorrect. Impeachment is discussed in this section of the Constitution, but impeachment refers to when a president is brought to trial for his/her wrongdoings as a leader.

3. **A) is correct.** As discussed in this section of the Constitution, senators serve six-year terms.

   B) Incorrect. Supreme Court justices hold lifelong terms, but senators only serve six-year terms.

   C) Incorrect. The president of the United States has a four-year term, but senators have a six-year term.

   D) Incorrect. Members of the House of Representatives serve two-year terms.

4. **A) is correct.** As the text mentions, the vice president of the United States also serves as the "President of the Senate."

   B) is incorrect. The president of the United States has many duties, but "President of the Senate" is not one of them.

   C) is incorrect. The attorney general of the United States has many roles and responsibilities, but he or she is not listed as the "President of the Senate."

D) is incorrect. The secretary of state is an important member of the president's cabinet but does not act as the "President of the Senate."

5. **A) is correct.** The "anti-war" sign and the youthful characteristics of the protesters indicate that it is likely a student protest. The casual clothes and acts of nonviolent protest contextualize the photograph in the late 1960s, during the era of the Vietnam War.

   B) is incorrect. Many protests over civil rights occurred in the South during the 1960s, but the exclusion of African-American boycotters/protesters in the photo helps test-takers to categorize the protest as one that likely exists outside of the direct civil rights movement.

   C) is incorrect. Although there are plenty of women participating in the protest, the "anti-war" sign ties the photo directly to the Vietnam protests rather than feminist marches.

   D) is incorrect. The Black Power movement was an urban phenomenon led by radical black activists. Most of the participants in this photo are white, and the "anti-war" sign indicates a direct correlation to the Vietnam War and its domestic protests.

6. A) is incorrect. There are no visible symbols of direct violence in the photograph, even with the direct threat of military force.

   B) is correct. The protest, as depicted in this photo, is generally peaceful/non-violent, as symbolized by the extension of the flower toward military forces, but there is also the imposing presence/force of the military police who form a phalanx in front of the protesters.

   C) is incorrect. Again, there is only the *threat* of military force, but there are no visible signs of direct violence.

   D) is incorrect. While the photo is generally peaceful, there are no acts of violence depicted.

7. **A) is correct.** The painting entitled *Spirit of the Frontier* is founded on this larger notion of *manifest destiny*, the historical belief that it was the United States of America's God-given right to expand west and "civilize" Native American lands. The woman in the painting represents liberty moving westward, bringing technology and light to the "uncivilized lands" of the West.

   B) is incorrect. The Native Americans in the photo are moving westward. Also, in most instances, Native Americans were actually victims of manifest destiny rather than leaders of manifest destiny. Many white American settlers violently took over Native American lands as a result of westward expansion.

   C) is incorrect. The incorporation of telegram lines and railroads indicates that this painting was created well after the American Revolution.

   D) is incorrect. The expansionist components of America's manifest destiny complicated the tensions between North and South leading up to the Civil War, but there are no symbols of the Civil War in this painting, and manifest destiny is typically not pinpointed as a major driving force in the conflict.

8. **A) is correct.** In 1898, the United States was at its peak as an imperial state. Following the Spanish-American War, the empire had grown to include enclaves in the Caribbean and the Pacific. The wide-reaching wings of the eagle convey a sense of not only protection, but also expansion.

   B) is incorrect. Although Germany also uses the eagle as a historical symbol, there is no indication that this cartoon is referencing Germany. Also, World War I occurred later in history.

   C) is incorrect. There are no signs of instability; although the cartoon did emerge just after the Spanish-American War, the strength and reach of the eagle convey stability rather than instability.

   D) is incorrect. Analyzing this cartoon, some may argue that the eagle represents a *realization* of manifest destiny rather than a failure of manifest destiny.

9. A) is incorrect. The eagle would have shrunk in size if this was the case. But the size of the eagle has clearly grown from 1798 to 1898, indicating the expansion of the US territorial boundaries over a 100-year period.

   B) is correct. The smaller eagle (labeled 1798) protects a smaller United States. But the larger eagle (labeled 1898) protects an entire American empire. The message here is that the United States has expanded dramatically into a global empire in as little as 100 years.

   C) is incorrect. The image does not convey any signs of nostalgia or imminent decline. Instead, it appears to be saying that the United States is much better off in 1898.

   D) is incorrect. Just the opposite: the eagle's growth in size indicates a coinciding growth in American political and military power.

10. A) is incorrect. Although Roosevelt was known as a trust-busting president, there are no signs of trusts, big business, or industry in this political cartoon.

    B) is correct. One of Roosevelt's famous quotes about US diplomacy in Latin America was that his goal was to "speak softly and carry a big stick" as he reinforced the "big brother" contingencies of the Monroe Doctrine. The phrase "The Big Stick in the Caribbean" is even included on the cartoon. He is also tiptoeing with a club, or a "big stick."

    C) is incorrect. Roosevelt was a firm believer in conservation and the National Parks system, but there is no mention of nature, parks, or conservation in this political cartoon.

    D) is incorrect. Roosevelt did survive an assassination and even formed the Bull Moose Party later in his life. Yet there are no references to that namesake or its historical relevance in this political cartoon.

11. **A) is correct.** This is the best answer because it accounts for all of the symbolism embedded in the political cartoon. Roosevelt, a president who invoked the power of the Monroe Doctrine, believed that the United States should police Latin America and care for it as a "big brother." The larger-than-life, giant depiction of Roosevelt conveys a sense of power and authority in

the region. The US Navy is even smaller than him, but also towed/controlled by him. He is carrying a "big stick" to symbolize his assertive power, but he is also tiptoeing around the coast of the region in order not to disrupt relationships too much.

B) is incorrect. Although the boats are smaller than Roosevelt, the cartoon indicates that they are being towed by the president in an effort to monitor the coasts of Latin America. There are no signs of inferiority. The main message is that Roosevelt is a political personality that is larger than life, and in control of the US Navy.

C) is incorrect. Every symbol in the cartoon indicates that Roosevelt had no qualms with leading and protecting the region as if it were his own land.

D) is incorrect. Just the opposite: the cartoonish Roosevelt appears to have a vested interest in policing and ruling over the region.

12. **A) is correct.** Lincoln's "house divided" speech is about the divisions created by debates about abolition and slavery prior to the American Civil War. He even references North and South in the speech. He also discusses divisions between "opponents of slavery" and "advocates of slavery."

B) is incorrect. The major conflicts between the United States and Great Britain had been resolved by the time of the Lincoln-Douglas debates. Most of these conflicts dwindled following the conclusion of the War of 1812.

C) is incorrect. The Texas Revolution divided the United States and Mexico during the 1830s and 1840s, but these tensions had calmed by 1858, and Lincoln does not directly mention Mexico or Texas.

D) is incorrect. These divisions continued to exist in 1858 but gained more notoriety in the years following the Civil War. Lincoln does not mention Native Americans in this speech, and his attention is focused on slavery.

13. A) is incorrect. The Third Amendment, which disallows the quartering of soldiers, is in the Bill of Rights.

B) is correct. The Thirteenth Amendment, which abolished slavery, was not added until after the Civil War.

C) is incorrect. The Fourth Amendment, which protects citizens from unlawful searches and seizures, is in the Bill of Rights.

D) is incorrect. The Sixth Amendment, which protects the right to a speedy and public trial, is in the Bill of Rights.

14. A) is incorrect. The right to a speedy and public trial by jury is protected by the Sixth Amendment, not the Second Amendment.

B) is incorrect. The right to freedom of speech is protected by the First Amendment, not the Second Amendment.

C) is incorrect. The right to protection from unreasonable searches and seizures is presented in the Fourth Amendment, not the Second Amendment.

D) is correct. Citizens often quote the Second Amendment to protect their "right to bear arms," which is justified by the Bill of Rights as being "necessary for the security of a free state."

15. **A) is correct.** The First Amendment, which also protects freedom of speech, protects freedom of religion.

B) is incorrect. The Second Amendment focuses on the right to bear arms but does not mention the freedom of religion.

C) is incorrect. The Eighth Amendment highlights the unconstitutional nature of excessive bail, fines, and cruel and unusual punishment; it does not mention religion.

D) is incorrect. The Tenth Amendment protects the decision-making powers of the states, or the people, but does not discuss religion.

16. A) is incorrect. The man in the portrait shows no signs of cowardice. He is standing before modern military machinery that is much more powerful than he is, and he does not appear to be fearful.

B) is correct. The single speck of humanity placed in front of such military force indicates that the power of this portrait is its juxtaposition of the bravery of humanity against the backdrop of unnecessary military force.

C) is incorrect. The long line of physically imposing tanks signifies military strength rather than military weakness.

D) is incorrect. Although the portrait does capture some historical anxiety—and it may even *induce* anxiety—there is no sign of military weakness. The tanks look like they are in control.

17. A) is incorrect. The poster paints Germany as a barbaric "enemy" rather than a hero or ally.

B) is incorrect. The use of the monkey signifies that German culture is uncivilized.

C) is correct. The use of a brutish monkey is telling: it sends the message that German culture is like a militaristic beast that will ravage women upon the shores of America if not taken seriously.

D) is incorrect. Again, the poster paints Germany as a barbaric "enemy" rather than a hero or ally.

18. A) is incorrect. The woman functions as a symbol of vulnerability in this poster, acting as a victim of the beast. The poster's message is not about women, but about the German threat to peace.

B) is incorrect. Just the opposite: the message of the poster is that the US is not aggressive enough, and if Americans sit back, they will be destroyed by the militarism of German culture.

C) is incorrect. The goal of the poster is to encourage the heroism and militarism of US citizens so that men will join the US Army.

D) is correct. Every symbol in this poster is pointing to the aggressive, threatening, and overly militaristic nature of Germany during World War I.

19. A) is incorrect. There are no visual signs of hope in this poster, nor are there any signs of harmony between the United States and Germany.

B) is incorrect. While the poster does suggest that German culture might land upon the shores of America, there is no indication that this invasion would be wished for or welcomed.

C) is correct. The brutish nature of the German monkey is meant to instill fear about the reach of Germany's militarism. The damsel in distress adds to this fear, symbolizing the ravaging capabilities of German culture.

D) is incorrect. The poster is focused on recruiting US soldiers to fight the Germans. Germany is the clear "enemy" in the poster, not the US Army.

20. **A) is correct.** Child labor laws were not in effect at the time of the cartoon. Later labor laws banned child labor before a certain age to protect children from exploitation.

B) is incorrect. The cartoon appears to be attacking the exploitation associated with child labor, signifying that laws were likely not yet in place to protect children from child labor.

C) is incorrect. Since the cartoon depicts Big Business squashing children, the core message of the cartoon is that child labor is exploitative and wrong.

D) is incorrect. While the cartoon depicts Big Business as a powerful force, there are no signs that the cartoonist supports the child labor that props up Big Business. Again, the core message of the cartoon is that child labor is exploitative and wrong.

21. A) is incorrect. Control and power seem to be in the giant hand of Big Business in this cartoon, not in the hands of the struggling child laborers. The child laborers look weak and unable to destroy Big Business.

B) is incorrect. Just the opposite: the diamond-studded ring represents the wealth of the child labor employers, not the employees.

C) is correct. The diamond-studded hand, which represents the "big business" of employing child labor, is trying to crush the feeble child laborers beneath it. At the same time, these laborers seem to be propping up the large hand, a symbol of the children's backbreaking work, which props up Big Business.

D) is incorrect. It is clear in this cartoon that the hand of Big Business is still reaching out to child labor, even if its goal is to crush the workers.

22. A) is incorrect. The use of the phrase "JOIN, or DIE" describes a need for union, not loose organization.

B) is incorrect. The poster is calling for the opposite; it is saying the colonies should come together in battle.

C) is incorrect. The term *alliance* means to "join together for military reasons." The goal of the poster was to join the colonies together so they did not perish in separation.

D) is correct. The phrase "JOIN, or DIE" hints at a dire need for union or alliance. The chopped-up snake symbolizes a death in separation.

23. A) is incorrect. Integration means "a union of two groups or races." It is the opposite of exclusion and segregation. The sign calls for both exclusion and segregation when it declares that the public premises are "reserved for the exclusive use of white persons."

B) is incorrect. Apartheid promoted division in society, which caused instability and harmed many South Africans.

C) is incorrect. The sign also runs counter to modern-day calls for diversity, in spite of its inclusion of multiple languages. The sign is trying to exclude people of color from white spaces.

D) is correct. The phrase "reserved for the exclusive use of white persons" signals that this sign is mostly about separation by race, or racial segregation.

24. A) is incorrect. The sign features two languages: English and Afrikaans. Since both languages were used on the sign, it is not reasonable to assume that most people spoke English; otherwise the sign would only be in English. Furthermore, many South Africans spoke other languages besides English and Afrikaans.

B) is correct. The inclusion of two languages on the sign shows that South Africa had more than one widely spoken language. During apartheid, the government only recognized Afrikaans and English as official languages, even though many South Africans spoke other languages such as Zulu and Xhosa. After apartheid, the government recognized eleven official languages, more accurately reflecting the population of the country.

C) is incorrect. It can be assumed that the provincial secretary wanted to reach multiple audiences due to the inclusion of two languages.

D) is incorrect. From the information given, it should be assumed that the intended audience of this sign is anyone who can read English or Afrikaans, which could be anyone in the general public. Even though whites were more likely to speak English or Afrikaans as a first language, many South Africans spoke and read both languages. What is most likely is that the government simply did not acknowledge at all the languages more widely spoken as first languages among people of color. Choice B is a better answer here.

25. **A) is correct.** The apartheid in South Africa and the Jim Crow segregation laws in the United States were very similar: they both banned blacks and other people of color from entering white spaces in public. These spaces were typically labeled with signs like the one pictured.

B) is incorrect. The apartheid in South Africa and the Jim Crow segregation laws in the United States were largely racialized efforts. Although linguistic differences sometimes compounded the bigotry in each country, both historical phenomena were largely about race, not language.

C) is incorrect. Although there was certainly an intersection of oppression that shadowed race and class during these times, global perceptions of race were the largest factors contributing to the apartheid in South Africa and the Jim Crow segregation laws in the United States.

D) is incorrect. Women remained oppressed in both contexts, especially if they were women of color. But the apartheid in South Africa and the Jim Crow segregation laws in the United States were mostly about race, not gender.

26. A) is incorrect. The cartoon speaks of a "holy" war and a sign in the picture mentions the "name of God." However, the women on horseback in the image do not wear any religious insignia or clothing. The movements might be somewhat associated with religion, but they are not necessarily led by religious leaders.

B) is correct. The political cartoon shows an alliance between feminism and temperance, symbolized by the powerful women soldiers in the cartoon.

C) is incorrect. Some women, like Carry Nation, were known for destroying containers of alcohol and damaging property as part of the temperance movement. The women do wield axes in this image, possibly alluding to these stories. However, they are not harming anyone. There is a stronger association between women's rights and temperance, making choice B a better answer.

D) is incorrect. There is no indication from the cartoon that the women are being forced to participate. Actively wielding axes and riding horses, they seem enthusiastic. Historically, women were leaders in the temperance movement, which emerged with the early women's rights movement in the United States.

27. **A) is correct.** The heroically destroyed barrels of alcohol show that temperance refers to an anti-alcohol movement.

B) is incorrect. Temperance actually means the opposite of alcohol consumption; it means to avoid the sale and consumption of alcohol. There is no sign of alcohol sale and consumption in this political cartoon—there is only the destruction of alcohol.

C) is incorrect. The temperance movement emerged in reaction to chronic cases of public drunkenness in urban environments. Women especially were alarmed at the growing rates of alcoholism in their working or unemployed husbands. There is no sign of alcoholism in this political cartoon; there is only the symbolic destruction of barrels of alcohol.

D) is incorrect. The temperance movement was believed to be a pro-American movement, symbolized by the stars and stripes on the shield of the female soldier in this political cartoon.

28. A) is incorrect. There is no reference to civil rights in this political cartoon. In fact, the temperance movement reinforced aspects of racial segregation.

B) is incorrect. Xenophobia was still rampant at the time this political cartoon was created; however, there is no direct reference to xenophobia (i.e., the fear and exclusion of certain immigrant groups) in this cartoon.

C) is incorrect. Some may argue that the political cartoon is actually pro-feminist because it depicts women as powerful historical agents capable of making changes in society.

D) is correct. The key word here is *God*. The temperance movement, which was tied to the progressive Protestant-Christian values at the time, believed it was destroying societal ills (such as alcohol) in the name of God.

29. A) is incorrect. Fort Larned is located around the midpoint of the entire trail, and Fort Dodge is located several miles away in the state of Kansas. These stops were important points, but not the beginning and ending points.

B) is correct. As illustrated by the map, the famous Santa Fe Trail extended from Independence, Missouri, in the east to Santa Fe, New Mexico, in the west.

C) is incorrect. Santa Fe is the end of the trail, but the beginning of the trail extends farther past Council Grove into Independence, Missouri.

D) is incorrect. While Independence, Missouri, is indeed the trailhead, the Santa Fe Trail extends farther than Fort Union, the second-to-last stop on this map.

30. A) is incorrect. Council Grove is hundreds of miles away from the trail split that separates the Santa Fe Trail into the Mountain Branch and Cimarron Cutoff.

B) is incorrect. Fort Leavenworth is another trailhead located several miles from the trailhead in Independence, Missouri. It was an alternative starting point that was hundreds of miles away from the trail split that separates the Santa Fe Trail into the Mountain Branch and Cimarron Cutoff.

C) is incorrect. According to the map, Bent's Fort is located *after* the trail split, which occurs at Fort Dodge. It is the halfway point on the Mountain Branch portion of the Santa Fe Trail.

D) is correct. At Fort Dodge, the Santa Fe Trail separates into two sections: the Mountain Branch and Cimarron Cutoff.

31. A) is incorrect. The Santa Fe Trail did not pass through Texas. Moreover, it passed through five states in total.

B) is incorrect. Again, the Santa Fe Trail did not pass through Texas, and it covered more states than those listed.

C) is correct. The Santa Fe Trail extended from Independence, Missouri, to Santa Fe, New Mexico, crossing through five states: Missouri, Kansas, Colorado, Oklahoma, and New Mexico.

D) is incorrect. All states listed are correct except Texas, which the Santa Fe Trail did not cross. The only state missing is Missouri, the state in which the trail began.

32. A) is incorrect. Texas was not only part of the Confederacy, and not the Union, but it was also staunchly pro-slavery because of its cotton industry.

B) is incorrect. Although Texas was staunchly pro-slavery, it was not part of the Union.

C) is correct. All Confederate states permitted slavery, and Texas, a southern state shaded in light gray with stars on the map, was part of the Confederacy.

D) Incorrect. As the map key mentions, all Confederate states permitted slavery.

33. A) is incorrect. Florida was part of the Confederacy and consequently permitted slavery.

B) is incorrect. Kentucky may have been part of the Union, but it was one of the "border states" that were pro-Union in character by 1865 but still permitted slavery.

C) is incorrect. Oklahoma was not officially a state at this time. It was a western territory that permitted slavery.

D) is correct. Most textbooks focus on the North-South dichotomy along the Atlantic coast when discussing the Civil War. Some test-takers may overlook California's role in the war, but as the map illustrates, California was pro-Union and therefore anti-slavery.

34. **A) is correct.** Arizona was not a state at this time in history. It was, however, a pro-Union territory that also permitted slavery within its boundaries.

B) is incorrect. All Union territories that did not permit slavery are located above the 36°30′ parallel, the anti-slavery–pro-slavery boundary established by the Missouri Compromise. These territories are solid gray on the map.

C) is incorrect. Arizona was not a state (it was a territory), and it had no affiliation with the Confederacy.

D) is incorrect. Arizona was still a territory at this time. It was pro-Union, but not a full-fledged state in the Union.

35. A) is incorrect. The graph shows a clear increase from 1790 to 1860. This is indicated by the sharp heightening of the dark bars (i.e., the number of slaves in the United States) from 1790 to 1860. If the number of slaves had decreased, then the dark bars would decrease from one year to the next.

B) is incorrect. There is no indication that the number of slaves ever leveled off from one time period to the next.

C) is correct. The graph shows a clear increase from 1790 to 1860. This is indicated by the sharp heightening of the dark bars (i.e., the number of slaves in the United States) from 1790 to 1860.

D) is incorrect. Not only are there no signs of decrease, but all increases shown are pretty consistent.

36. **A) is correct.** According to this graph, in the decades leading up to 1860, the number of slaves always outpaced the number of cotton bales produced. But around 1860, with the help of mechanized machinery, the number of cotton bales produced skyrocketed to a point in which the bales produced outpaced the number of slaves.

B) is incorrect. According to this graph, in the decades prior to 1860, the number of slaves always outpaced the number of cotton bales produced. This is true for 1840.

C) is incorrect. According to this graph, in the decades prior to 1860, the number of slaves always outpaced the number of cotton bales produced. This is true for 1820.

D) is incorrect. According to this graph, in the decades prior to 1860, the number of slaves always outpaced the number of cotton bales produced. This is true for 1810.

37. A) is incorrect. This answer is incorrect for two reasons. First, it ignores the bar graphs provided on the chart. Second, slavery did not end in the United States until 1865, at the end of the Civil War. Thus, the number of slaves could not be 0 in 1840, a time when battles over slavery were at their peak.

B) is incorrect. This is a trick answer. It switches the number of slaves and number of cotton bales in an attempt to fool the test-taker.

C) is correct. In 1840, according to the graph, there were almost exactly 2,500,000 slaves in the United States who helped produce roughly 1,250,000 bales of cotton.

D) is incorrect. The graph does not show that the number of slaves in the United States ever equaled the number of cotton bales produced.

38. A) is incorrect. At one time, Spain did have authority over the Louisiana Territory, but eventually the region fell back into the hands of France. The United States purchased the territory from France in 1803.

B) is incorrect. The United States had full control of the Oregon Territory after a series of meetings and treaties with the UK in the 1840s.

C) is incorrect. The United States purchased Alaska from Russia in 1867. It was initially called "Seward's Folly" in an attempt to poke fun at the US secretary of state who supported the purchase, William H. Seward. Citizens believed it was a folly because they did not think the land was worth anything. Today Alaska is one of the most resource-rich states in the Union.

D) is correct. Florida had long been a southern buffer between the United States and the Spanish empire. In 1819, the Adams-Onis Treaty between the United States and Spain legitimized the cession of East and West Florida from Spanish control to US control.

39. **A) is correct.** The Louisiana Territory was purchased in 1803, making it one of the first major post-Revolution land acquisitions for the United States of America. The Jefferson administration purchased it from France, and it nearly doubled the size of US territory in North America.

B) is incorrect. The United States annexed Texas in 1845, about forty-three years after the Louisiana Purchase.

C) is incorrect. The Mexican Cession occurred in 1848 at the culmination of the Mexican-American War.

D) is incorrect. The United States purchased Alaska from Russia in 1867.

40. A) is correct. Before Texas was a state in the Union, it was its own country. Specifically, it was a republic. On the map, the area that includes what became the state of Texas is labeled "former Republic of Texas," which indicates that Texas was independent prior to annexation.

B) is incorrect. Mexico did indeed have authority over the land that is now the state of Texas. However, years before the annexation of Texas, the United States helped Texas gain its independence from Mexico during the Texas Revolution. This answer is consequently inaccurate.

C) is incorrect. Russian colonization only played a very minor role in the history of North America. The only major region granted to the United States by Russia was Alaska, which, as the map shows, was purchased by the US government in 1867. The Russian empire never had any geopolitical influence over territories as far south as Texas.

D) is incorrect. By 1845, the year of Texas's annexation, Spain's authority in the New World was all but void. At one time, Spain did maintain authority over Texas. But during the Mexican Revolution, that authority passed from Spain to the new Mexican government. Authority then passed from Mexico to the Republic of Texas. In cities such as San Antonio, there is still evidence of Spain's influence in the region, but Texas was its own independent state by the time the United States wanted to annex it.

41. A) is incorrect. The image is from a periodical, so the mass media was investigating and publicizing the Ghost Dance movement.

B) is incorrect. Civilians, including a woman and a young child, are clearly visible in this image.

C) is incorrect. The Ghost Dance movement was a spiritual movement. There is no sign of violence in this image; the people are dancing, appear to be civilians, and there are no weapons.

D) is correct. In this image, a large group is participating in the Ghost Dance. The crowd stretches far into the distance; the scale provided by the mountains and structures clarifies how big it is.

42. A) is correct. Although the United States has been trying to be more independent when it comes to energy in recent years, it is still very dependent on OPEC's price-setting process for oil and gas. The United States is not part of OPEC, as the map shows, but it is still a top oil consumer. This means it has to work with OPEC in order to navigate its oil dependency.

B) is incorrect. The map clearly shows that the United States is not part of OPEC and therefore does not have much of an impact on its price-setting procedures.

C) is incorrect. While the map shows that the United States is not part of OPEC, it does not indicate that the United States is not reliant on OPEC. The question states that the United States is one of the top consumers of oil, so the United States must be impacted by OPEC's price-setting procedures.

D) is incorrect. Although the United States has had some tension with OPEC throughout history, the map and information provided do not indicate that the two are enemies. In fact, the United States maintains strong relations with some OPEC countries.

43. A) is incorrect. Gasoline is an important resource, so OPEC is an important organization since it controls world gas prices.

B) is correct. Since most OPEC countries are located in the Middle East and North Africa, those regions are important in determining world gasoline prices.

C) is incorrect. While most OPEC countries are located in the developing world, it is not safe to assume they are all impoverished countries from this information alone. In fact, several OPEC countries are considered high-income and middle-income countries.

D) is incorrect. There are fewer OPEC members in South America than there are in Africa, but that does not necessarily mean that there are lower oil reserves in South America than in Africa. The map only shows countries, not quantities of petroleum.

44. A) is incorrect. According to the diagram, the legislative branch creates the laws, not the judicial branch. Congress—which is composed of the US Senate and US House of Representatives—is responsible for making (and voting on) US laws. The judicial branch interprets the laws that are created by the legislative branch and enforced by the executive branch.

B) is incorrect. As the diagram indicates, only the president of the United States has the power to veto laws.

C) is correct. According to the diagram, the judicial branch interprets the laws that are created by Congress and enforced by the executive branch.

D) is incorrect. The judiciary interprets the law. The executive branch enforces the law. While the executive branch appoints judges to the federal courts that compose the judiciary, these judges do not have the power to enforce the law.

45. A) is incorrect. Not only do district courts have less power than the Supreme Court, but they are also far removed from the impeachment process because they belong to the judicial branch. The judicial branch can only declare presidential acts unconstitutional; it cannot impeach the president. Only Congress can impeach the president.

B) is incorrect. Like the district courts, the courts of appeals also have less power than the Supreme Court. Likewise, they belong to the judicial branch and so are removed from the impeachment process. The legislative branch is the only branch of government that can impeach the president.

C) is incorrect. The Supreme Court is the highest authority on matters of constitutionality. However, it does not have the power to impeach the president. Only Congress can impeach the president.

D) is correct. As the diagram illustrates, Congress is the only governmental entity that is able to impeach the president.

46. A) is correct. The diagram shows that only the president has the power to nominate judges. The black arrow in the diagram that is labeled "The president nominates judges" stems from the executive branch.

47. A) is incorrect. At the First Continental Congress, colonial delegates did not declare independence; they met to coordinate a boycott of British goods.

B) is incorrect. Delegates at the First Continental Congress met to coordinate a boycott, not to threaten independence.

C) is incorrect. Thomas Jefferson wrote the Declaration of Independence in 1776 at the Second Continental Congress, once delegates had given up hope of effecting change through boycotts and negotiation.

D) is correct. At the First Continental Congress, delegates intended to use economic pressure—boycotts—to push for reform.

48. A) is incorrect. The boycotts did the exact opposite; they ignited the military uprisings rather than quelling the American-led opposition.

B) is correct. The economic effects of the American-led boycotts created more tension between the colonies and the Crown, paving the way to the violent conflicts of the American Revolution.

C) is incorrect. The British tried to use military force to stop the boycotts; they did not welcome the economic opposition.

D) is incorrect. The American-led boycotts strained all political relations between the colonies and the Crown. Peaceful agreements did not occur until well after the American Revolution.

49. A) is incorrect. Montana is one of the larger states. Although it has a small population, it clearly has a lot of territory, according to the map.

B) is incorrect. Although Montana clearly has a large amount of territory, it only has one US representative and three electoral votes. Larger states like California have more electoral votes to account for their larger population size.

C) is correct. According to the map, Montana is one of the largest states but has the lowest number of electoral votes. With only three votes, it is evident that Montana has just one US representative (and two senators). This is the lowest number a state can have, which means that Montana must have a small population.

D) is incorrect. New Jersey would be the best example of a small state with a large population. Montana is not only much bigger than a state like New Jersey, but its electoral votes indicate that it has a smaller population.

50. A) is incorrect. In order to answer this question, test-takers must recognize Texas on a map. This answer provides the number of electoral votes in New York, not Texas. Moreover, it does not subtract the proper number of US senators (two) from the total electoral votes in New York.

B) is correct. This correct answer subtracts the proper number of US senators (two) from the total number of electoral votes in Texas to arrive at the correct number of US representatives: thirty-six.

C) is incorrect. Texas has thirty-eight electoral votes; however, electoral votes account for the number of US representatives *and* the two US senators per state. The thirty-eight electoral votes account for these US senators.

D) is incorrect. According to the map, California has fifty-five electoral votes. That means it has fifty-three representatives. This number is unrelated to Texas.

51. A) is incorrect. It is clear that New Jersey is a small state in territory, especially compared to bigger states like Alaska, California, Texas, and Montana. While this answer correctly notes New Jersey's large population, it completely misses the mark on the size of its territory.

B) Incorrect. New Jersey is similar in geographic size to states such as Vermont and New Hampshire. Yet New Jersey has more electoral votes. However, North Carolina has more territory than New Jersey but close to the same number of votes. This illustrates that New Jersey packs a lot of electoral votes in a small space. This means that New Jersey likely has a large population, not a small population.

C) is incorrect. According to the map, New Jersey is one of the smallest states in physical size but has a relatively high number of electoral votes. With a total of fourteen votes, New Jersey has twelve representatives who cover its small territory (and two senators). Compare it to North Carolina—which has more territory but close to the same number of votes. Again, it can be concluded that New Jersey likely has a large population, not a small population.

D) is correct. This answer correctly notes New Jersey's small territorial size and also accounts for the fact that New Jersey has a similar number of electoral college votes as much larger states like North Carolina. This, again, illustrates that New Jersey packs a lot of electoral votes in a small space.

Made in the USA
Monee, IL
01 July 2021

72771068R00105